Information Seeking

Information Seeking

AN ORGANIZATIONAL DILEMMA

J. David Johnson

QUORUM BOOKS
Westport, Connecticut • London

Library of Congress Cataloging-in-Publication Data

Johnson, J. David.
  Information seeking : an organizational dilemma / J. David
Johnson.
    p. cm.
  Includes bibliographical references and index.
  ISBN 0–89930–999–2 (alk. paper)
  1. Management information systems.   2. Information resources
management.   3. Office information systems.   I. Title.
  HD30.213.J64   1996
  658.4'038—dc20   95–50745

British Library Cataloguing in Publication Data is available.

Library of Congress Catalog Card Number: 95–50745
ISBN: 0–89930–999–2

First published in 1996

Quorum Books, 88 Post Road West, Westport, CT 06881
An imprint of Greenwood Publishing Group, Inc.

Printed in the United States of America

∞

The paper used in this book complies with the
Permanent Paper Standard issued by the National
Information Standards Organization (Z39.48–1984).

10 9 8 7 6 5 4 3 2 1

Copyright Acknowledgments

The author and publisher are grateful for permission to reproduce portions of the following
copyrighted material.

Figure 2.3 is drawn from Reynolds, E. V., & J. D. Johnson (1982). Liaison emergence: Relating
theoretical perspectives. *Academy of Management Review*, 7, 551–559. Reproduced by permission of the Academy of Management.

Figure 4.2 is drawn from Johnson, J. D., Donohue, W. A., Atkin, C. K., & Johnson, S. H.
(1995). A comprehensive model of information seeking: Tests focusing on a technical organization. *Science Communication*, 16, 274–303. Copyright 1995 by Sage Publications. Reprinted by
permission of Sage Publications. Inc.

To Sally, who ended my search.

CONTENTS

FIGURES AND TABLES

FIGURES

TABLES

PREFACE

I wrote this book for a combination of personal and professional reasons. Recently, I have engaged in sponsored research focusing on cancer-related information seeking (e.g., Johnson & Meischke, 1993), a matter of some importance to my family. Individuals increasingly find that they must choose between an array of alternatives based on often very limited knowledge. Thus, information seeking, literally, is an important survival tool for individuals.

As I became more interested in the general concept, I began to see the pervasiveness of issues surrounding information seeking to almost every aspect of our social lives, especially to modern organizations. This book highlights the importance and pervasiveness of information seeking in organizations, and develops models and analytic frameworks to promote a comprehensive understanding of information seeking. Information seeking often represents a dilemma, balancing many negative and positive aspects, for the organization. Indeed, the forces promoting ignorance in organizations often outweigh imperatives to seek information.

This book explores both sides of the information-seeking dilemma, examining reasons why people do and do not seek information. While the benefits of information seeking are well known, we know very little about the processes that have led to the failure of most information technologies designed to support it. Since literally billions of dollars are spent inappropriately on information technologies, a greater understanding of strategies that promote information seeking is needed. This book specifies general strategies that management and workers can employ to enhance information seeking.

As I investigated information seeking in greater depth, I was struck by how little was known about such an important issue. Especially lacking were systematic, in-depth theoretical treatments and associated rigorous empirical tests. Personally, given my traditional interest in communication structure and network analysis (Johnson, 1993a), information seeking provides a compelling focus for explaining individual action and the theoretical underpinnings of individual relationships in informal structures in organizations. Fortunately, with a grant from the Michigan Department of Public Health, my colleague Hendrika Meischke and I conducted a series of research studies that provide the empirical foundation for the arguments presented in this book. Simultaneously, I have been investigating information seeking within a governmental organization that provides technical services (Johnson et al., 1995) and I recently completed a network analysis of advice seeking within a university office (Johnson & Meyer, 1995).

Currently, I am an outside expert to the Evaluation Task Force of the National Cancer Institute's Cancer Information Service. Most importantly, for the last two years I have been evaluating a four-year $7.3 million program project grant focusing on the Cancer Information Service as an information provider to the public. Thus, in recent years, I have had the opportunity to look at information seeking both from the seeker's and provider's perspective.

This book is intended for three primary audiences. First, it can be used by practitioners in the fields of decision science, management consulting, management information systems, information technology, and information science. To make the book more accessible to these diverse audiences, I have knowingly circumvented some standard academic conventions (e.g., citing authorities for commonplace ideas). The interested academic reader can turn to my more traditional articles listed in the Bibliography for a more exhaustive (and exhausting) citation of academic works. Second, this book is still intended for a scholarly audience and should be of interest to those in the academic fields of communication, information systems, library science, psychology, management, marketing, accounting, and computer science. As a result of the variety of professionals who are interested in this topic, I have tried to write this work to appeal to as many of them as possible, perhaps in the end not really completely satisfying any one of them. Third, this book would be most useful as a text (or supplement) for graduate-level courses in information science, organizational communication, or organizational behavior.

Unfortunately, it is beyond the scope of this book to pursue specific "how to do it" issues related to the application of many of its ideas, although I do specify general strategies which managers and others may want to use. The interested reader can consult this book's Bibliography for many excellent introductions to such pragmatic issues as how to conduct an Internet search in very concrete terms. This book focuses on general issues, providing readers with analytic frameworks that should be useful across specific information-seeking situations, as well as being applicable to the future in a way that discussions of specific technologies are not.

Several people have helped me in the writing of this book. I would like to thank Eric Valentine for believing in this project. I would especially like to thank Sally Johnson for reviewing earlier drafts. I would also like to thank Franklin J. Boster and Vernon Miller for their comments on earlier sections of this work. Needless to say, I assume ultimate responsibility for what follows.

Information Seeking

ONE

INTRODUCTION AND OVERVIEW

In an information economy, organizations compete on the basis of their ability to acquire, manipulate, interpret and use information effectively. (McGee & Prusak, 1993, p. 1)

Increasingly, individual information seeking has become a critical determinant of the success of organizational members and of the organization as a whole. In many service industries, such as banking and insurance, about 25 percent of personnel expenses are related to creating and maintaining information needed for business operations. But, disconcertingly, up to 25 percent of a knowledge worker's time is spent on marginally productive tasks related to inefficient information seeking (e.g., looking in the wrong places for information) and processing (Marchand & Horton, 1986).

Not too long ago, information in organizations was the exclusive preserve of management. Still today, in many organizations, information is kept from people. In part, organizations are designed to encourage ignorance through specialization and rigid segmentation of effort (Kanter, 1983). So there is a constant dilemma for organizations: the imperative (in part stemming from efficiency needs) to limit the availability of information, and the recognition that structural designs are flawed and circumstances change, requiring individuals to seek information normally unavailable to them. How organizations resolve these conflicting imperatives is a critical question for the modern organization. Unfortunately, while volumes have been written on formal organizational design, comparatively little is known about the forces that shape individual information seeking within organizations.

The comfortable world, where one's supervisor provided authoritative directives concerning organizational activities, is gradually changing to one where organizational members must make decisions about what goals should be emphasized and how they should be accomplished. (This general trend in institutions also has the important by-product of allowing them to shift blame for bad outcomes to the individual who is making the decision.) In this context, individual information seeking becomes a pivotal force in explaining the handling of communication related to technical problems in an organization. Not only is the necessity for information seeking increasing, but the technical possibilities for it are also increasing at an exponential rate.

While "Man's very survival depends on paying attention to aspects of the environment that change" (Darnell, 1972, p. 61), individuals have free access to an often bewildering wealth of information. They have to choose between a variety of information sources, including the new sources represented by the Internet. There are literally millions of articles published every year in the organizational and technical literature, making it nearly impossible for even the most dedicated individual to keep abreast of recent advances (Gould & Pearce, 1991). This overload of information forces decentralization of effort, with increasing responsibility passing to individuals, and organizational effectiveness determined by its ability to gather, then intelligently act on, information (Davidow & Malone, 1992).

In effect, lower-level employees must often do the traditional work of management, who cannot possibly keep up with the in-depth information related to specific technical issues. Baldridge award-winning companies recognize this in their total quality efforts, believing that empowering workers to solve problems is critical to their success (Hanson, Porterfield, & Ames, 1995). In fact, increasingly, managers are irrelevant to the information-seeking concerns of technical employees whom they supervise, because they lack the requisite technical knowledge (Johnson et al., 1995). Recognition of the limits of management and other sources also requires individuals to confirm and corroborate information by using multiple sources. Paradoxically, in this age of information, there may never be enough information to answer specific questions. For example, how long will highway pavement developed in Tahiti last in the exotic climatic conditions found in Duluth?

The decline of middle management and the leaner/meaner organizations associated with downsizing have contributed to these trends, resulting in quicker response times and reduced coordination and relay costs because of the linkages that have been removed from the hierarchy. These changes are made possible by advances in computer technology. The information context of the modern organization is rapidly evolving. Information technologies, including databases, new telecommunications systems (e.g., the information superhighway), and software for synthesizing information, make a vast array of information available to an ever-expanding number of organizational members. These trends put increasing responsibility on individuals to become active seekers, rather than passive recipients, of information, especially for decision support and problem solving (Rouse & Rouse, 1984). For technical and managerial positions, the most adept at identifying sources of information and developing approaches to acquiring it will be the most successful in these new organizational environments. Active information seekers are also more likely to assess their own performance and to take proactive steps to address any deficiencies with existing organizational standards (Ashford, 1989). More generally, increased competition and new technologies have led to a resurgence of interest in how people network to obtain information (Nohria, 1992).

Geertz's spider web metaphor, which is often drawn in studies of organizational culture, is quite appropriate here. At the same time, a spider web constrains and enables action. A spider can weave new strands into a web to meet new needs; but, until it does so, there are some things it won't be able to do, since the web constitutes a real boundary to action. Some have argued that, in this age of telecommunication, using the metaphor of "being wired," which also directly relates to the spider web metaphor, may be the most compelling way of thinking of the modern organization. Information is indeed the glue that holds organizations together.

Regrettably, academic approaches to these secular trends have lagged, partly because of the traditional focus on management and controls over information. Like communication research more generally, with the notable exception of Allen's (1977) work on research and development laboratories, our focus has been on how authoritative sources develop messages that can inform and persuade employees concerning management's vision of the organization and their participation in it. Comparatively little research has focused on the forces that shape an individual's active acquisition of information.

BENEFITS OF INFORMATION SEEKING

A central assumption underlying this book is that information seeking is a key moderator between perceived threats and likelihood of taking action (Thomas, Clark, & Gioia, 1993). Information seeking is often the first step in both individual and organizational change efforts, with heightened awareness of a problem often leading to increased readiness to change (Armenikas, Harris, & Mossholder, 1993). Information technology is at the root of many organizational changes either as a cause or an enabler (Hoffman, 1994). Information seeking can also provide individuals with a feeling of control over events: reducing their uncertainty (Freimuth, 1987); providing effective support; inducing attitude change; and increasing compliance with organizational directives.

Information seeking can provide individuals with critical assistance that enables them to also deal on an affective level with organizational life. Information itself can be considered a form of social support (Freimuth, 1987). This is reflected in the three fundamental conclusions Albrecht and Adelman (1987a) draw from the literature on social support in both organizational and non-organizational settings. First, supportive interactions are a search for human contact as well as a search for meaning to interpret the world. Second, social support reduces uncertainty-producing feelings of control and mastery. Finally, support occurs within an individual's communication network.

Networks are the infrastructure of social support, as they are also for information seeking. In particular, ties to others who are outside the immediate work unit are more likely to reduce burnout and stress. These networks facilitate coping, role transition, and access to needed information. They also contribute to a greater sense of personal control, since individuals are not dependent on any one group of others (Albrecht & Adelman, 1987b).

Information adequacy has been associated with commitment, identification, absenteeism, and turnover (Penley, 1982). Information seeking by newcomers has been positively related to satisfaction, performance (Morrison, 1993b), role mastery, cultural learning, and social integration (Morrison, 1993a), and negatively related to intention to leave the organization (Morrison, 1993b). Many organizations have found that providing organizational members with information concerning their performance has a very positive impact on enhanced levels of effort (Peters & Waterman, 1982; Burt, 1992).

A focus on information seeking develops a true receiver's perspective and forces us to examine how an individual acts within an information field containing multiple information carriers. Some of these carriers may be actively trying to reach individuals, while others contain information awaiting retrieval by an active individual. Managerial communication outlets such as newsletters may result in felt needs, but the individual and his/her placement in a particular social context will determine how these needs are acted upon. Managers need to know where individuals will seek information, since what they acquire will have a direct effect on their work performance, a relationship commonly recognized in the Total Quality Management movement (McGee & Prusak, 1993). But managers seldom understand the world from their worker's perspective, especially in terms of the information environment of individuals and what source of information they are normally exposed to. Knowledge of these sources can lead to strategic placement of information, which the seeker may find to be more authoritative than information that is spoon-fed to them.

A true picture of the impact of communication in organizations needs to contain elements of both sender and receiver perspectives. However, because most of the literature in this area tilts in the direction of understanding sender-oriented formal communication, here the focus will be primarily on how individuals acquire the information that helps them make sense of the information fields within which they act. This focus on receivers dovetails nicely with the renewed focus on the customer in most organizations. Emerging new organizational forms, such as virtual organizations, are also built upon the information processing skills of key integrators who facilitate close relationships between customers, suppliers, and the organization (Davidow & Malone, 1992; Galbraith, 1995).

DYSFUNCTIONAL CONSEQUENCES

In our view, actors operate in information fields where they recurrently process resources and information. This field operates much like a market where an individual makes choices (often based on incomplete information, often irrationally) that determine how they will act. This contrasts directly with the view of formal approaches to organizations that tend to view the world as rational, known, and that concentrate on controlling individuals to seek values of efficiency and effectiveness (e.g., Johnson, 1993a), particularly regarding the timeliness of decision making.

In spite of (or maybe because of) the abundance of available information, organizational members' lack of knowledge about important issues is a significant problem confronting the modern organization (Johnson, 1993a; Downs, Clampitt, & Pfeiffer, 1988). There is a growing recognition that information channels used by management can be easily avoided by certain groups within the organization, since they are not as captive an audience as they once were. As we will see, the forces preserving ignorance may be far more compelling than those resulting in information seeking.

Most treatments of information seeking tend to focus on the benefits of information seeking. Yet, information seeking can be viewed as having many negative consequences. Most threatening to management is their loss of control, since information seeking may be inherently destabilizing. Enhanced information seeking for one group in the organization also increases the possibility of collusion between members of informal coalitions, to the detriment of other organizational members, much as occurs with classic insider traders in financial markets.

Still, the more control that managers have, the less effective their organizations may ultimately be, especially in terms of obtaining the critical answers that they need for pressing questions. Kanter (1983) has argued that a major barrier to innovation in American organizations comes from a narrow focus on departmental/unit/division concerns. Imbalances in the distribution of information in organizations are a key consequence of this differentiation which often benefits the interests of individuals in privileged or specialist positions (Moore & Tumin, 1949). Organizational power structures, particularly management, reap benefits from hoarding information, since it is widely thought that information is power.

Segmented concern, as opposed to a concern for the good of the entire organization, is a direct result of the differentiation of the organization into specialized groupings which focus on particular tasks. In the classic formal organization, substantial barriers arise to the integration of organizational effort. This effect is often related to the development of silos or chimneys around different organizational functions. These barriers include informal rules that discourage individuals from developing cross-unit relationships. But these relationships are the most critical ones for innovation since they are the vehicle for sharing information and perspectives. Diverse perspectives result in the development of synthetic ideas and approaches that are holistic and concerned with the organization and new directions for it.

On the other hand, with their increasing responsibility for information seeking, there is also an increasing burden on individuals. It may be unfair to make employees responsible for every aspect of their performance, especially in these highly uncertain times. In this new world, individuals must confront the world very much as a scientist, constructing practical theories upon which they must act. This may be establishing a set of expectations that only the best educated can achieve. Will people make the right choices? Do they know enough to weigh and decide between the often conflicting pieces of information they will receive? Human beings are far from optimal information seekers (Rouse & Rouse, 1984). While information is a multiplying resource, attention, by implication, is a zero-sum resource (Smithson, 1989).

All of this also raises the question: Whose information is it, anyway? Information that to an employee is necessary for the accomplishment of his/her job may be seen by management as an intrusion into its prerogatives. In addition, the same piece of information may be irrelevant to one organizational member who has it, but critical to another organizational member who does not. Information seeking is truly a multidimensional construct when viewed from a variety of perspectives (Rouse & Rouse, 1984).

INFORMATION SEEKING DEFINED

Naturally, before we define information seeking, we must discuss the more basic concept of information. The word information is ubiquitous; it has even been used to define our society as a whole (Doctor, 1992; Rouse & Rouse, 1984). By 1977, one-half of our gross national product was associated with information processing activity (Bellin, 1993). As with any such central concept, several senses of the word are frequently used in the literature. Unfortunately, several of these are also mutually contradictory.

Perhaps the most appealed-to source for a definition of information comes from Shannon and Weaver's (1949) seminal work on telecommunication systems. Their central concern was how to send messages efficiently, with minimal distortion, over mediated communication channels (Darnell, 1972). Yet, this work has always been troublesome because of its mechanistic, engineering transmission focus, which slights the meaning of messages (Darnell, 1972; Littlejohn, 1992; Rowley & Turner, 1978; Stonier, 1991).

Shannon and Weaver developed an abstract definition of information based on the concept of entropy. Total entropy would represent complete randomness and lack of organization in messages. With greater entropy you also have higher levels of uncertainty, so that the more familiar a situation is, the less information it generates. In this sense, something is information only if it represents something new, thus a measure of information is the "surprise value" of a message (Krippendorf, 1986). However, it is quite possible that only an experienced person can recognize the unfamiliar in the most seemingly familiar of messages (Cole, 1994; Rowley & Turner, 1978). This also leads to the expert's paradox: The greater one's expertise, the more likely they are to be successful in finding information, but the less likely that information is to be informative in this sense of information (Buckland, 1991a). Since most people associate information with certainty, or knowledge, this definition can be somewhat counterintuitive (Littlejohn, 1992).

Much more globally, information is sometimes equated with any stimuli we register or recognize in the environment around us (Miller, 1969). In this view, information involves the recognition of patterns in the basic matter/energy flows around us (Farace, Monge, & Russell, 1977). The other side of this view focuses on the nature of an individual's perceptual processes, arguing that they shape what we consider to be information, what we will perceive, and how we will perceive it (Miller, 1969). In this work we will not focus on these cognitive questions: rather, we will focus on the gathering of information.

But there is also a sense—a very important one for communication structures in organizations—that information is what you use to develop a higher level of comfort, perhaps even more of a feeling of familiarity with a situation. The more confident and sure you are about something, the less uncertain it is (Farace, Monge, & Russell, 1977). Thus, information can also be viewed as the number (and perhaps kind) of messages needed to overcome uncertainty (Krippendorf, 1986). In this view, information is of value if it aids in overcoming uncertainty; the extent to which information does this also defines its relevancy (Rouse & Rouse, 1984).

Associated with the concept of information load, a critical problem that most organizations must confront, is yet a fourth sense of the concept of information, and one that encompasses in some ways the previous two definitions. In this fourth sense, information load is a function of the amount and complexity of information. Amount would refer to the number of pieces (or bits) of information. Complexity relates to the number of choices or alternatives represented by stimuli. In a situation where all choices are equally probable, entropy is at its maximum. This fourth sense of information reflects the close association of information with decision-making processes (Krippendorf, 1986).

The senses and properties (e.g., timeliness, depth, breadth, specificity, quality, accuracy, quantitative/qualitative, hard/soft, etc. [Dervin, 1989]) of information are many. In this work we will use information in its most general sense, that is, the discernment of patterns in the world around us. The patterns themselves may often represent the material world, but some of the most interesting implications of an information society are in how it differs from the economies that preceded it. Cleveland (1985) has offered several interesting distinctions in this regard. First, information is expandable, that is, new knowledge often interacts with old knowledge to produce an exponentially increasing wealth of new information while leaving the old intact (Buckland,

1991a). The limits to expansion are primarily in the users of information systems, not in the systems themselves. Second, information is typically not resource-hungry; it does not deplete a finite store of material resources, like mineral extraction industries. Third, information is substitutable; it can replace itself and it can be readily exchanged. Fourth, information is transportable by mediated means (e.g., telecommunications systems) that can overcome the limits of time and space of the material world. Fifth, information diffuses. It is hard to hoard information—to prevent its spread to others who have an interest in it. Increasingly, we are living in a world where there are no secrets, at least not for long. Sixth, information is sharable, especially so because different parties may have considerably different uses for the same piece of information (Buckland, 1991a). Cleveland (1985) goes on to suggest that these characteristics of information are inevitably going to lead to the decline of hierarchies in organizations, just as they have led to the decline of authoritarian states.

The intention to seek information has a relative salience within an individual's other intentions. So, for example, while an individual may vaguely know that he/she needs to possess more information related to project management software, he/she may not act on this concern because of more pressing ones (e.g., declining market share, angry customers, etc.). In addition, an individual's intention to act may be further constrained by a myriad of other factors in his/her environment, which we will discuss in later chapters.

One such constraint is the information field within which the individual is embedded. This field encompasses the sources of information an individual is normally exposed to and the sources an individual would normally consult when confronted with a problem. For technical staff, this information environment might be incredibly rich, including access to sophisticated databases, advanced satellite systems, and "search engines" for computerized information retrieval. The arrangement of an individual's information field limits the degree to which that individual can act on his/her predispositions. The information field an individual is located in constrains the very possibility of selecting particular sources of information.

I may seek answers to my questions from a variety of channels, from a variety of sources within channels, and from a variety of messages provided by these sources. These information carriers may provide me only partial answers. These answers, in turn, may stimulate additional questions, the answers to which I may not be immediately able to get because of constraints that exist in my immediate information environment. For example, for financial reasons I may be limited by the extent to which I can directly consult experts. I may not be aware that the Commerce Department supports a telephone hotline that can provide responses to many of my queries. I may be fortunate and have a neighbor, who has purchased the product, whom I can informally approach with my concerns.

The act of information seeking can take an amazing array of forms. I can be cued by an advertisement in a trade publication to seek information on a new product. This might lead to an additional act of information seeking, talking to a salesperson. This might be a positive interaction, leading to more specific information seeking centering on securing answers to particular questions: How much training will I need? Do I have the money in my budget to purchase it? How will upper management react?

Information seeking can be related to a variety of purposes that it serves for individuals. First, it can enhance an individual's general knowledge of a particular subject. It has been argued that one of the distinguishing features of human beings is their curiosity. Individuals become fascinated with particular subjects for a variety of reasons. They will seek information about an area even though it is not directly related to immediate planned actions, merely because they are curious. Second, individuals can gather information to make a particular decision. Obviously, this type of information seeking is much more tied to a direct event. So, individuals gather information about their organization's history, informal cultural norms, fringe benefits, work practices, new technologies, and so on. Third, individuals engage in residual information seeking related to decision making; that is, an individual has already made a decision and needs to rationalize it to others or to further confirm it to him/herself. In more extreme forms, this can lead to "information hounds" and "hyper-information seekers" who become obsessed with gathering information about a particular topic. Fourth, individuals can gather information to share with others—either as a topic of conversation or to help them in some way. For example, a mentor might gather information helpful to his/her student's career advancement. In this book we will focus primarily on information seeking related to decision making, although reference will be made to information seeking in all of its variety (e.g., surveillance, connecting with others, stimulation, getting direction, education, socialization, etc. [Dervin, 1989]).

Information seeking can be defined simply as the purposive acquisition of information from selected information carriers. Traditional definitions of communication have often foundered on the issue of intentionality (Dance & Larson, 1976). However, here it is assumed that information seeking is primarily intentional. This intentionality is related to the accomplishment of a particular goal that the individual has in mind. Since individuals determine the value of information acquired in relation to a particular goal, information seeking is inherently a receiver-oriented construct. So, for example, I might want to gather information about various widgets so that I can make an informed choice of which widget I will propose as part of an innovative new production process I have developed. Since this activity is goal-related, it also may be more rational than communication as a whole. So, the individual may formulate an initial plan of information seeking. Some individuals may engage in what could be termed meta-information seeking. That is, they seek information about information seeking. In part that is what this book is all about: the choices individuals make in determining their information-seeking behavior.

So an individual may consult sources about what sources they should consult. At times this occurs before the start of a search, but it also may occur in a parallel fashion. That is, I initially consult some carriers, I find that they don't have enough information, then I formulate a plan for further searches. This process may continue until the individual becomes satiated, exhausted, or the time for that particular search expires.

PLAN OF THE BOOK

As we have seen, the study of information seeking is one of great pragmatic importance for individuals, organizations, and our society. It is also one that is more complex than it might at first appear, presenting many dilemmas for organizations. Individuals need to gather information on multiple contents from an ever-increasing array of carriers. In doing this, they face the limits of their past knowledge base and their ability to process information. They also must wrestle with denial and fear of the answers that may result from their search, and organizational restrictions on what kinds of information they can gather.

We will examine these issues in the chapters that follow. Chapter 2 describes the communication structure of organizations in which individual information seeking is embedded. While traditional views of structure focus on the need to restrict information access to reduce information load, more modern views try to capture how organizations can process ever larger volumes of information in increasingly complex environments. Chapter 3 describes the information fields outside the organization that an individual can draw upon. Chapter 4 develops a more complete picture of the ever-increasing number of information carriers that individuals have to select from. Chapter 5 describes the barriers to information seeking that often result from the benefits of ignorance.

The next two chapters discuss strategies for seekers and for management, given the foundation developed in the preceding chapters. Chapter 6 details strategies individuals can use in their search for information, particularly when they confront new situations. Chapter 7 discusses what management can do to facilitate searches for information. Managers typically have operated in the role of very active providers (and sometimes hoarders) of information to often obstinate audiences. However, increasingly managers must promote the information seeking of others by ensuring that they operate within rich information fields. In summary, Chapter 8 weaves the themes of the book together in discussing the importance of developing a theory of information seeking and the pragmatic implications of information seeking for our society as a whole.

TWO

HIERARCHIES, NETWORKS, AND MARKETS

In a market each element (individual, firm) pursues its own interest and the interaction between elements produces a collective outcome—the market coordinates the separate activities. Coordination by hierarchy is different in that the actions of similar elements (individuals, firms) are to some extent constrained. Hierarchy presupposes an already determined outcome or purpose; the underlying idea of hierarchy is that such an outcome can be broken down into a set of sub-processes. So hierarchy depends upon ideas of organization, task specialization and rationality. (Mitchell, 1991, p. 104)

Communication structure research, which encompasses hierarchies, markets, and networks, has always been a central area of organizational communication inquiry. Structure has five central dimensions: relationships, entities, configurations, context, and temporal stability (Johnson, 1993a). Hence, the following definition of structure: "Organizational communication structure refers to the relatively stable configuration of communication relationships between entities within an organizational context" (Johnson, 1992, p. 100). Structure provides the basic framework within which information seeking can occur in organizations.

As an example, let us look at the formal and informal communication structures of Conundrum Corporation found in Figures 2.1 and 2.2. The organizational chart in Figure 2.1 specifies the formal division of roles and the official relationships within this organization. Following the formal organizational chart, there are official rules and protocols governing the seeking and giving of information. If the Vice President of Staff Services (#3) wanted information concerning the future supply needs of Group 2 of Product A, s/he would know where the information could be found and would channel his/her request through managers 1, 2, and 4. Needless to say, this would be cumbersome

Figure 2.1
Organizational Chart for Conundrum Corporation

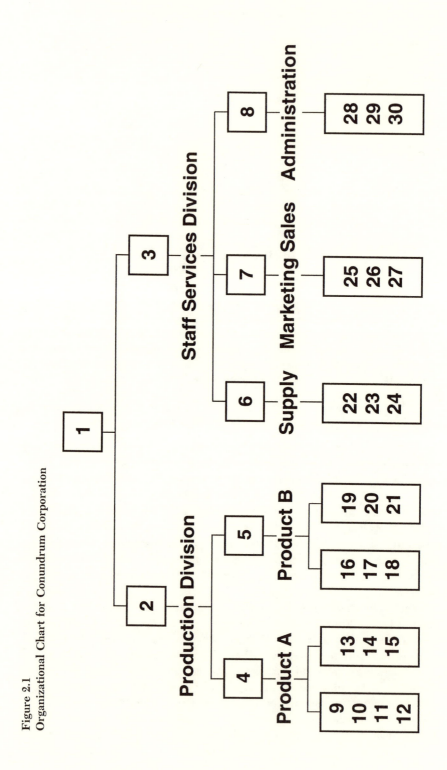

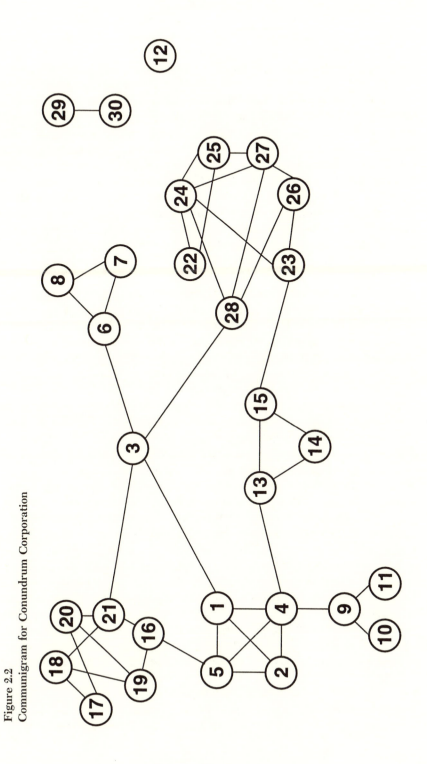

Figure 2.2
Communigram for Conundrum Corporation

and time consuming, and any one of these individuals could gatekeep information, deciding there really wasn't a need for #3 to have it.

Figure 2.2 represents the network of informal relationships in this organization in a communigram where circles represent individuals and lines show relationships among them. Gathering information within a set of informal relationships requires a different approach and set of skills than those for formal structure. Suppose that vice-president #3 has a nephew who is looking for work. S/he has heard rumors of potential marital problems involving #'s 25 and 27 in marketing that could potentially lead to 27 transferring to another division of the corporation. Number 3 remembers that 28 is on the same bowling team as these two members and asks 28 for information on the status of 25 and 27's relationship. While 28 has heard 27's side of the story, s/he usually doesn't discuss personal matters with 25. So 28 turns to 24 for information on 25's perspective. After synthesizing the information from the various sources, 28 then reports to 3 that there is a high probability that 27 will be leaving the unit soon.

In contrast to the formal structure, more idiosyncratic sources of information characterize the informal structure, which often require a certain level of experience and history in the organization. The rules governing the transmission of information are also different, with informal rather than formal norms governing what are appropriate topics of conversation. These examples illustrate that there can be considerably different approaches to seeking information within different communication structures.

Communication structure determines what is possible in large organizations since it enables action. "Networks make the achievement of output goals (such as production) possible" (Farace, Monge, & Russell, 1977, p. 179). The existing communication structure of an organization limits what is possible, if only by inertia, and at times quite formally. Without a predictable pattern of recurring relationships, coordinated activity within the organization would be impossible. The more constraints that exist, the more things occur in known, predictable patterns, the more information people have concerning the organization. "Structure is a fundamental vehicle by which organizations achieve bounded rationality" (Thompson, 1967, p. 54); structure provides organizational members with the limits within which efficiency may be a reasonable expectation.

While definitions of structure are taken for granted in the literature, a closer examination of the key components of the definition of structure is central to examining the importance of the concept and the value of the various approaches that are available for exploring it. These approaches, such as network analysis for informal structures, almost inevitably focus on one or another of the key dimensions of organizational communication structure. As such, they inherently provide only a limited perspective on the construct of the communication structure.

Relationships have been the primary focus of most recent investigations into communication structure within the field of organizational communication, since structure refers fundamentally to "a definable set of relationships which hold together a number of elements or objects in juxtaposition one with another" (Clayton, 1974, p. 221). Relationships are central to the network analysis approach that in essence views structure as a pattern of recurring communication relationships. These surface communication relationships are often manifestations of other more fundamental ways that individuals relate (e.g., status, work dependencies, roles, power, authority, influence, positions, norms). These more fundamental factors form the deep structures of interaction, with acts of communication revealing their surface manifestations (Johnson, 1993a; Richards, 1985). Thus, while people may ask each other specific questions, the underlying motivation for these questions reflects the deeper needs of the individual.

Organizations, to meet demands from their environment and to become more skilled, specialize their labor (Katz & Kahn, 1978). As a result, more and more entities emerge within the organization and, in turn, the increased number of units implies increasingly rich and diverse relationships among these entities, and greater variety in potential sources of information. These entities can range from objects to units of a system. How entities are defined determines the level of analysis of communication structure research—an increasingly important issue in management (see Dansereau & Markham, 1987 for an exhaustive discussion) and communication research (Berger & Chaffee, 1987; Monge, 1987). Information seeking can be expected to differ at various levels: intrapersonal, dyadic, and group. Task specialization within hierarchies ensures that each entity is a repository of unique information. How this information is shared with others in ongoing work processes provides a delicate balancing act that is critical to organizational success. If too much is shared, then individuals cannot appropriately specialize. If too little is shared, then there may not be a general understanding of what needs to be done. This is the fundamental dilemma for information seeking within organizations.

Structure is often viewed as an information processing tool, in part because of its role in promoting coordination between organizational entities. One clear dysfunctional aspect of a lack of structure is its effect on information load. Structure permits an organization to process more information. Since a lot of information is processed by means of specialization, it is filtered and/or condensed before it is transmitted to other units. Thus, more information can be processed, since some responsibility is delegated to particular units, so that everyone does not have to handle the same information. As a result, structure reduces information overload in organizations (Rogers & Agarwala-Rogers, 1976) and thereby increases the efficiency of their operations. Ironically, in reducing information overload, organizations reduce the availability of information, which can reduce organizational effectiveness, particularly in terms of effective decision making.

Context provides meaning and direction to the activities embodied in a particular structure. For example, Monge and Eisenberg (1987) discuss national character, socioeconomic contexts, and type of industry as among the environmental factors that can shape emerging communication networks. In this book our focus is primarily on the intraorganizational context of information seeking.

The preceding three dimensions result in an overall configuration. The various relationships between entities result in an overall pattern that forms a gestalt of the total structure within the organizational context. Examining structure moves us beyond the inherent reductionism of separate relationships to the holistic patterning of an entire system (Blair, Roberts, & McKechnie, 1985).

Structure also implies some degree of temporal stability or permanence, a relatively enduring set of linkages: "This structure gives regularity and stability to human behavior in a social system; it allows us to predict behavior with some degree of accuracy" (Rogers, 1983, p. 24). This predictability inevitably results in a reduction of uncertainty among organizational members. Temporal stability is important in increasing predictability, since organizational relationships that are enduring are also more predictable. Thus, our first choice for information will often be the individuals with whom we have a recurring relationship.

In this chapter we will explore in more detail the role that structure plays in information seeking. First, we will examine the traditional perspectives on structure represented by hierarchies. Next, we will consider network analysis, which represents an inherently more flexible approach to understanding information seeking. Finally, we will examine more modern conceptions of information seeking related to the emerging application of market concepts to organizational settings.

HIERARCHIES

If intelligence is lodged at the top, too few officials and experts with too little accurate and relevant information are too far out of touch and too overloaded to cope. On the other hand, if intelligence is scattered in many subordinate units, too many officials and experts with too much specialized information may engage in dysfunctional competition, may delay decisions while they warily consult each other, and may distort information as they pass it up. (Wilensky, 1968, p. 325)

The challenge faced by managers is how to restrict great amounts of upward communication that may result in overload, and at the same time ensure that relevant and accurate information is transmitted up the hierarchy. (Glauser, 1984, p. 615)

Early approaches to studying formal communication structure in organizations concentrated on the organizational chart and the flow of messages vertically and horizontally within it. The formal organizational chart is embedded in the assumptions of the classical approach to rational management (Morgan, 1986). It specifies very clearly who reports to whom and, in effect, constitutes a map for the routing of communication messages and for repositories of key information for those interested in information seeking (see Figure 2.1).

Recent reviews suggest (Dow, 1988; Jablin, 1987; McPhee, 1985, 1988) that formal approaches focus on the configurations resulting from the following characteristics of structure: formal authority relationships represented in the organizational hierarchy; differentiation of labor into specialized tasks; and formal mechanisms for coordination of work among these tasks. These characteristics, with the notion of goal or purpose, have been seen by some to represent the very essence of what an organization is (Schein, 1965). Indeed, hierarchies can be viewed as inevitable features of social organization (Frances et al., 1991). They provide a basic framework for information seeking by reducing the possibilities for communication. Thus, a formal structure specifies who is the official source of particular types of information.

The central impetus underlying the development of formal structures, then, is the differentiation of entities into specialized subtasks who depend on each other and must communicate to coordinate their activities. In general, information load is determined by such factors as size, transmission rules, and degree of interdependence (Downs, 1967). Organizations which severely constrain their structures substantially reduce their level of information load. The more severely constrained the structure, the more the organization is divided into autonomous groups, the less the general distribution of knowledge in an organization. Some have gone as far as to suggest that the classic forms of bureaucracy "are invitations to intelligence and communication failures" (Lee, 1970, p. 101), because of this rigid segmentation of information sources.

There are also a host of problems with downward formal communication, with management often guilty of distorting downward communication messages. Downward messages often do not arrive in a timely fashion nor are they sufficiently well targeted to ensure distribution to the proper mix of individuals. Shortcomings in downward communication often set the stage for active information seeking by lower level organizational members who want to rectify critical shortcomings in the information they receive.

Besides direct monetary benefits (e.g., withholding information about dental plans), and the presumed benefits of keeping people on edge, organizational power structures reap several other benefits from hoarding information. It is widely recognized that knowledge is power. It is no accident that those higher in the hierarchy are typically more well informed than those who are lower (Brenner & Sigband, 1973; Jablin, 1987). The purposive exclusion of groups in the organization from information deprives them of the information necessary to participate successfully in organizational decision making; interestingly, Marshall and Stohl (1993) found supervisors give lower ratings to groups who are more knowledgeable. So, for example, a common response of management to workers pressing ideas for change is that you do not have all the facts, and if you did you would hold the same position that we do. Thus, information is purposively manipulated to maintain the relative power of various groups. Lower level employees, especially skilled technicians, also accumulate power by not sharing information with management (Eisenberg & Whetten, 1987).

Probably the two biggest failures in downward communication content lie in feedback about performance and in information about organizational procedures and practices. Often organizations fail to adopt systematic means of providing members with feedback (such as appraisal interviews) or perform miserably at them (Longenecker, Gioia, & Sims, 1987). Employees are often uncertain and anxious about how well they are doing. Manipulative managers will exploit this uncertainty, feeling that the resulting stress and tension will produce higher performance. Ignorance can result in anxiety that can be manipulated to cause higher levels of effort (Moore & Tumin, 1949). These information deficits in formal communication also stimulate individuals to seek information in informal communication channels that they feel is more complete and trustworthy.

Organizations often have powerful motivations to keep employees in the dark concerning procedures and practices as well. This area raises many potential ethical questions concerning organizational behavior. For example, the cost of medical insurance is rising astronomically. Is it in the profit-making organization's best interest financially to send out complete and detailed information concerning health insurance if this is going to increase its costs? Or should its humane concern for workers offset any considerations of the cost involved? The more complete the information provided to workers, the more likely it is that they will take advantage of these costly fringe benefits.

As uncertainty reaches high levels, the traditional hierarchical approach runs into difficulty and the organization is confronted with strategies that involve a departure from traditional perspectives of coordination. Essentially the major choice an organization faces is whether to reduce the need for information processing or to increase its capacity for processing it (Galbraith, 1973; March & Simon, 1958). Organizations can be improved not by producing more information, but by reducing the amount any one subsystem must handle (Johnson & Rice, 1987). Reduction in need depends primarily on the strategies of creation of slack resources and creation of self-contained tasks, which are both aimed at reducing communication between units (Galbraith, 1973), and by implication increasing their ignorance of the operation of other units.

Increasing the capacity for information processing requires investments in vertical information systems, such as computer-based management information systems, and the creation of lateral relations that require a heavy investment in human resources. The creation of lateral resources involves much more personalized integrating mechanisms such as liaisons, task forces, and teams. These integrating devices result in a greater awareness by organizational members of each other's activities. Yet, they are extremely costly in terms of communication (Cheng, 1983; Hage, Aiken, & Marrett, 1971) and in some contexts may be inefficient (Lawrence & Lorsch, 1967).

In fact, there may be a natural tendency for organizations to develop hierarchical communication structures which segment the organization. In reviewing the literature on small group communication network studies, Shaw (1971) found clear evidence of a relationship between effectiveness in the performance of particular types of tasks and the relative degree of centralization. Shaw (1971) adopts the concept of saturation to explain these findings. For complex problems, the most central person quickly becomes overloaded with information and distracted by the burden of relaying information to other group members. However, when the group has a simple task, the volume of communication can be easily handled and there is a benefit to having a central repository of information. The independence possible in decentralized groups permits sharing the relaying burden of information among group members and also results in a better "match" of individual capabilities to the group's task.

Guetskow and Simon (1955), in an interesting twist on these experiments, speculated that one reason centralized groups were more efficient was that they had in effect been provided with a plan of action for making decisions. They discovered that if decentralized groups had an opportunity to discuss group organization after some experience with the task, they became just as efficient as more centralized groups in performing simple tasks. They became more efficient by reducing the number of communication linkages between group members. Other research studies have also suggested that there is a general trend over time for efficient groups to reduce the number of communication linkages used; in effect, to become more structured or to match their structure to the task (Katz & Kahn, 1978). Indeed, some have argued that these processes can be generalized to a broad range of systems, that hierarchies are inevitable (Krackhardt, 1989). While recent economic trends have brought hierarchies under increasing criticism, they are likely to persist for some time to come, albeit in substantially modified form (Galbraith, 1995).

Without a predictable pattern of recurring relationships, coordinated activity within the organization would be impossible. Without formal structure there would be chaos. Sometimes a little chaos is useful, but nothing can be achieved without some framework, just as not very much can be done in a totally constrained system, except what it is specifically designed to do. Formal structure reduces uncertainty, thus lending predictability to organizational activities. For organizations, this predictability is critical to the smooth functioning of day-to-day operations. Organizational members must feel confident that certain messages will flow to certain locations at certain times. Management in particular abhors unpredictability; as a result, it often spends considerable time designing organizational structures (e.g., formal organizational charts) that contribute to a subjective feeling of certainty. One reason that informal structures remained hidden in management thought for so long is that awareness of their existence inevitably diminished management's feeling of control over organizational operations. Structures are designed to minimize, or at least regulate, individual variation in organizations (Dalton et al., 1980).

The classic principle of management by exception states that managers only deal with deviations from established procedures and policies. It is natural and expected that management will not know everything that is occurring below them in the hierarchy, because if management knew everything, they would quickly become overloaded with information and unable to function. For example, if the manager of even a small, 100-person assembly plant knew everything that was going on beneath him or her, the manager would have to do the work of 100 people. So it is critical that information be condensed and removed before being given to an upper level manager. The central problem for upward communication (communication from workers to bosses) is how this can be done while retaining the critical information management needs to control current organizational activities and to direct future operations of the organization. So the flow of information needs to be restricted, even to managers, and by implication managers will be unaware of some organizational activities.

Yet, the transmission of regular, negative feedback to upper management is essential if subunits of an organization are to be integrated into the system and work to desired organizational goals (Glauser, 1984). Like all vertical communication, upward communication usually is formal, in writing, and flows along the chain of command represented by the organizational chart. Upward communication is more important for control than for coordination of organizational activities. Without adequate upward communication from workers, management cannot react to change quickly enough to prevent major problems from developing. For example, if a salesperson does not tell managers that customers are dissatisfied with the organization's product line, then the organization will not have a new product line in place when the customer's dissatisfaction becomes a decision not to buy.

Further, without feedback (workers providing management with their reaction to messages), the impact of downward communication is unknown, although many managers wrongly assume that just because an order is given, workers will do what they are told. Upward communication is also critical if an organization is to react to the problems and concerns of its workers. If workers have input into decision making through upward communication, they are more likely to react positively when decisions are implemented (Fidler & Johnson, 1984).

The context of formal structure lies in the "official world" of the organization. Most often it can be conceived of as embedded in the formal authority structure of the organization, usually associated with bureaucracy. In this context, communication is conceived as flowing along the proscribed pathways of the organizational chart, and the content of communication is limited to those production-related matters that concern the organization. While this formal approach constitutes a limited view of the role of communication in organizations, this still may be, especially operationally, the most important role of communication, and certainly one that management must at least try to control. Perhaps most importantly, the traditional view of communication structure reinforces some dangerous assumptions that managers often hold; that messages flow along the conduits represented by the organizational chart without blockage or interruption, that management is in charge, and that messages actually reach their destinations (Axley, 1984). It also suggests that information will be provided to individuals who need to know, and that therefore individuals should play a more passive role and not engage in active information seeking.

So there is a constant dilemma for organizations: the imperative, in part stemming from efficiency needs, to limit the availability of information, and the recognition that structural designs are often flawed and circumstances change, requiring individuals to seek information normally unavailable to them. However, at least in the short term, the design of the formal structure, and the rewards associated with it (e.g., promotion) often are designed specifically to discourage the sharing of information (Powell, 1990). Thus, within formal structures there are conditions that eventually require it to change (Blau, 1955). Some might argue that "to extract information from those who have it typically requires the bypassing of regular organizational structures" (Wilensky, 1968, p. 324). As we will see in the next two sections, the less formalized and centralized the structure, the easier it is for individuals to acquire information (Menon & Varadarajan, 1992).

NETWORK ANALYSIS

Because of its generality, network analysis is used by almost every social science to study specific problems, and it has been the primary means of studying communication structure in organizations over the last decade (Johnson, 1993a). It is particularly useful for analyzing information seeking because it can specify the individuals someone turns to for information, and, in turn, the sources of information for these individuals.

Network analysis is a very systematic and complete means of looking at the overall pattern of communication linkages within an organization. One way this is done is through graphic representations, such as those found in Figure 2.2. This form of graphic portrayal is very flexible, since the nodes (circles) can be any type of entity, and the linkages represented by the lines can be of any kind. These elements of graphic representations are essential to most network analysis definitions: "In general, the term "network" is taken to mean a set of *units* (or *nodes*) of some kind and the *relations* of specific types that occur among them" (Alba, 1982, p. 42).

In recent years, a critical issue facing network analysis has been the consequences of an individual's membership in multiple networks of relationships of different kinds. Multiplexity classically refers to the nature of overlap, or correspondence, between differing networks (e.g., friendship as opposed to work) (Farace & Mabee, 1980; Rogers & Kincaid, 1981). The nature of overlaps between networks is of great pragmatic concern, since it can suggest the inherent capabilities of individual actors within systems, and it also has rich implications for the understanding of social systems generally (Reynolds & Johnson, 1982; Roberts & O'Reilly, 1979). At its heart, multiplexity refers to the extent to which different types of network relationships overlap: "The relation of one person to another is multiplex to the extent that there is more than one type of relation between the first person and the second" (Burt, 1983, p. 37).

The degree of multiplexity has been related to such issues as the intimacy of relationships (Minor, 1983), temporal stability of relationships (Minor, 1983; Mitchell, 1969; Rogers & Kincaid, 1981), reduction of uncertainty (Albrecht & Ropp, 1984), status (Albrecht & Ropp, 1984), the degree of control of a clique over its members (Rogers & Agarwala-Rogers, 1976), performance (Roberts & O'Reilly, 1979), redundancy of channels (Mitchell, 1969), and the diffusion of information within networks (Minor, 1983). The breadth of someone's linkages might serve to provide an individual with a variety of information sources, as well as repetition of certain effects, such as attitude change.

The strength of weak ties, which is a special case of multiplexity, is perhaps the most well-known concept related to network analysis. It refers to less developed, uniplex relationships that are limited in space, place, time, and depth of emotional bonds (Adelman, Parks, & Albrecht, 1987; Weimann, 1983). This concept has been intimately tied to the flow of information within organizations, and by definition is removed from stronger social bonds, such as influence and multiplex relations (Weimann, 1983).

Weak ties notions are derived from the work of Granovetter (1973) on how people get information related to potential jobs. It turns out that the most useful information comes from individuals in a person's extended networks—casual acquaintances and friends of friends. This information is the most useful precisely because it comes from infrequent or weak contacts. Strong contacts are likely to be people with whom there is a constant sharing of the same information, as a result, individuals within these groupings have come to have the same information base. But information from outside this base gives unique perspectives and, in some instances, strategic advantages over competitors in a person's immediate network.

Weak ties are also crucial to integrating larger social systems, especially in terms of the nature of communication linkages between disparate groups (Friedkin, 1980, 1982; Weimann, 1983). Granovetter (1982) maintains that this bridging function between different groups is a limiting condition necessary for the effects of weak ties to be evidenced. However, weak ties may be discouraged in organizations because of concerns over loyalty to one's immediate work unit and questions of control of organizational members. Strong ties also are preferred because of their stability, accessibility, and heightened responsiveness (Granovetter, 1982).

Weak ties provide critical informational support because they transcend the limitations of our strong ties, and because, as often happens in organizations, our strong ties can be disrupted or unavailable (Adelman, Parks, & Albrecht, 1987). They may be useful for: discussing things you do not want to reveal to your close work associates, providing a place for an individual to experiment, extending access to information, promoting social comparison, and fostering a sense of community (Adelman, Parks, & Albrecht, 1987). Naturally, when individuals need unique, novel information, processes associated with weak ties have great significance for information seeking.

The Liaison Role

An individual's network communication role is determined by the overall pattern of his/her communication relationships (or linkages) with others. Some individuals, labeled nonparticipants (e.g., isolates), have few communication contacts with others (e.g., 12, 29, and 30 in Figure 2.2). Participants, on the other hand, form intense patterns of linkages that represent communication groups and linkages between these groups (e.g., 5, 15, and 18). Several research studies have found key differences between these two kinds of individuals, with participants being more outgoing, influential, satisfied (Goldhaber et al., 1978) and having more coherent cognitive structures (Albrecht, 1979), and nonparticipants deliberately withholding information, having lower satisfaction with communication (Roberts & O'Reilly, 1979), reporting less identification, variety, feedback, and required interaction (Moch, 1980). Obviously these patterns of findings have interesting implications for the pattern of information seeking within organizations.

The most important communication role is that of a liaison (3 in Figure 2.2) (see Reynolds & Johnson, 1982, for a systematic review). The liaison links two or more communication groups, while not being a member of any one group. This strategic positioning of liaisons has earned them the label of "linking pins," who, through their promotion of more positive climates and successful coordination of organizational functions, serve to hold an organization together (Likert, 1967). The role of the liaison in the coordination and control of organizational activities is closely tied to the concepts of integration and differentiation. That is, as the organization divides into more and more groups, greater efforts have to be made at pulling these groups together through integrating mechanisms (Galbraith, 1973; Lawrence & Lorsch, 1967). These integrating mechanisms are crucial to organizational survival since, without them, the organization would be a collection of groups each going off in its own direction. Typically, liaisons are the most efficient personal integrating mechanisms because of their strategic positioning. Due to their centrality and their direct linkages with others, liaisons reduce the probability of message distortion and increase the timeliness of communication. They are also likely to be the most skilled information seekers within organizations, as well as the primary target of initial information seeking for others.

Unfortunately, liaisons are rare in organizations; this is reflected in the generally low level of communication between diverse groups in organizations (Farace & Johnson, 1974). Given their central role in organizational operations, it is important to understand the factors that make it more likely that an individual will come to assume this role. These factors, summarized in Figure 2.3, also relate directly to the capacity of individuals to seek, secure, and process information.

Relational factors often cause liaison emergence. Since network analysis is essentially a means of representing patterns of linkages, the quality of these relationships becomes an important determinant of the patterns of linkages for individuals. For a liaison, one such relational factor that is of critical importance is openness, or a willingness to impart or accept information. If information is to flow freely in an organization, then it is critical that network participants maintain open communication relationships. The research results summarized in Reynolds and Johnson (1982) suggest that liaisons are more open in their communication with other organizational members; with liaisons being more receptive to differing types of communication encounters, and often sought out by others in their communication networks. Indeed, liaisons may emerge because others initiate contact with them. Blau (1955) found in studying a government agency, for example, that more competent agents did not initiate more communication with others, but were sought out much more often by others. Liaisons are sources of scarce and valuable information, which results from the wide diversity of their contacts.

Another set of factors relating to a liaison's emergence is his/her cognitive abilities. Because the liaison stands at the center of organizational groups, this role has unique information processing demands. Liaisons must process information from diverse sources whose messages are couched in different technical languages. In organizational contexts, the liaison's information processing abilities have been associated with cognitive complexity. The highly cognitively complex individual can recognize important differences between bits of information (differentiation); perceive the relative significance of these bits (discrimination); and, finally, assimilate a great variety of information into coherent and/or novel perspectives (integration) (Schroder, Driver, & Streufert, 1967). Several empirical studies have found a relationship between cognitive complexity and network positions (Albrecht, 1979; Schreiman & Johnson, 1975; Zajonc & Wolfe, 1966).

While relational and cognitive factors are essential to a liaison's role performance and are necessary for liaison emergence, motivational factors determine whether or not an individual will aspire to such a role and perform effectively within it. The emergent nature of network linkages is in part a picture of the more voluntary and spontaneous choices that organizational

Figure 2.3
A Model of Factors Related to Liaison Emergence

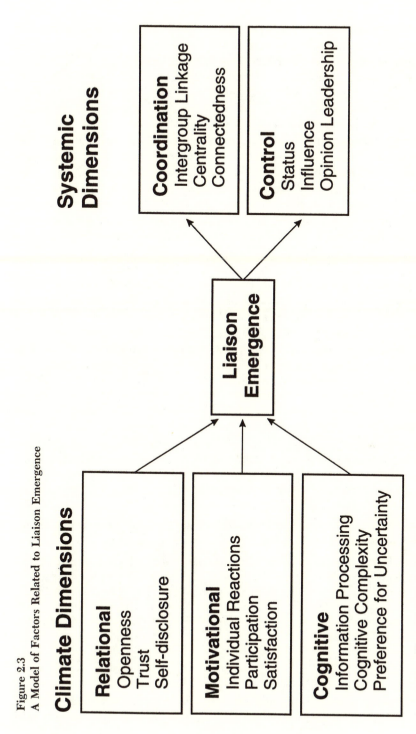

Climate Dimensions

Relational
Openness
Trust
Self-disclosure

Motivational
Individual Reactions
Participation
Satisfaction

Cognitive
Information Processing
Cognitive Complexity
Preference for Uncertainty

Liaison Emergence

Systemic Dimensions

Coordination
Intergroup Linkage
Centrality
Connectedness

Control
Status
Influence
Opinion Leadership

Source: Reynolds & Johnson, 1982, p. 588.

members make in their communication relationships. Linkages also describe, in part, the need-fulfillment strategies of organizational members. Typically, liaisons in production communication networks can be said to fit into the classification of upwardly mobile individuals in organizations (Presthus, 1962). The needs of upwardly mobile individuals are fulfilled within the organization. They are active seekers of information, who constantly monitor the organization for information useful to their advancement.

Traditionally, control in organizations has been viewed as occurring within the formal communication structure. Roberts and O'Reilly (1979) have argued that effective control in an organization corresponds to the extent to which networks link critical task groups. Increasingly, management functions can be viewed as similar to those of a liaison, a factor reflected in the finding that liaisons tend to be managers. An effective manager must perceive coherent patterns from diverse information inputs and must form clear judgments that can serve as the basis for organizational action. Yet only a minority of managers occupy liaison positions in informal communication networks.

The liaison role points to the convergence of network analysis and formal approaches. In new organizational forms, new demands are placed on formal integrators who must link several interdependent organizations who are acting together as a coalition (Galbraith, 1995). The liaison role is a precursor of the growing interests in markets, which makes critical assumptions about the motivations for voluntary interactions and the basic relational qualities necessary for the functioning of social systems.

MARKETS

Markets are arrangements which coordinate the actions of large numbers of people automatically, and on a lateral basis, through the operation of the price mechanism, without infringing their freedom or requiring inequalities of status. (Beetham, 1987, p. 136)

Prices embody a crucial information system that suits a decentralized decision making environment. (Frances et al., 1991, p. 9)

[I]n the bazaar information is poor, scarce, maldistributed, inefficiently communicated, and intensely valued. . . . The level of ignorance about everything from product quality and going prices to market possibilities and production costs is very high, and much of the way in which the bazaar functions can be interpreted as an attempt to reduce such ignorance for someone, increase it for someone, or defend someone against it. (Geertz, 1978, p. 29)

Recently, yet another view of structure—a market approach—which shares much with both network and formal approaches, and rests on economic and exchange assumptions, has begun to emerge (Nohria & Eccles, 1992). Markets, through the mechanisms of exchanges, operate to diffuse information rapidly to interested parties (von Hayek, 1989). Some have suggested that the opposite of centralization is not decentralization (which still keeps a focus on traditional hierarchical relationships) but rather the forces of mutual adjustment characteristic of the market (Cleveland, 1985).

By focusing on exchanges, it provides a compelling theoretical focus for the development of relationships between interactants, who may otherwise lack compelling motives to interact. We may seek exchanges with others because they are not like us and they have resources that we do not possess. This view also suggests a broader conception of information as something that can be shaped and modified in exchanges, then interpreted in different ways in the collectivity as exchanges proceed. Markets have an inherently dynamic view of information exchanges, with individuals compelled to change their ideas because of the reactions of others. This contrasts directly with the view of information in a hierarchical approach as an unchanging commodity that should be passed with minimum transformations from one part of the organization to others (Powell, 1990).

While markets have been viewed as occurring outside the context of formal organizations, they have been recognized as containing many authority properties found in organizations, and organizations with complex, multidivisional structures take on market characteristics (Eccles & White, 1988). "The internal operations of real-world firms are controlled by a blend of authority and market-like mechanisms" (McGuinness, 1991, p. 66). Thus, internal organizational equivalents of the Securities and Exchange Commission may be put in place to enforce rules of fair trading and to ensure that everyone in an organization is on an equal footing. In part, organizations that have ethics boards, such as Dow-Corning, are protecting the nature of relationships between interactants within organizations.

The rules governing interactions primarily are in place to ensure fair trading. The best outcomes in a market perspective are thought to occur from individuals pursuing their self-interest in a welfare maximizing manner. However, this also suggests that individuals can operate in an unscrupulous manner. Trust is an essential ingredient of long-term collaborative relationships in collectivities (Powell, 1990), and may be the most important attribute of network relations (Burt, 1992; Frances et al., 1991). Trust has also been strongly related to both the frequency and the accuracy of upward communication (Glauser, 1984). In markets, individuals come to depend on a limited range of others who they can trust to provide them information concerning various market conditions; but, paradoxically, these others also can be competitors who seek competitive advantage within the limits of desiring to maintain a continuing relationship (Geertz, 1978). The delicate balancing act between competition and cooperation in information exchange also goes to the heart of interpersonal relationships in new organizational forms such as the virtual organization (Galbraith, 1995).

Of course, trust may have many bases: process-based trust results from recurrent transactions; characteristic-based trust results from social similarity; and institutionally based trust is tied to formal social structures (Bradach & Eccles, 1989). Thus, organizational members would be more likely to trust individuals with whom they have had past successful relationships, who are like themselves, within an organization that has strong norms of conduct and associated penalties.

In a pure market, with a multitude of other traders, protection against malfeasance would not be essential, since individuals could quickly replace "unfair" relationships with fair ones (Granovetter, 1985). Still, very few intraorganizational contexts can be said to be characterized by unlimited choices; so mechanisms must be in place to protect the weak from the powerful. For example, in the natural sciences, within university settings, professors who are principal investigators on grants have enormous fate control over graduate students. The graduate students in turn have very limited options in terms of faculty members with whom they can work. Without strong mentoring norms and procedures to protect them, graduate students are literally at the mercy of faculty members.

The nature of these relationships is determined by notions inherent in exchange, achieving a fair price for a good or service. Price is an extremely effective summary means of communicating knowledge, indicating such things as what is valued and how scarce a commodity is (Gurbaxani & Whang, 1991). In pure market exchange relationships, the only thing that may matter is the value of the goods exchanged. Yet determination of the price for any piece of information is an intractable historical problem in economics (Bates, 1990; Stigler, 1961).

While information can be considered a commodity, it is one whose value depends greatly on its scarcity; thus, open access to it, or differential access, can cause wide fluctuations in price. So, by increasing the barriers to information seeking and privacy, organizations may be paradoxically increasing its value, ensuring that someone will expend the effort to acquire it (Smithson, 1989). Often there is also considerable uncertainty about the value of information and its applicability to various organizational problems (Bates, 1990). One indication of the level of organizational ignorance is wide fluctuation in prices (Stigler, 1961). A benefit of effective information seeking is driving down the costs of any information that is gathered—a considerable benefit of the search process (Stigler, 1961).

In network-based exchanges, normative controls also can be operative in the relationship (Powell, 1990; Lorenz, 1989) and the consequences of untrustworthy behavior may cloud concurrent and future interactions. For those organizational members who are unscrupulous in their relationships, the possibility of their behavior being sanctioned internally provides a positive incentive to interact outside the firm (Eccles & White, 1988). For example, the unscrupulous principal investigator on a large grant may develop relationships with others outside the normatively controlled departmental or invisible college setting.

Networks of information exchanges, which also contain market elements, are particularly useful structures for organizations composed of highly skilled workforces who possess knowledge not limited to particular tasks (Powell, 1990). More generally, it has been argued that knowledge flows may be best done within informal organizational structures because of problems in recognizing the significance of information and communicating it effectively and efficiently (Gupta & Govindarajan, 1991). This form of decentralization often reduces the possibility of information overload, and attendant delays and imperfect planning orders. Especially in organizations with substantial research and technology emphases, it may be better to minimize intrusive formal structures and promote wide-ranging interactions, while providing a framework in which trading relationships can occur.

The availability of information concerning costs and beneficial exchanges is critical to the operation of a pure market, since inadequate information is one source of market failure. Thus, markets place a premium on information seeking. Inadequate information can take many forms. One set deals with problems in price and trust that go to the heart of exchange relationships (Levacic, 1991). Sellers are likely to know more about the quality of information they provide, thus creating information asymmetries that rules in markets are designed to overcome (Nayyar, 1993). Opportunistic sellers selectively reveal, distort, and withhold information, if they perceive they can do so without penalty (Lorenz, 1989; McGuinness, 1991). Another set of issues deals with uncertainties, especially concerning future (and often unknown) contingencies (Levacic, 1991). Of course, acting in a market (and observation of the actions of others) produces essential feedback and critical information that can be used dynamically to refine future market behavior (Krizner, 1973). Information technologies also play an increasingly critical role in the operation of internal organizational markets (Gurbaxani & Whang, 1991).

The market approach, especially as it relates to transaction costs, has been used to specify those conditions under which an organization will try to subsume certain relationships under its formal umbrella. Uncertain transactions that recur frequently and require substantial investments of money, time, or energy are more likely to occur within a hierarchy. These transactions offset the "costs" of bureaucracy because they provide a means (e.g., formal structure) for adjudicating unforeseen problems in the relationship and the naturally opportunistic impulses of actors are controlled by authority relationships (Granovetter, 1985; Powell, 1990, discussing the work of Williamson). In this view, organizations are islands of planned coordination relationships embedded in a sea of market relationships (Powell, 1990).

Structural Holes as an Exemplar

Ron Burt (1992) recently has articulated the concept of structural holes in such a way that he brings together the themes developed in this chapter, explaining in more detail such phenomena as weak ties. He argues that much of market-oriented competitive behavior can be understood in terms of the access of individuals to "holes" in network structures. Holes are discontinuities in a social structure that create opportunities for information access to certain actors. For example, if two formal divisions that need to interact (e.g., product development and engineering) do not have formal integration links, then the individuals in these units who establish informal bridge or liaison linkages have a competitive advantage over their peers. While these ties may be weak, adding to the arguments presented earlier, they are also positioned in such a way as to provide unique information. Individuals can turn such relationships into "social capital" that gives them strategic advantage in the competition for scarce resources in an organization, such as promotions.

The information benefits of structural positioning revolve around the classic question of who knows about opportunities, who participates, and when do they participate. Individuals who are correctly positioned (e.g., 3 in the communigram in Figure 2.2) know about key pieces of information earlier than others because of their unique pattern of ties. They also can gatekeep the distribution (or at least slow the progress) of this information to others, and they may have an idea of when and how the information is likely to diffuse to others in the social system.

They also can refer the information to targeted others who serve as their allies. Thus, if there is a training program associated with a key new technology in the organization, an adept individual can alert his/her subordinates, who will then be in the forefront of developments and can keep their mentor informed. Taking these active steps moves an actor beyond the acquisition of information to the active control and manipulation of organizational resources based on the information acquired. Thus, players can be "pulled" into entrepreneurial action by the promise of success.

Perhaps the most interesting application to date of the structural holes arguments comes in its implication for promotions. Burt (1992) has found that managers with networks rich in structural holes get promoted faster and at a younger age than their competitors. This is partially because the higher one goes in organizations, the more promotion rests on what can be accomplished with others. Not only do these managers have the benefits described earlier, but they also are known to others in the organization, and may develop champions in unlikely places that are critical to their career paths. In this connection, one of the least effective strategies is to build strong, redundant relationships with one's immediate supervisor. When a supervisor does praise a worker, s/he is often by implication praising him or herself ("Look what a brilliant employee I have developed"). The supervisor also has a vested interest in protecting his/her investment by not advertising this unique resource to competitors. So, by building relationships with diverse others for information seeking, an employee also may be indirectly accomplishing other, more personal, ends as well.

INFORMATION SEEKING AND STRUCTURE

Together, these three models (hierarchies, networks, and markets) are the major competing explanations for the coordination of all social life, including life within organizations (Frances et al., 1991). Market perspectives essentially argue that coordination occurs automatically because of the self-interest of individual actors; in hierarchies, control is consciously and overtly exercised. Yet both these approaches neglect the informal forces characteristic of networks of interdependent relationships (Frances et al., 1991).

In many ways, hierarchies, markets, and networks are idealized concepts that may not exist anywhere in pure form (Bradach & Eccles, 1989). With formal structure, a market approach shares a concentration on central rules governing relationships between interactants, and, with network analysis, market approaches share a focus on emergent relationships between actors in a collectivity. In much of the literature on the interrelationship between markets, hierarchies, and networks, hierarchies are fairly close to the meaning of formal approaches developed earlier; yet networks have a much more narrow meaning, coming to reflect primarily the more informal trusting relationships that develop in ongoing associations (Thompson et al., 1991). Formal structure also can be encompassed within network conceptions (Monge & Eisenberg, 1987), so both hierarchical and market approaches could be considered to be special cases of networks (Frances et al., 1991).

Since network analysis is the more general technique, it can cover a wider range of phenomena than either formal or market approaches. Inherent in the idea of networks is also a greater range of flexibility in relationships and entities examined. For example, the context of formal approaches is the official world of the organization, while the context of markets is limited by the nature of the substances exchanged between parties. Network analysis subsumes both these contexts and other contexts as well, including political coalitions, friendship networks, etc. Thus, both formal and market approaches examine a limited set of information-seeking behaviors.

Table 2.1 describes the relative strengths of each approach to communication structure for various dimensions of information seeking. For formal approaches, the constraints on information seeking are determined by official rules and job requirements. On the other hand, information seeking in markets is determined by what can be exchanged, trust factors, and the few central rules governing the relationship. Thus, a supervisor might compel subordinates to share information in a formal perspective, or a supervisor could give a subordinate a piece of information valuable to the subordinate (e.g., you can apply to a new training program in a month, get your materials ready), and in exchange the subordinate might give the supervisor information about a work problem developing in another team. All three frameworks—formal, network, and markets—provide unique perspectives on processes of information seeking within organizations.

Table 2.1
Relationships between Structures and Information Seeking

Information Seeking Dimensions	Formal	Structure Network	Markets
Context	Official	Varied	Limited
Motive Force	Work Demands	Many	Information Exchange Needs
Constraints	Many Formal Rules	Informal Norms	Limited Set of Central Rules
Bases of Exchange	Attempts to Rationalize, Legalistic	Many Types of Relationships	Information
Individually Negotiated Relationships	Minimal	Pluralistic, Subgroups	Idiosyncratic
Sentiments	Minimal	Cliques, Localized Group Structures, Personal Ties	Trust Develops in Ongoing Relations

THREE

INFORMATION FIELDS

Information seeking can be broadly related to two major sources of influence on the individual. First, there is a set of utilitarian imperatives that demand certain levels of information seeking by the individual that relate to task requirements. These requirements often transcend the embedded, physical elements of the organization and compel individuals to seek information wherever it might be.

Second, there is a set of forces embedded in an individual's immediate physical and social environment, called their information fields, which stimulate an individual to seek certain types of information and that also incidentally expose individuals to ambient information they were not actively seeking. This type of accidental exposure may cue people to more active searches.

An individual's information field provides the context and the starting point for individual information seeking. Thus, information fields represent the typical arrangement of information stimuli to which an individual is daily exposed. Information fields contain resources, constraints, and carriers of information that influence the nature of an individual's information seeking (Hagarstrand, 1953; Archea, 1977). For an upper level manager this information field might be incredibly rich, including access to computerized information retrieval, specialists, other managers the individual knows personally, and subscriptions to a wide array of publications. On the other hand, a lower level organizational employee, in a remote outpost of the organization, might be limited in the sources he/she can easily consult for information.

Individuals are embedded in a physical world that involves recurring contacts with an interpersonal network of managers and co-workers. They are also exposed to the same mediated communication channels (company news bulletins, local newspapers, television news, etc.) on a regular basis. Typically, an individual's local information field consists of an interpersonal communication network and information terminals (e.g., fax machines), both of which are embedded within a physical context. This physical context serves to stabilize an individual's information fields, and in large part determines the nature of the information individuals are exposed to on a regular basis.

The constraints of an individual's information field limit the degree to which that individual can act on his/her predispositions to seek information. The information field an individual is located in constrains the very possibility of selecting particular sources of information. Yet individuals can, if they so desire, arrange elements of their information fields to maximize their surveillance of professionally related information. They can regularly scrutinize company memoranda and subscribe to trade magazines with high proportions of professionally related content. In other words, individuals who are more concerned with their jobs are likely to mold their information fields to include a richer mixture of organizationally related information sources.

How they shape this field over time determines not only their knowledge of general organizational issues, but also their incidental exposure to information that stimulates them to more purposive information seeking. Thus, in a sense, individuals are embedded in a field that acts on them; this is the more traditional view of organizational communication. Yet individuals also make choices about the nature of their fields: the types of media they attend to, the friendships they form, and their professional specializations, which are often based on their information needs.

The nature of an individual's stable information field can shape his/her more active information seeking, since it provides a starting point for more active information searches. Naturally, an information field can change to reflect changes in an individual's life, which at times are also directly related to changing information seeking demands. For example, when an individual is assigned to an ad hoc group focusing on a major new organizational product line, his/her interpersonal network changes to include other workers who are proximate during the project. S/he also may be exposed to a greater array of mediated communication (e.g., pamphlets, videotapes, etc.) concerning the nature of this project. Thus, as individuals become more focused in their information seeking, they change the nature of their information field to support the acquisition of information related to particular purposes. In this sense, individuals act strategically to achieve their ends, and in doing so construct local, temporary communication structures and fields that mirror these interests.

This chapter will focus on three key elements of information fields. First, we will examine the physical factors that provide the initial context for information seeking activities. Second, we will discuss the interpersonal networks in which the individual is embedded; the relative diversity of these networks determines the success of searches for novel information. Third, we will focus on the increasingly turbulent and rich world of information outside the organization.

PHYSICAL FACTORS

Physical factors associated with location and mobility constrain who we can easily access for information. Physical space also influences the meanings given to interactions within it. The physical environment is rich in symbolic artifacts (Davis, 1984) that can be the object of information seeking. So, while office arrangements with closed doors promote the sharing of confidential information, they also promote the perception that there are secrets within the organization for only the privileged few.

The primary force underlying physical structure is the effect it has on spatial relationships between interactants. Particularly important initially is the dispersion of locations of actors throughout an organization. While physical locations may be attributable to many factors (e.g., cultural), in organizations these locations are largely tied to technologies. Location can determine the information one is privy to and thus one's inclusion or exclusion from other organizational processes (Davis, 1984). It provides a static framework within which interaction is embedded.

Two variables reveal contrasting dimensions of spatial relationships and their impact on an individual's information seeking: social density, or the number of interactants in a space; and proximity, which refers to the spatial distances between interactants. Social density affects the opportunities for communication (Form, 1972). An optimal array of interactants within one's physical environment can promote growth and intellectual stimulation (Sundstrom, Burt, & Kamp, 1980) and at least moderate levels of social density are essential for a rich information environment (Szilagyi & Holland, 1980). In addition, members of a culture who share the same physical space are exposed to the same ambient stimuli, thus providing them with a common experiential base and opportunity to jointly interpret events (Hackman, 1983).

Proximity is the spatial factor that has traditionally been most clearly related to communication processes (Guetskow, 1965). Generally, proximity relates to task-related information seeking by increasing information exchange, coordination linkages, and feedback (Szilagyi & Holland, 1980). One direct way of determining an individual's interpersonal information field is by the probabilities of communicating with others at various distances from an individual's physical location. These probabilities sharply diminish with distance from an interactant's position (Hagarstrand, 1953). Allen (1977) describes access in research and development laboratories as determined by gradually diminishing communication up to 50 feet away from an interactant, with communication beyond that characterized by a dramatic dropoff. Both Allen and Hagarstrand suggest that individuals typically interact with others who can be found within a very limited physical radius.

The physical environment of the organization also can be seen as a space containing a set of locations or places each differing in their access to information (Canter & Kenney, 1975), particularly information from outside an immediate physical location. To fully understand information seeking, we should be concerned with the means by which the environment transduces, amplifies, contrasts, or otherwise mediates the appearance of available information (Archea, 1977). "An information *terminal* is a point within an informal social setting at which information is either entered into or retrieved from a formal communication network or information storage system" (Archea, 1977, p. 126).

Information terminals are technological features that considerably increase communication levels at particular locations. They also can serve to expand someone's access to information. If a terminal is proximate, then the range of interactants that individuals can contact is expanded and spatial limitations can be overcome to a certain degree. Enhanced information access through a rich information field also raises the probability that individuals will be stimulated to seek out information. Increasingly, open areas that promote access to information are being used in R & D settings. These areas provide an informal setting for face-to-face interaction, and they also often provide teleconferencing facilities for interactions with others off-site. So, an individual whose office opens onto this area can easily keep track of the ongoing activities of others in their unit, and might be stimulated to ask questions concerning aspects of it that relate to their projects.

While both social density and proximity act to determine the access of individuals to each other, access is also affected by the relative mobility of individuals, which is also directly related to channel selection. Increasing mobility can be a direct result of technologies, but the necessity for this mobility can stem from utilitarian imperatives associated with problem solving as well. Information-seeking imperatives often demand that individuals transcend their local physical environment to seek out others on whom they depend for information. At this point, utilitarian concerns result in individual's seeking alternative pathways or channels for reaching distant others (Culnan, 1983).

Spatial factors can determine the method by which we reach other interactants. The dramatic dropoffs in communication contacts, related to distance, may be the point at which an individual chooses to go to another plane, such as electronic channels in his/her interaction with another. While increases in social density and in proximity increase our physical access to others, we are, of course, not limited in our information seeking to just those in our immediate physical environment. Access can be enhanced by various mediated technologies that, in effect, create electronic propinquity in Korzenney's (1978) terms. Thus, differing technologies (e.g., telephones, faxes) profoundly affect the spatial dispersion of communication activities across physical spaces. Therefore, spatial factors affect channel selection in determinant ways (Reinsch & Beswick, 1990) and mediated channels can be viewed as the communicative surrogate of mobility. In this second sense, then, an individual's information field can expand to meet special needs. As we will see in the next chapter, the choice of channels is often the first, and perhaps the most important, step in information seeking.

INTERPERSONAL ENVIRONMENT

The nature of an individual's interpersonal environment, or social fields (Perin, 1991), has important consequences for information seeking (Lenz, 1984). An individual's effective network consists of friends, family members, and other close associates, while an extended network of weak ties is composed of casual acquaintances and friends of friends, who, because they have different contacts than the focal individual, can provide him/her with unique information.

The human environment of organizations provides another basic element of the context for information seeking. Recently, several new approaches to research in this area have developed. For example, organizational demography examines the composition of the human membership of the organization in terms of basic attributes like sex and age (Pfeffer, 1982). The distribution of attributes in an organization's population has important consequences for organizations and their members. This is particularly so in terms of communication, because of the natural tendency of people to communicate with others like themselves (Rogers, 1983; Tsui & O'Reilly, 1989; Zenger & Lawrence, 1989). As a result, minority groups have special difficulties in their information seeking that could be attributable primarily to the proportion of their members in an organization.

There is some suggestive evidence that demographic factors, particularly those associated with larger societal trends (e.g., competitiveness stemming from a particularly large age cohort), impact dyadic relationships, such as the supervisor–subordinate communication relationship, in several ways (Jablin & Krone, 1987). First, demographic factors may affect recruitment practices and the degree to which an organization will defer to members once recruited. Second, they may affect modes of control. For example, a large number of new members represented in a growing organization may ensure bureaucratic versus cultural forms of control, since the new members have not had the time to be properly socialized. In any event, the higher the ratio of new members to old, the greater the proportion of communication that needs to be directed to the socialization of new members (McNeil & Thompson, 1971) and, in turn, much of the new members' information seeking reflects their concern for finding out what the organization is "really" like (Miller & Jablin, 1991). A third issue related to demography is intercohort conflict. If a supervisor is a member of a different demographic grouping, as well as in a privileged position, this might further impede the development of relational qualities such as openness and sharing of information in his/her relationships with subordinates.

A common theme related to demographic research, which bears directly on information seeking, is the relative isolation of certain groups. For example, Allen (1977) has found in research and development laboratories that non-Ph.D.'s were isolated from Ph.D.'s. This isolation was due primarily to status differences; while non-Ph.D.'s could enhance their status by communicating with Ph.D.'s, Ph.D.'s would suffer a decrease in their status. Similarly, non-Ph.D.'s communicating with each other reinforced their low status position. As a result, non-Ph.D.'s did not communicate widely in these organizations and felt limited in selecting individuals as sources of information.

The most researched issues related to organizational demography focus on proportional imbalances in organizational membership. Kanter (1977) has argued that the integration of organizational members whose attributes were different from the work group majority was a function of their relative minority status. Tokens who represent a small minority (say 15 percent of organizational members) are subject to considerable pressures because of their visibility and uniqueness. However, as the balance becomes more even, the impacts of different attributes become less pronounced.

One of the most important impacts of tokenism is the isolation of token individuals from informal communication networks composed of majority members (Fairhurst, 1986). For example, Brass (1985) found in a newspaper publishing company, with roughly equal numbers of men and women, that men and women were not well integrated into each other's communication networks, and that women were not well integrated into the dominant coalition. A follow-up indicated that, in this organization, promotions were significantly related to an individual's centrality in departmental, men's, and dominant coalition interaction networks.

While Kanter's ideas related to proportional imbalances are provocative, they have been systematically criticized. For example, Fairhurst and Snavely (1983) argue that power and status attenuate these relationships and decrease the potential impacts of token status. Tokens can offset numerical disadvantages by increasing the importance of their power bases, their influence on decision making, and increasing their individual power skills (Fairhurst & Snavely, 1983). In research designed to assess their critique of Kanter, Fairhurst and Snavely (1983) found that male tokens were not isolated communicatively from their organizational networks.

Another central question related to proportion concerns the impact of the distribution of relational states (see Kanter, 1977; Pfeffer, 1982). For example, can I be open and share information when all others in my environment are closed? This issue could also be related to a variety of relational characteristics (e.g., trust and credibility). Although openness is crucial to organizational effectiveness generally—and to information seeking specifically—there is considerable evidence that subordinates are unwilling to be open (Jablin, 1978), with recent arguments that openness may not be beneficial in all circumstances, especially in terms of individual consequences (Eisenberg & Whetten, 1987).

If individuals enter the organization with an essentially open approach to their relationships with others, what factors can cause this approach to change? One factor that might lead to change is the experience of asymmetry, that is, some others with whom the person has relations act in a closed manner. Now the key issue is at what point does the perception of closed relationships cause an individual to change his/her behavior? Does just one particularly devastating experience cause change, or is it likely that a substantial proportion of relationships with others have to be closed to lead to a negative reaction? Or is the person more discriminating? Does s/he reciprocate and behave toward others as these others behave toward him/her? Does the person have closed relationships with only those people with whom he/she is at risk (e.g., I want something from them, or they can punish me in some way)? This guardedness might dissipate over time if a certain level of trust has been built up.

Issues of proportion, both of relationships and of prior experience, can have a substantial impact on the formation of informal networks and resulting information seeking. Naturally if a person has had consistently negative experiences, or consistently positive ones, s/he can be expected to respond with less or more openness, respectively, and contract or spread their contacts narrowly or widely. The really interesting issue is at what point between these extremes does the individual tendency to react become more negative.

Jablin's (1978) study, which examined the content of messages within the supervisor–subordinate communication relationship, suggests that only a minimum amount of negative messages, especially those concerning the underlying relationship between the two parties, can act to close off a supervisor–subordinate communication relationship. Jablin (1978) argues that reciprocal acceptance by both parties is crucial to an open relationship. The individual must perceive that both their messages and who they are as a person will be responded to positively before they will choose to be open. In an atmosphere of closed relationships, the individual may not feel that this essential precondition is being fulfilled. Subordinates are more likely to distort information when they perceive their supervisors are actively withholding information or are politically motivated (Jablin, 1981). This, of course, has substantial implications for information seeking and the broader issue of sharing information, and may compel individuals to seek information beyond the confines of their organization.

INFORMATION ENVIRONMENTS

While the primary focus of this book is on information seeking within organizations, naturally the information environment represented in the world outside the organization is also important. The information environment affects internal organizational information seeking in several ways. First, the world outside the organization is often the primary source of highly technical, specialized information, especially for professionals like engineers. Cosmopolitan organizational members often consider organizational boundaries to be artificial and do not, often to the consternation of upper level managers, view information as proprietary.

Professionals in different organizations share information with each other informally (e.g., TGIFs, association meetings) and formally (e.g., trade journals). Scientists also form invisible colleges that share information and act as a resource for their members in information searches. The most productive scientists are often those who communicate most outside the boundary of the organization (Allen, 1966). These invisible colleges then cut across the membership of more formal organizations localized in particular geographic areas. In many ways, information seeking in this context is a special case of intraorganizational information seeking since the invisible college has many characteristics of an organization. In this instance, the individual is really a member of multiple networks with different information-seeking functions.

Second, environments create imperatives for organizations to seek certain kinds of information (Wilensky, 1968). It has often been noted that more complex organizational environments require more complex internal organizational relationships, especially communicative ones. These environments also provide a critical stimulus for information seeking among organizational members (Huber & Daft, 1987). The environmental scanning that results is a special case of information seeking (Choo & Auster, 1993; Thomas, Clark, & Gioia, 1993).

Of course, not all organizations will feel the same imperatives to seek information. Emery and Trist (1965) have developed a very useful category scheme for analyzing different organizational *information environments*. They argue that there are four different types: placid, randomized; placid, clustered; disturbed reactive; and turbulent field. *Placid, randomized* organizations have the simplest organizational environment, with no direct competitors or interest groups. Organizations in this category are becoming increasingly rare, and may be only represented by a very few governmental organizations, such as some elements of the Office of Civil Defense, which are no longer relevant to today's environment.

A *placid, clustered* organization has groups in their environment who are interested in their performance, but they do not have direct competitors. Electric utilities, which need to be responsive to customers, government, and environmental groups, would be characteristic of this type of organization. The internal structural arrangements of these organizations change to reflect their environment, with customer relations units, for example, charged with relating to customers. These relationships often cue information seeking within the organization, with customer service representatives serving as *boundary spanners* who need to broker queries from customers to the internal organizational environment. These boundary spanners become the mechanism that operationalizes environmental cues to the internal organizational structure (Spekman, 1979).

The integration and commitment of boundary spanning personnel have always been problematic for organizations. Boundary spanners are individuals who, while members of one social system, have links to another. Usually these linkages are discussed in terms of individuals who have communication ties to people outside their organization because of their formal organizational position. Central to the definition of boundary spanning is the idea that these individuals process information from diverse sources and they represent the organization externally (Womack, 1984). These positions are critical to innovations and the diffusion of ideas between and within organizations (Czepiel, 1975; Daft, 1978). One problem they can create is imbalances in information within the organization, with some units of the organization reacting to customer concerns, for example, while others ignore them (Marchand & Horton, 1986).

The next two types of organizations identified by Emery and Trist (1965) not only need to react to the environment in which they find themselves, they need to become much more proactive in their strategies to uncover information outside their environment and discover means of assimilating it into internal organizational operations. Beyond the structures characteristic of placid, randomized organizations, *disturbed reactive* organizations have to deal with the presence of direct competitors. They must create strategic planning capabilities to optimize their efforts in relation to their environment and potential competitors. They also must create more active ways of discovering what their competitors are doing and what their customers want (e.g., marketing surveys). These organizations are in the exceedingly tricky business of seeking information about the future, so that their current plans and operations can be positioned to prosper not only today, but also in the near and far term. This concern with reacting and adapting, with an eye to future survivability, naturally puts additional force behind an organization's information-seeking efforts.

If an organization is not successful in these efforts, then it may find itself in a *turbulent field* situation, where the organization finds its ultimate existence directly threatened. Two types of situations are characteristic of turbulent fields. The first is when the environment of the organization has changed so that the organization's goals are no longer meaningful. For example, while the March of Dimes succeeded in its original goal of fighting polio, if it had not reformulated itself to focus on birth defects, its existence as an organization would have been threatened. In this context, an organization must search its environment for information that will help it, while it is rediscovering who it is and searching the environment for niches in which it can prosper. Obviously, the intensity level of this search is high, since the very survival of the organization is at stake.

Competitive organizations threatened with takeover or bankruptcy are the second case where elements of the environment are directly threatening the existence of the organization. In this situation, organizations, such as Chrysler in the late 1970's and early 1980's, find that the line separating them from their environment becomes increasingly blurred, with elements of their environment increasingly intrusive in internal organizational operations. Chrysler placed a union official on its Board of Directors, and government agencies and banks had effective veto power on decisions relating to the development of product lines. Information seeking for organizational employees in this context becomes increasingly complex, with the familiar sources and pathways for information no longer the place to seek definitive answers to their questions. In fact, a form of meta-information seeking involving answers to questions such as "Who is in charge here?" and "What constitutes an authoritative answer?" often precedes any searches for substantive answers to questions.

The proactive strategies necessary for the survival of organizations in disturbed reactive and turbulent field environments generally fall into two classes: placing sensory apparatus into the environment to collect information, and deciding what categories of information it is vital for the organization to collect. Thus, organizations play a very active role in enacting their environment.

The first means by which they do this is in their placement of sensory apparatus, scanning and search mechanisms, used to apprehend the world outside. All of us have a *noosphere*, a layer of information that surrounds us, which can be apprehended by our senses (de Chardin, 1961). Similarly, organizations place sensors in their environment that allow them to process information. So a competitive organization may: reach out to customers through marketing tools such as telephone or face-to-face mall intercept interviews; have lobbyists roaming the halls of the legislature; have lawyers talking to regulators; have observers outside another organization's research facility; have buyers on site purchasing commodities, and so on. These individuals act as the eyes and ears of the organization; they enable it to experience its environment, and when coupled with correct interpretation, permit an organization to respond adaptively to its environment.

The arrangement of an organization's noosphere rests on an organization's interpretation of what are important elements of its environment. Based on this interpretation, the organization decides on the placement of resources needed to experience these elements. How the environment is enacted by organizational members determines how information is brought into the organization, but even more importantly it determines what is brought in and how it is likely to be evaluated (Weick, 1969). An organization's members are likely to only recognize information that they have identified *a priori* as important and to categorize the information based on their understanding of the world.

If we could reconstruct how the great railroad barons at the turn of the century reacted to the advent of flight, it would provide a useful example of an organization's interactions with its environment. They probably read about it in the newspapers with some curiosity, but did not perceive it to be the start of a new transportation system that would eventually supplant their thriving passenger railway systems. In short, they failed to define adequately what was important in their environment, to conceive of alternative ways of doing their business, and to expand their noosphere to gather detailed information about this phenomenon. An adequate recognition of what was important would have led inevitably to much greater information seeking related to the future development of this new means of transportation. In sum, the world outside the organization has many implications for the internal information field of the organization and the urgency of information seeking.

SUMMING UP

In sum, then, individuals are embedded in an information field that shapes the context of their information seeking. The nature of this field determines their exposure to information that triggers a desire to seek more information. For example, weak ties may expose an individual to information that suggests changes should be explored, triggering an expansion of the individual's information field. In addition, the mediated channels in information terminals may incidentally contain information that causes them to seek more information. Of course, an organization's information environment can also cause individuals to expand their information field to obtain information concerning potential threats to them or to their organization. The expansion of the individual's field is often determined by their knowledge of, and beliefs concerning, the efficacy of various information carriers, which is the focus of the next chapter.

FOUR

INFORMATION CARRIERS:
A FOCUS ON CHANNEL SELECTION
AND USAGE

Developments in communication technology have made the modern organization possible. They have permitted the geographic dispersion of organizations across the world and the development of organizations of enormous size. But these developments in organizations over the last 150 years have also meant that the possibilities for face-to-face interactions have decreased, and that decision making, messages, and action are often separated from sources of information. As a result, the common core of meanings in organizations has been reduced, so that only simple messages (e.g., numbers in MIS reports) are commonly understood. In short, technology has had an enormous impact on communication in organizations historically, and this impact is accelerating with the development of new electronic forms of communication (e.g., e-mail). These trends have resulted in considerable research and theoretical interest in channel selection and use.

Nohria and Eccles (1992) suggest that several factors related to new technologies make entirely new organizational forms, such as networked organizations, possible. First, they increase the possibilities for control and decrease the need for vertical processing (e.g., condensation) of information (Galbraith, 1995). Second, new technologies facilitate communication across time and space. Third, they increase external communication, blurring traditional lines of authority within the firm. A professional in an organization is as likely (if not more likely) to seek answers to questions from professionals outside the organization as from his/her supervisor within it. Somewhat relatedly, easier access to top management through e-mail increasingly makes middle-management intermediaries superfluous (Contractor & Eisenberg, 1990). Fourth, information technologies enhance flexibility within the firm by decreasing the reliance on particular individuals for specialized information. Computer-mediated communication makes organizational communication more egalitarian, diminishing status differences and promoting access to a wide range of others.

Interest in channel selection also stems from pragmatic issues of efficiency, particularly related to the claims of proponents of new technologies. Communication and computing are increasingly merging, offering enormous possibilities for organizations. New media enhance efficiency by: transforming, translating one medium to another (e.g., voice to data); reducing shadow functions (e.g., busy signals on telephone calls); overcoming temporal unavailability through asynchronous communications (e.g., telephone tag); communicating more rapidly and efficiently to targeted groups; selectively controlling access to communication; increasing the speed of transmission of information; increasing user control; creating more specialized content; permitting multiple addressability, computer searchable memory; reducing the number of links used by individuals in decision making; and enhancing individual perceptions of being informed (Culnan & Markus, 1987; Huber, 1990; Huff, Sproull, & Kiesler, 1989; Markus, 1994; Perse & Courtright, 1993; Rice, 1989). Although, at times, what appears at first to be efficient merely adds complexity to the organization's information fields. So, for example, increased e-mail use often leads to a desire for more face-to-face communication (Contractor & Eisenberg, 1990).

While information technologies make a vast array of information concerning technical problems available to an ever expanding number of organizational members, conversely management's exclusive control over information resources is steadily declining, in part because of the downsizing of organizations and the decline of the number of layers in the organizational hierarchy. These trends make our knowledge of communication channels, especially new media, increasingly critical for understanding how organizational members seek information.

The dynamics underlying the frameworks used to explain channel selection, detailed in this chapter, as well as needs and use studies in information science (e.g., Dervin & Nilan, 1986; Hewins, 1990), often implicitly rest on the assumptions of uses and gratifications theory, a classic mass communication theory. Unfortunately, studies focusing explicitly on uses and gratifications within organizational settings have been sparse (e.g., Dobos, 1988). This is partly because the focus of organizational communication research has generally been on the source of the message, although more and more attention has shifted to the receiver (Contractor & Eisenberg, 1990). Indeed, some have argued that the failure of many information systems can be traced to designers ignoring the value of information to end users (Dervin, 1989; Rouse & Rouse, 1984).

Fundamentally, uses and gratifications theory suggests that individual receivers differentially select and use communication vehicles to gratify felt needs (Katz, Gurevitch, & Haas, 1973; Rubin, 1986; Tan, 1985). The specific substantive assumptions of uses and gratifications are particularly important for a renewed focus on receivers and information seeking. First, uses and gratifications assumes that media use is goal directed. Second, it assumes receivers select differing media and content to fulfill felt needs. Third, uses and gratifications theory assumes that individuals initiate media selection, suggesting that people are active information seekers. Fourth, there are multiple sources of need satisfaction and any one communication channel must compete with other channels for satisfaction of individual needs. Fifth, "people are aware of communication alternatives and select channels based on the normative images those channels are perceived to possess" (Perse & Courtright, 1993, p. 501).

Uses and gratifications suggests that people are active information seekers who are goal directed, selecting differing media and content to fulfill felt needs, thus initiating media selection. Individuals will make their choices of channels in a way that will maximize their gratifications obtained, especially in relation to gratifications sought (Dobos, 1988). For organizational information seeking, people want answers to questions that may literally mean the difference between profit and loss for corporations and the relative success of individuals in their careers.

Uses and gratifications theory, by suggesting that individuals will turn to specific media channels to fulfill specific cognitive or effective information needs, helps us to understand why individuals differentially expose themselves to channels and contents. It stresses the functions which media serve for users. Recently, several researchers examining new technologies have articulated different frameworks for categorizing the functions of new media. Heeter (1989), for example, suggested a functional categorization of new media technologies determined by the extent to which they are used for information retrieval (e.g., video disk), information processing (e.g., word processing), or messaging (e.g., e-mail). Rice (1989), on the other hand, focused on the more abstract categories of allocution, the system-wide offer of information (e.g., MIS systems, processing forms and records); registration, collection of information at the individual level (e.g., on-line polling); consultation, selective use of information (e.g., expert diagnostic systems); and conversation, the exchange of information (e-mail).

In this chapter we will focus first on the broader concept of information carriers, which represents sources, messages, and channels. Then, since channels are the primary focus of most research and theoretical development in this area, we will focus on channel selection and usage. Perhaps the most telling theoretical weakness of a uses and gratifications approach is its failure to specify the initial motivating conditions for information seeking (Rubin, 1986; Tan, 1985). In organizational settings, these motivating conditions have usually been couched within the framework of organizational imperatives, drive reduction, or reaction to social forces. In comparing perspectives of channel selection, we will particularly focus on six major theoretical expla-

Figure 4.1
Information Seeking Matrix

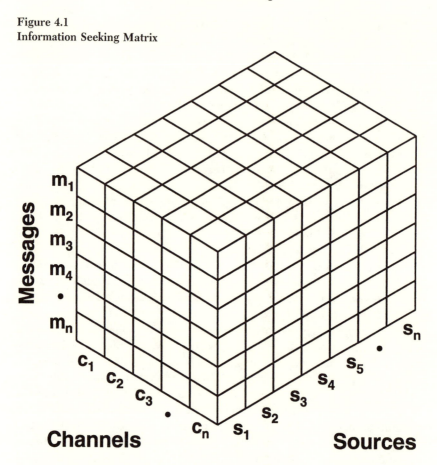

nations: social information processing, decision making, cost minimization, social presence, uncertainty reduction, and media appraisal. Finally, we will
focus on explanations of the level of usage of a channel once selected.

INFORMATION CARRIERS

Information carriers are the primary repositories of information available to
individuals within their information fields. The communication literature has
traditionally focused on three primary classes of information carriers: channels,
sources, and messages (see Figure 4.1). There are multiple channels (e.g.,
trade publications, meetings) from which information can be acquired; within
each of these channels there is a wide variety of sources, and each of these
sources can contain a variety of messages. So, while the *Wall Street Journal*
and *National Enquirer* share many channel similarities (e.g., lack of immediate
feedback between source and receiver), each of us would recognize critical

differences between them as sources (e.g., credibility). Similar differences in characteristics might occur for different messages emanating from the same source. So I might trust my supervisor to give me advice on work-related problems, but not on nutrition.

The relationship between these different carriers is somewhat akin to the relationship between compounds, molecules, and atoms in chemistry. Messages are the essential building blocks of which the other units are composed—the irreducible component of all carriers. Sources, somewhat akin to molecules, contain relatively stable combinations of messages. So, over time, we become very familiar with the repeated stories and themes of our close associates. Channels, like compounds, consist of more complex structures of sources that share similar attributes. So, there may be inherent similarities (e.g., preferences for new technologies, willingness to change) in individuals who use a channel like e-mail. By and large, communication researchers have focused their efforts within each of these classes of carriers, with organizational communication researchers most often focusing on differing channels, rather than assessing the things that are in common across them or processes like information seeking that may underlie them. While each information carrier has its own unique properties, there are also some dimensions (e.g., perceived utility) that transcend the differing types of carriers.

Channels have been variously defined as: "an information transmission system" (Goldenson, 1984, p. 137) or "the means by which the message gets from the source to the receiver" (Rogers & Shoemaker, 1971, p. 24). Channels are also often seen as constraints, as in the conduit metaphor; thus a message has to stay within channels (Axley, 1984). As the preceding illustrates, and as Berlo (1960) has noted, channels have become one of the more ephemeral communication concepts. This confusion is exacerbated by the frequent use of media as a term to refer to channels (e.g., by Daft & Lengel, 1986). Relying on the metaphor of a person on one shore trying to reach another on the opposite shore, Berlo distinguishes between three senses in which channels are used: "modes of encoding and decoding messages (boat docks), message-vehicles (boats), and vehicle-carriers (water)" (p. 64). Here we will stress mainly the sense of channels as message-vehicles, the contrivances by which messages are delivered. Thus, "a channel is a medium, a carrier of messages" (Berlo, 1960, p. 31).

Channels, because of their encompassing nature and because of the large volumes of recent research in this area, will be our primary focus throughout the rest of this book. Since channels are the largest aggregate of the different types of information carriers, they are usually the first branch of an individual's decision tree (i.e., how they should pursue their information seeking). So, my first decision when confronted with a work-related problem might be to consult co-workers, manuals, or trade publications.

General properties of channels can impact on individuals' relative evaluations of them as disseminators of information. For example, television is the most influential medium in this country, followed by newspapers, radio, and magazines. Each of these media possesses specific advantages and disadvantages. Television's greater intrusiveness compels exposure, while readers of newspapers and magazines can readily ignore messages they encounter. The print media such as newspapers and magazines are more appropriate for detailed, lengthy, and technical material, while brief, simple ideas are more effectively communicated via broadcast channels (Atkin, 1981).

Mass mediated channels tend to provide information of a general nature with considerable efficiency for reaching large audiences quickly with a message (Schramm, 1973). Interpersonal channels are more effective in reducing uncertainty because they provide social support, enhance confidence in suggested outcomes, and are tailored to individual needs and questions because of their immediacy of feedback and the situation specificity of their communication (Schramm, 1973). For these reasons, interpersonal channels are seen as more useful in presenting complex, serious information and are generally preferred by seekers of information.

Sources are particular nodes/locations of information. "A *source* is an individual or an institution that originates a message" (Rogers & Shoemaker, 1971, p. 251) or "A person or place that supplies information" (American Heritage Dictionary, 1976). While interpersonal sources, such as supervisors, may share many similar attributes, they also differ along dimensions, such as personal dynamism, trustworthiness, and credibility, that have been the classic concerns of persuasion research. Some have found that the source of information is more important than the type of information a message contains (Hanser & Muchinsky, 1978).

Messages consist of the words, symbols, or signals used to transmit a particular content emanating from a particular source within a particular channel. For example, Berlo (1960) distinguishes between a message's code, content, and treatment. Codes are groups of symbols that can be structured in meaningful ways. Treatment refers to the decisions sources make in arranging both content and codes. To Berlo (1960, p. 169): "Messages are the expressions of ideas (content), expressed in a particular way (treatment), through the use of a code."

As Figure 4.1 reveals, individuals can pursue their information seeking within an information matrix formed by channels, sources, and messages. Thus, for example, I may start my search with a decision to consult a mediated communication channel, but I also may decide that I want this channel to contain authoritative information, as well as a personal touch. This unique hybrid of properties is represented by the customer support hotline of my computer software supplier. After placing a call, I might decide that a particular operator is inexperienced, so I might then decide to call again or to link up with the computer bulletin board focusing on this product. This new source I evaluate to be more credible, partially because of the nature of the messages it contains. While I can accept the other user's message concerning the need for a particular macro, I consider the linkage she is suggesting between print-ers and textual representations to be farfetched and discount it. In other words, I move within this matrix making decisions about how I will go about pursuing the information I want related to particular topics, which information I will accept and discard, and whether I need to continue my search within the matrix. Typically, research related to carrier selection has ignored the dynamic nature of this process (Froehlich, 1994; Saunders & Jones, 1990).

The route I follow in pursuing my search within this matrix reveals a num-ber of characteristics of my search. For example, Lenz (1984) argues that search behavior can be characterized by its extent, or the number of activities carried out, which has two components: scope (the number of alternatives investigated) and depth (the number of dimensions of an alternative investi-gated). Lenz (1984) also identifies the method of the search, or channel, as another major dimension of the search. Applying this to the information-seeking matrix, an individual might choose the method of consulting the news-paper, decide to have a narrow scope by only consulting the local newspaper, but investigate every article about business within the paper, thus increasing the depth of the search.

Since the primary focus of this book is on information-seeking behavior, the nature of an individual's search, the factors that underlie it, and the charac-teristics of information carriers and fields that shape it will be explored in much more detail in the next several sections of this chapter. Next, we will focus on competing perspectives of channel selection, then we will develop the Comprehensive Model of Information Seeking (CMIS) to explain the rel-ative usage of a channel once it is selected.

COMPETING PERSPECTIVES ON CHANNEL SELECTION

As we have seen, there are a variety of potential information carriers within organizations. Research attention over the last decade has focused on the fac-tors that lead to some channels being selected for use, as opposed to others, by senders of communication messages. Central to these approaches is the assumption that there is an optimal match between channels and organiza-tional tasks that will lead to more effective performance (Sitkin, Sutcliffe, & Barrios-Choplin, 1992; Steinfield, Jin, & Ku, 1987). Increasingly, research in this area falls into two competing camps (Rice, 1993): one focusing on the characteristics of the channels themselves (Daft & Lengel, 1986), and the other focusing on the social context of communication (Fulk et al., 1987). However, other approaches are emerging, and there is an increasing need for meta-organizing schemes for this research, such as the one suggested in this section.

A major shortcoming of this research is that it focuses on the selection processes of senders of communication messages, almost totally ignoring re-ceivers (Sitkin, Sutcliffe, & Barrios-Choplin, 1992), although it has been sug-gested that a mirror image of many issues from a sender's perspective could

Table 4.1
Classification of Competing Perspectives on Channel Usage

	Level		
	Organizational	Individual	Communication Process
Formal	Social Information Processing	Decision Making	Cost Minimization
Informal	Social Presence	Uncertainty Reduction	Appraisal

apply to receivers as well (Trevino, Daft, & Lengel, 1990). For example, a receiver shouldn't choose a "lean" channel (e.g., numerical reports) to understand ambiguous information.

In this section we will selectively review differing approaches to explaining channel selection from the receiver's, or information seeker's, perspective. Table 4.1 organizes the six competing perspectives—social information processing, decision making, cost minimization, social presence, uncertainty reduction, and appraisal—by level or communication as a process, and by the formality of the communication. Issues of level of analysis are increasingly important in communication (Berger & Chaffee, 1987) and organizational research (Dansereau & Markham, 1987; Rousseau, 1985). They are generally similar to the familiar contexts (e.g., interpersonal) of communication research that can be contrasted with a focus on processes (e.g., conflict, decision making, information seeking) that cut across contexts (Littlejohn, 1992).

As we have seen in Chapter 2, an organization's communication structure has formal and informal elements, as well as other ingredients, and is not reducible to either (March & Simon, 1958). To most organizational researchers, this fundamental distinction captures two different worlds within the organization, worlds that have different premises and outlooks and, most importantly, different fundamental assumptions about the nature of interaction (Allen, 1977; Dow, 1988). Since this distinction is so fundamental, we will organize our discussion of competing perspectives on communication channels by those that are more formal in character, and then we will discuss more informal approaches.

Formal Approaches

Existing formal structures constrain channel selection, with the use of new media often forced into existing patterns within an organization's communication structure (Schmitz & Fulk, 1991). Often, for example, corporate management imposes formal rules on the use of electronic media that ensures that it more closely follows hierarchical structures, reversing what organizational members often consider to be very valuable access to a variety of information sources (Saunders, Robey, & Vaverek, 1994). Management must also sanction the purchase of new technologies, as well as "buy in" to their use in significant ways, for channels like e-mail to be used to their full potential (Markus, 1994).

Perhaps the most critical dimension of formal approaches is the relative hierarchical status of interactants. High-status people have access to an array of channels, while low-status people can be systematically deprived of access (Morris, 1988). Channel selection also impacts such status-oriented relational issues as showing respect and consideration for others (Morris, 1988). The content of messages, such as the delivery of bad news, and its potential impact on relationships also may have important implications for channel selection (Sitkin, Sutcliffe, & Barrios-Choplin, 1992; Markus, 1994). For example, face-to-face channels are more likely to be used in situations where authorization is doubtful, where there is ambiguity about status, and the decision is important (Saunders & Jones, 1990).

Social Information Processing. The key tenets of a social information processing approach (e.g., Fulk, Schmitz, & Steinfield, 1990) closely follows the work of Salancik and Pfeffer (1977, 1978) that assumes that workers within formal work units jointly construct interpretations of technology, and that an individual's social environment affects media selection. (See Table 4.2 for a comparison of the six approaches along several key dimensions.) Perhaps most importantly, communication is an activity that implies shared behaviors by workers (Fulk et al., 1987). It is impossible to communicate with a fellow worker by electronic mail if s/he refuses to use the medium (Markus, 1994). These effects appear to be heightened by the level of attraction of members to formal work groups (Fulk, 1993). In addition to normative pressures, individuals generally inform themselves of topics that they are likely to discuss with others (Allen, 1969; Chaffee & McLeod, 1973).

Another key tenet of this perspective is that channel selection is rule driven (Morris, 1988; Ruchinskas, 1983). To coordinate properly their interdependent relationships, individuals negotiate complementary role behaviors. One way that this is done is by the generation of rules governing relationships. The development of rules is a key "soft" technological factor which governs the development of particular communication structures. Thus, a perception of a strong information-sharing norm in an organization resulted in greater use of internal communication channels among scientists and engineers (Dewhirst, 1971). Similarly, media use is often a question of behaving appropriately, that is, selecting the channel that is the best representation of our roles and the social norms surrounding them (Markus, 1994).

Judgments of media are often based on the belief structures of individuals within organizations. This is most noticeable in the limits that an organiza-

Table 4.2
Constrasting Different Perspectives Along Key Dimensions

Dimension	Perspective					
	Social Information Processing	Decision Making	Cost Minimization	Social Presence	Uncertainty Reduction	Appraisal
Rationality	Determined by Social Norms	High	High	Affective	Disturbed by Ambiguity	Based on Perceptions
Importance of Social Context	High	Low	Low	High	Low	Low
Importance of Channels	One of Many Cultural Artifacts	Support Structure for Decision Making	One of Many Cost Factors	Mediator	Tool for Reducing Uncertainty	Primary Focus on Channel
Technological Determinism (substitutability)	None	Moderate	Moderate	High	Moderate to High	Moderate
Drive Reduction	No	High	No	Some	High	Some
Channel Selection Process	Determined by Social Norms	What Best Supports Decision	Most Cost Effective	Highest Closeness	Most Uncertainty Reduction	Most Authoritative, Stylish

tional culture places on the adoption and implementation of new information technologies. Generally, technical (how well the technology matches role requirements) and cultural factors play a crucial role in the level of adoption of information technologies (Kling, 1980; Rice & Manross, 1987). Often new information technologies threaten existing power relationships within organizations; for example, adoption of MIS systems permits workers access to information that traditionally is the prerogative of upper-level management. These threats can lead to decisions not to adopt or resistance to technologies adopted by others (Rogers, 1983). Strangely, reflecting the general top-down approach to channels, often users are blamed for the failure of communication systems, although the real problem lies in designers who do not consider their needs (Dervin, 1989).

One of the most detailed investigations of this topic to date is Johnson and Rice's (1987) exhaustive study of the early adoption of word processing technologies by organizations. Generally, they found that unsuccessful implementation was the rule, not the exception, largely because organizations insisted on implementing technology along the lines of the existing structure of the organization. "Efforts to implement word processing technologies using principles of the industrial bureaucracy *did not work*" (Johnson & Rice, 1987, p. 2). Technology, in spite of its linkage to rational values of efficiency, is heavily influenced by cultural factors and by existing formal power relationships within the organization (Sept, 1989).

Decision Making. Another general approach to channel selection has been to evaluate the appropriateness of the media for central organizational tasks, such as gathering the information needed for decision making (Rice, 1993). Decision making and uncertainty reduction have a predilection for rational explanations (Fulk & Boyd, 1991) and a focus on drive reduction (see Table 4.2). This approach has much in common with uses and gratifications research discussed earlier, and Chapter 5 will focus on information gathering in support of decision making.

Cost Minimization. In general, the communication literature has focused only in passing on factors underlying channel selection that relate to the accomplishment of pragmatic organizational goals such as cost effectiveness, accessibility, timeliness, development of appropriate information infrastructures, and productivity. But differing media also can be categorized by their ability to overcome situational constraints such as time, spatial factors, permanence of records, and so on (Rice & Shook, 1990). Reinsch and Beswick (1990), in a study focusing on voice mail in an organizational setting, found three areas in which organizational members might rationally analyze costs and associated probabilities of use: access, errors, and delays.

Access costs relate to the actual dollar cost of channel use. Relatedly, effort costs can be associated with such factors as the amount of physical space between two potential interactants, familiarity with technology, length of message, and complexity. In general, especially in technical areas, it has been found that issues related to accessibility override any other concern of information seekers, with individuals often choosing inferior sources of information just because they are accessible (Allen, 1977; Maguire & Kench, 1984).

Error costs reflect discrepancies in signals (Reinsch & Beswick, 1990). Impact discrepancies result in a difference between the actual and the intended impact of a message attributable to such issues as typos or critical omissions. Relationship disruptions can result from impact discrepancies and the selection of an inappropriate medium, which is a factor we will turn to in subsequent sections. Blame can be attached to the user of any media which results in these discrepancies. A preference for avoiding blame can result in preferences for media that promote the delivery of messages even in asynchronous situations and with multiple channels, since multiple channels enhance the likelihood that the intended party will receive a message. Relatedly, a media's capacity to produce documentation may be important for its selection.

Delay costs are associated with encoding delays and transmission delays. From the cost minimization perspective, channels are freely substitutable based on rational assessments of their capabilities for performing various organizational tasks.

Informal Approaches

Informal approaches (see Table 4.1) recognize that a variety of needs, including social ones, underlie communication in organizations and that, as a result, actual communication relationships may be less rational than those envisioned by formal structures (Johnson, 1993a). Informal structures facilitate communication, maintain cohesiveness in the organization as a whole, and maintain a sense of personal integrity or autonomy (Smelser, 1963).

Social Presence. As we have seen in discussing social information processing approaches, all communication occurs within a social environment with a minimum of agreement necessary on such basic properties of communication events as the symbol system and the channels used. In the area of new technologies, concepts like critical mass capture this fundamental precondition of their adoption (Markus, 1987). For new media to be successful, a minimum number of users must agree to communicate within it (Markus, 1994). Somewhat similarly, media also differ in the extent to which they reveal the presence of other interactants and can capture the human, feeling side of relationships (Daft & Huber, 1987; Markus, 1994). It has generally been accepted that individuals will be most receptive to channels that reveal the presence of other people (Sullivan, 1995). In fact, across a wide range of settings, interpersonal communication is still the preferred channel for access to information and stimulating ideas (e.g., Zuboff, 1988).

Early studies of the impact of teleconferencing technology were particularly concerned with issues like the absence of nonverbal components, the depersonalization of messages, and the presumed linearity of interactions (Acker & Calabrese, 1987). Because face-to-face communication can use all the senses, has immediate feedback, and is more spontaneous, it became the "standard" against which other channels were evaluated (Durlak, 1987). This emphasis on face-to-face communication was related to the notion of *social presence* of a particular medium. Social presence refers to the degree to which a channel approximates the personal characteristics of face-to-face interaction (Durlak, 1987) and enhances the psychological closeness of interactants (Sullivan, 1995). Social presence has been found to predict the perceived utility of media by managers (Ruchinskas, 1983).

Social presence perspectives essentially argue for the superiority of face-to-face communication because of the richness of the communication cues available, especially nonverbal cues that make more salient the presence of other interactants, that may be filtered out by new communication technologies (Walther, 1994). Yet the reduction of cues could conversely focus attention on tasks, promote enhanced possibilities of conflict resolution, and lead to quicker solutions of problems (Fulk & Boyd, 1991; Keyton, 1987). Others have suggested that managers who want to conceal their true purposes also may want to avoid rich media, since more cues are available which could lead to detection (Contractor & Eisenberg, 1990).

Increasingly, emerging technologies may be better than face-to-face communication because of their superior capabilities, particularly in terms of: memory, storage, retrieval, and participation/enhanced access to other sources (Culnan & Markus, 1987). So, interestingly, in a comprehensive study, across a number of organizations, other channels were often ranked more highly than face-to-face (Rice, 1993); these findings are increasingly repeated in studies focusing on e-mail, particularly its use by upper management for equivocal communication (Markus, 1994; Sullivan, 1995).

Uncertainty Reduction. Daft and his colleagues' (e.g., Daft & Lengel, 1986; Lengel & Daft, 1988; Trevino, Lengel, & Daft, 1987) *media richness* theory argues that the capacity of a channel to reduce uncomfortable psychological states associated with uncertainty determines channel selection. So, individuals will ultimately choose channels that match the level of uncertainty reduction they feel is required in any one information processing task (Sitkin, Sutcliffe, & Barrios-Choplin, 1992). If a problem is extremely complex, then face-to-face discussions may be the only way to address it. If it is simple, then a written memorandum may be the appropriate choice.

Prior research studies in organizations have found that the channels employed vary across different technologies, with a negative relationship found between technological certainty and use of verbal media (Randolph, 1978). As technology becomes more sophisticated, work is differentiated into more and more separate tasks, increasing the need for coordination (Hage, 1974; Jablin, 1985). As we proceed from pooled to reciprocal interdependence, coordination, and relatedly communication, becomes more costly and complex and the impact of coordination on output quality and quantity increases (Cheng, 1983). When problems are unusual and difficult to analyze, more interactive modes of coordination—although costly—are more effective (Dunegan, Green, & Baker, 1987). In general, complex, nonroutine tasks require more information processing than simple, routine tasks (Daft & Macintosh, 1981). As task uncertainty increases, more personal, "rich" forms of communication substitute for more impersonal modes (Hiemstra, 1982; Picot, Klingenberg, & Kranzle, 1982; Van de Ven, Delbecq, & Koenig, 1976). These research findings form the basis for the uncertainty reduction perspectives of media use in organizations.

Media richness theory argues that the information processing requirements of individuals depends on equivocality and uncertainty. As a result, additional uncertainty increases the need for interpersonal communication (Daft & Lengel, 1986). Communication media or channels differ in their inherent capacity to process rich information, assumed to be an objective characteristic of the media. "Information richness is defined as the ability of information to change understanding within a time interval" (Daft & Lengel, 1986, p. 560). Thus, media of low richness (e.g., impersonal written documents) are effective for processing well-understood messages and standardized data, while media of high richness (e.g., face-to-face meetings) are necessary to process information high in equivocality and uncertainty. Rich media can increase the capacity of an organization to learn, especially interpretively (Daft & Huber, 1987).

Appraisal. A model of Media Exposure and Appraisal (MEA) that has been tested on a variety of channels and in a variety of international settings (Johnson, 1983; 1984a; 1984b; 1987; Johnson & Oliveira, 1988) suggests that receiver evaluations of a channel's characteristics predict usage. Characteristics, such as editorial tone and communication potential, primarily relate to message content attributes. *Editorial tone* reflects an individual's perception of the credibility and intentions of a source. If individuals perceive that a source has motives other than the mere provision of information, then this will weigh heavily in their exposure decisions. Credibility and trustworthiness are important source characteristics in communication processes related to anticipatory socialization (Jablin, 1987) and the upward flow of information in organizations (Glauser, 1984).

Communication potential, the other dimension examined in prior research, refers to an individual's perception of the manner in which information is presented. This dimension relates to issues of style and comprehension. For example, is an article in a company newsletter visually stimulating and well written? Comprehension is a critical factor in determining the selection of technical reading material of engineers (Allen, 1977). It often depends on the match of cognitive and syntactic structures of source and recipient (Hayes, 1993). A media appraisal approach focuses on perceptions of the attributes of communication channels as the primary determinants of first selection, then usage, as we will see when we discuss the Comprehensive Model of Information Seeking.

Summary

While empirical research directly comparing these contrasting perspectives is minimal, the few studies that have been conducted have not been unequivocally supportive of any of the above positions (e.g., Fulk & Boyd, 1991; Markus, 1994; Rice, 1993; Rice & Aydin, 1991). Media richness perspectives have often faced contradictory findings in empirical research, in part attributable to the unexpected impacts of new media of communication (Fulk & Boyd, 1991). Steinfield, Jin, & Ku (1987), in reviewing the literature on social presence, found some moderate support in laboratory contexts, but, in general, found that social presence only accounts for a small proportion of the variance in media behavior. Theoretical work is still evolving in this area, demonstrating a commendable capacity to incorporate new research findings and theoretical arguments. One question, however, that this literature fails to address is: once a channel is selected by a receiver, what factors will determine the level of usage associated with it?

CHANNEL USAGE

In this section we will outline a basic model of channel usage related to information seeking that has been tested in a variety of settings. While selection of particular channels has critical effects on the ultimate outcomes of a search, a basic tenet of communication research is that repetition reinforces and enables knowledge gain and attitude change. As we have seen, repetition also affects such basic relational issues as trust, which only develops in ongoing relationships.

The Comprehensive Model of Information Seeking (CMIS) (see Figure 4.2) seeks to explain usage. It has been empirically tested in health (Johnson, 1993b; Johnson & Meischke, 1993) and organizational situations (Johnson et al., 1995). It contains three primary classes of variables. The Antecedents determine the underlying imperatives to seek information. Information Carrier Characteristics, referred to in the preceding section when we discussed the MEA, shape the nature of the specific intentions to seek information from particular carriers. Information Seeking Actions reflect the nature of the search itself and are the outcomes of the preceding classes.

Antecedents to Information Seeking

Antecedents to information seeking in organizations largely focus on the imperatives that motivate someone to seek answers to questions. These factors determine an individual's natural predispositions to search for information. This model focuses on four primary antecedents: salience, demographics, personal experience, and beliefs.

Salience. "Information is valued to the degree it is salient. Salience to an individual means the perceived applicability of information to a problem that he or she faces" (Evans & Clarke, 1983, p. 239). Thus, an individual might wonder: Is it important that I do something? While the force of salience may be determined by the interaction of a number of variables, our concern is with the outcomes of these processes that can be said to drive a certain level of information seeking. Thus, salience provides the underlying motive force to seek information.

Individuals have a variety of motives for information seeking (e.g., curiosity), including some intensely personal ones, such as securing information related to advancement and merit increases, which we focus on in more detail in Chapter 5. Indeed, Ashford and Tsui (1991) have found that seeking negative feedback is associated with performance. Information seeking, especially seeking feedback about performance, can be seen as an instrumental response by employees who want to achieve their goals within an evaluative context; the

Figure 4.2
Comprehensive Model of Information Seeking (CMIS)

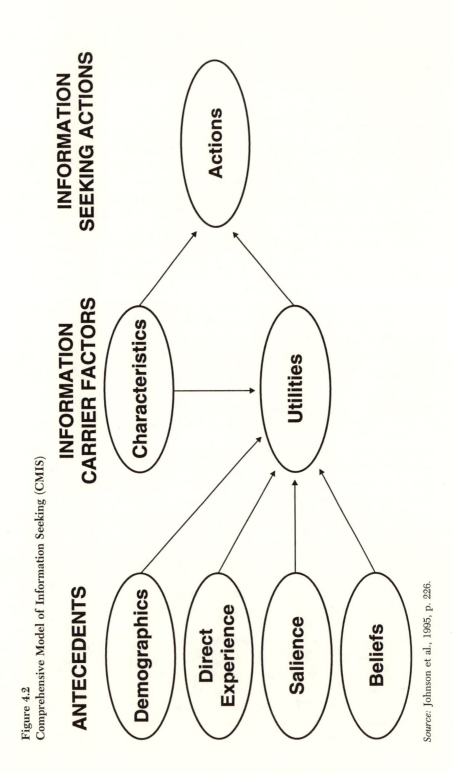

Source: Johnson et al., 1995, p. 226.

more involved an individual is, the more likely it is the individual will seek feedback (Ashford & Cummings, 1985). The less easily available this information is, the more uncertainty there is related to it, the greater the variety of strategies individuals may engage in to secure it (Miller & Jablin, 1991). The more skilled an individual is at seeking feedback related to performance, the more likely it is s/he will ultimately be successful (Ashford & Cummings, 1985). Indeed, high performers within research and development laboratories were much more likely to communicate widely within their organizations (Allen, 1977).

Task requirements associated with technologies also establish a framework for various types of information seeking. For example, Allen (1966) has found that different professional specialties have different preferences for channels, with scientists in R & D laboratories more likely to use journals, and engineers more likely to use personal sources. More recent studies suggest that scientists in different specialties have unique patterns of needs for differing channels of information (Gould & Pearce, 1991).

A particularly useful framework for examining the interrelationships between information seeking and salient organizational task factors is Thompson's (1967) classification of differing types of interdependencies associated with technology. Interdependence is a necessary consequence of the division of labor in an organization (Victor & Blackburn, 1987). Thompson (1967) sees structure as facilitating coordinated action among interdependent elements of the organization, thus providing an imperative for information seeking. In his view, the three different types of interdependence implied by differing technologies are particularly important for organizational functioning. In *pooled interdependence*, each part of a system renders a discrete contribution and is supported by the whole (e.g., a bowling team). When one entity within the organization must act before another can, you have *sequential interdependence* (e.g., an assembly line). *Reciprocal interdependence* is found when the outputs of each element of the system become inputs for others (e.g., a basketball team or maintenance unit). The need to seek information in a position based on pooled interdependence is minimal; on the other hand, the need to seek information in a position based on reciprocal interdependencies is quite high.

Demographics. A number of demographic factors, such as gender and age, have important consequences for information seeking in organizations (Tsui & O'Reilly, 1989; Zenger & Lawrence, 1989). An individual's education level, and associated professional status, probably has the most important consequences for information seeking. Education has three direct effects on an individual's information-seeking capabilities. First, it provides a critical substantive base for deciding what information, if any, is needed. Second, it provides a set of criteria for evaluating the nature of information that can be acquired. Third, a large part of modern technical education involves a familiarization of the individual with effective search strategies: what knowledge bases are most useful, what sources are the most authoritative, what is a sufficient answer, and so on. For technical positions, such as engineers, within organizations, education may be the one central demographic variable.

Personal Experience. An individual's degree of direct experience, in part because it relates directly to an individual's base of knowledge, also affects information seeking. Generally, tenure within an organization has been negatively related to information seeking, especially with seeking proactive feedback (Ashford & Cummings, 1985). Prior direct experience, and experience through others, affects an individual's information seeking related to organizational assimilation processes, with experienced individuals less needful of general information about the organization (Jablin, 1987), but perhaps more aware of specialized information sources relating to salient technical topics (Allen, 1977).

Beliefs. An individual's beliefs about the outcomes of information seeking are also important. The question individuals pose to themselves here is: Can I do something? A corresponding belief that there is no procedure available for effectively confronting his/her problems would impede information seeking. Somewhat relatedly, if an individual believes there are costs (e.g., loss of self-esteem) associated with particular information-seeking strategies, this will reduce the level of information seeking (Baliga & Jaeger, 1984; Miller & Jablin, 1991).

Information Carrier Factors

While antecedents, such as salience, provide the initial motivating force for interaction, the nature of the search itself is determined by the Information Carrier Factors. The Information Carrier Factors discussed in this section are drawn from a model of Media Exposure and Appraisal (MEA) that has been tested on a variety of information carriers, including both sources and channels, and in a variety of cultural settings. Studies focusing on magazines were conducted in India (Johnson, 1983), in Nigeria (Johnson, 1984a), and in Germany (Johnson, 1984b). In addition, studies were conducted in the Philippines on films (Johnson, 1987) and on more generalized perceptions of television, radio, and print channels in Belize (Johnson & Oliveira, 1988).

Research on the MEA focused on three dimensions—editorial tone, communication potential, and utility—which have been clearly related to exposure and evaluation decisions across many communication channels. The first two dimensions, editorial tone and communication potential, primarily relate to message content characteristics; the third dimension, utility, represents a judgment of how these attributes serve individual needs (Atkin, 1973). This research relates attributes of the medium to the functions they serve for the user, a focus shared by other programmatic media research (e.g., Burgoon & Burgoon, 1979, 1980; Burgoon, Burgoon, & Wilkinson, 1981).

Following the MEA, the CMIS (Johnson, 1993b; Johnson & Meischke, 1993; Johnson et al., 1995), posits determinative relationships between two

Information Carrier Factors—characteristics and utility—and Information Seeking Actions. The CMIS in many ways represents the "bare bones" of a causal structure. Fundamentally, it suggests that the Antecedent Factors provide the motive force for Information Seeking Actions that are shaped by Information Carrier Factors (see Figure 4.2).

Information Carrier Characteristics

Editorial tone reflects an audience member's perception of the credibility and intentions of a channel. If individuals perceive that information is disseminated for reasons other than the mere provision of information, this will weigh heavily in their evaluation of channels and in their usage decisions. In a comprehensive examination of newspapers in the United States, Burgoon and Burgoon (1979) have found this dimension, particularly as it relates to fair-mindedness, to be the critical factor in determining satisfaction with a channel.

Another component of editorial tone is perceived accuracy, despite motives. Burgoon and Burgoon (1979) have found that an editorial production index that included accuracy was positively related to satisfaction and in some cases to exposure. Somewhat relatedly, they have found that a trustworthiness/competence dimension related positively to an individual's evaluation of newspapers (Burgoon et al., 1981). Studies focusing on the media generally have found that television is perceived as the most credible media channel (Wallack, 1989; Doctor, 1992).

Communication potential refers to an individual's perception of the manner in which information is presented. This dimension relates to issues of style and comprehension. For example, is a television program visually stimulating and well paced? Burgoon and Burgoon (1980) have found for newspapers that such indicants as the quality of visuals and of organization, contained in an editorial production index, related to exposure in some communities. They also found that an inability to comprehend a medium was related to nonreadership. In a companion study, their results also indicated that this index was a very important contributor to satisfaction with newspapers (Burgoon & Burgoon, 1979). In addition, Burgoon et al. (1981) have found that the more colorful and stimulating the newspaper, the greater the frequency of use and the higher an individual's satisfaction. Manager's clear preferences for face-to-face verbal communication is in part based on the communication potential of this channel, which offers rich detail (e.g., stories, gossip) that can provide triggers to particular actions (Mintzberg, 1975a, 1975b).

Visual attractiveness of magazines has also been related to exposure cross-nationally (Johnson & Tims, 1981). Additionally, the specific targeting of most magazines makes it more feasible to write in a style that is understandable as well as attractive to a particular audience. Although local, daily newspapers have a more distinct readership than national newspapers, the audience is likely to be less homogeneous than magazine audiences. This may make it more difficult to adapt writing and style to the tastes of the readers. In general, broadcast channels such as television and radio appear to be best suited for carrying stylistically entertaining messages that engage the tastes of the audience, assuring closer attention to the informational content (Atkin, 1981). Similarly, to have value for a manager, information must be timely, accurate, and relevant (McKinnon & Bruns, 1992).

Utility

The preceding dimensions involve a direct evaluation by an individual of a particular channel. The final dimension, utility, relates the characteristics of a medium directly to the needs of an individual, and thus shares much with the uses and gratifications perspectives discussed in the preceding sections. For example, is the information contained in the medium relevant, topical, and important for the individual's purposes? Atkin (1973) has argued that mass media exposure will result from a combination of such needs of the receiver and the attributes of a message. Indeed, perceived utility of information has been related to newspaper readership (Wang, 1977) and a satisfaction index, which included a current information measure, had the strongest relationship with newspaper readership in a variety of communities (Burgoon & Burgoon, 1980). For the print media, it has been argued that indicants of this dimension, such as interest, usefulness, and importance for achieving one's goals, are interrelated and they have been associated with exposure (Carlson, 1960). In sum, communication research in a variety of contexts demonstrates a direct relationship between utility and use (Dervin, 1980).

Utility is a central concern in determining formal structures that filter the upward flow of information in organizations, since reducing information overload requires choices about which information should be provided to decision makers (Glauser, 1984). The relevance of information, which is the central concept in information science (Froehlich, 1994; Schamber, 1994), is often intertwined with its utility. As Thayer (1988) has observed, we cannot be moved by the "truth" of information, we can only be moved by its relevance. Relevance and utility judgments are typically not absolute ones when individuals engage in information seeking, rather they are comparative ones (Wilson, 1977). Ultimately, relevance is based on a mental calculation of the relationship between an individual's need and any one piece of information (Schamber, 1994).

Information-Seeking Actions

Naturally there are several types of Information-Seeking Actions that can result from the impetus provided by the foregoing set of factors contained in the CMIS. For example, as we have seen, movement within the information carrier matrix might differ in terms of the number of different sources from whom information is sought, and depth, in terms of the number of different messages involved. Diversity in the number of people contacted and the depth of each contact have both been found to be very important to successful performance within research and development laboratories (Allen, 1977).

Results of Empirical Tests of the CMIS

The results of the various tests of the CMIS suggest it represents a general framework for examining information seeking, but that further work needs to be done to incorporate contextual, and underlying factors in the model. This is a subject we will return to in Chapter 8. Most importantly, the various tests of the model have focused on vastly different information-seeking situations for respondents. Two of the prior research studies have focused on cancer-related information seeking by the general population (Johnson, 1993b; Johnson & Meischke, 1993). Needless to say, for most individuals this is a nonrecurring problem, which is focused, novel, and fraught with emotional complications. These tests suggested that the model works best with authoritative channels, which are the object of intense, goal-directed searches, such as doctors.

The third study, which focused on information seeking in the defined context of a technical organization, yielded some critical differences in this more rational and programmed task (Johnson et al., 1995). The most important variables in this test were those related to an individual's existing information base, those associated with an individual's need for recurrent, programmed information seeking, and those drawn from Johnson's model of Media Exposure and Appraisal. These results suggested that information seeking might be less influenced by motivations and individual cognitions than previously thought, and may be more correctly viewed as a beginning and end, in and of itself, done often to fulfill the requirements of someone's role in a social system.

In addition, as in prior tests of the MEA, only a minimal relationship was found between appraisal/utility variables and exposure ones, thus calling into question the current academic literature's fascination with processes of channel selection in organizations (Rice, 1993; Sitkin, Sutcliffe, & Barrios-Choplin, 1992). Tests of the model suggest that barriers and various irrational processes may be more important than was initially thought, which is a problem we will turn to in more detail in Chapter 5. We will also return to the CMIS when we discuss future directions of information seeking in Chapter 8.

CONCLUSION

As we have seen, a whole host of factors cause the selection of an exponentially proliferating array of channels. The focus on channels is somewhat akin to the classic demographic approaches to social research; it focuses on crude surface distinctions (e.g., e-mail versus voice mail) which mask more powerful underlying processes. A focus on selection, rather than on the effects of media, may be posing the wrong questions for research in this area (Walther, 1994). More recently, work has focused on the interpretation and meaning, dealing with issues like the symbol-carrying capacity of various media (Sitkin, Sutcliffe, & Barrios-Choplin, 1992). Unfortunately, underlying processes associated with context, the content of messages, and frameworks for understanding meaning are only tangentially addressed in this literature (Sitkin, Sutcliffe, & Barrios-Choplin, 1992).

A medium would be considered a good conduit of meaning to the extent that it can carry nuance, metaphor, and the deep structure of the organization (Sitkin, Sutcliffe, & Barrios-Choplin, 1992). Media themselves in this situation can become symbolic, and their use interpreted within the social framework of the organization (Sitkin, Sutcliffe, & Barrios-Choplin, 1992). Thus, if the president of the organization was to seek information from a middle manager about a work-related problem, his/her choice of the face-to-face medium carries rich symbolic significance for the manager and others in the organization. As a result, the meaning of media use is not invariant across situations, although its inherent capacity for carrying data might be (Sitkin, Sutcliffe, & Barrios-Choplin, 1992).

Returning to the problem of channel selection, historically we also must confront issues related to the growth and development of channels. While the Pony Express constituted a very interesting (some might even say romantic) conduit for messages in the 19th century American West, it was quickly supplanted by other channels that offered compelling competitive advantages. If channels are a tool, then it is easy to understand how they can be quickly discarded, if another channel, more useful for accomplishing the underlying function, comes along. So, channel specialization, not equivalence or substitutability, may be the critical issue (Reder & Conklin, 1987).

In this regard, it might be useful to apply some notions of the population ecology school to channel selection. Some channels may survive for a very long time, because they have established a unique niche function that is not easily supplanted. So, for example, since the dawn of the computer age, people have been advocating the benefits of the paperless office, but written documents and memos still exist in increasing volume. A combination of legal and bureaucratic imperatives, associated with the need for permanent records, makes this niche function remarkably resistant to the array of new (supposedly superior) technologies.

Increasingly, there is also a blending of functions for sources, messages, and channels. One sense of multimedia is to use differing channels to get the same message from the same source across to a greater range of audiences in a variety of ways, thus extending the reach and impact of channels. Organizational members also will often switch channels in the middle of communication events for reasons of convenience, record keeping, efficiency, and so on (Markus, 1994). So, I may have a brief telephone conversation with a subordinate and insist s/he follow up with an e-mail message documenting the actions taken.

As we have suggested, channels may only be the tip of the iceberg for information seeking. The question is not which channel we choose, but why. This question brings us back to the information-seeking matrix. For most of us, when we initiate a search, the issue is the answer, not the search process. There may be an infinite combination of sources and channels that will provide us with an answer. So, the real issue is what answers will satisfy our quest and how much time and effort we are willing to expend on it. The more important the problem, the greater the variety of sources and channels we will consult, and the more exotic and different from our normal information field they will be. In the next section, then, we turn to the issue of how motivated we are to seek answers to our questions, and how many barriers we are willing to overcome in their pursuit.

FIVE

BARRIERS TO INFORMATION SEEKING OR THE BENEFITS OF IGNORANCE

[T]hey [Americans] judge that the diffusion of knowledge must necessarily be advantageous and the consequences of ignorance fatal. (de Tocqueville, 1966)

[P]erfect knowledge is itself impossible, and an inherently impossible basis of social action and social relations. Put conversely, ignorance is both inescapable and an intrinsic element in social organization generally. (Moore & Tumin, 1949, p. 788)

Information has always been a source of power, but it is now increasingly a source of confusion. In every sphere of modern life, the chronic condition is a surfeit of information, poorly integrated or lost somewhere in the system. (Wilensky, 1968, p. 331)

Ignorance and information seeking are inextricably intertwined concepts (Stigler, 1961). Ignorance, as used here, refers to a state where an individual is not aware of information related to organizational life, including procedures, policies, cultural factors, and events. So, ignorance exists when knowledge resides somewhere in the social system of which an individual is a part, yet the focal individual just does not have it. Ignorance by itself is not a sufficient condition for information seeking. Classically it is argued that a perceived need for the information is a necessary condition for information seeking to occur. Ignorance is thus different from ignoring, which often happens in an organization when an individual consciously knows that a problem exists, but chooses not to confront it.

Kerwin (1993) has developed a very useful classification scheme for mapping ignorance in terms of various levels of personal and societal (also read organizational) awareness and/or knowledge (see Table 5.1). Fundamentally, we can make a distinction between the things that are accepted as knowledge, although they might be socially constructed and subject to future paradigm

Table 5.1
Mapping Ignorance

Personal Knowledge	Social System Knowledge	
	Known Things	Unknown Things
Known	Awareness Tacit Knowing	Known Unknowns
Unknown	Ignorance	Unknown Unknowns
Error	Error	False Truths
Proscribed Knowledge	Denial	Taboos

Source: Derived from Kerwin, 1993.

shifts (Berger & Luckmann, 1967; Kuhn, 1970), and things that are unknown. Typically, the number of unknown things is much larger than known things, but we have a tendency to focus on objects rather than their grounds (Stocking & Holstein, 1993), so we focus on what is known rather than what is unknown. While rare, it is possible for the individual to know things his/her social system as a whole does not yet accept; however, we will treat this as an exceptional case.

Usually an individual will know much less than any social system of which they are a part. Some observers are concerned with the ignorance explosion—the growing gap between that which an individual knows and that which is knowable—with 85 percent of the people in the United States functionally technologically illiterate, for example (Lukasiewicz, 1994). While we are steadily increasing our knowledge of specific subareas, we are also raising the dilemma of decreasing the possibility of any one person knowing enough about each of the parts to integrate the whole (Thayer, 1988). Of the things an individual knows, some will be in conscious awareness and others will be tacit knowledge, i.e., things we do not know we know. Much of what we do in our social worlds, how we react to each other's nonverbal expressions, for example, is tacit knowledge, beneath our level of conscious thought. Intuition often falls in this classification and, as we will see, it is often extremely important for how upper level managers make decisions (Simon, 1987).

There are also things we know we don't know, i.e., the known unknowns. They have also been termed conscious ignorance or meta-ignorance (Smithson, 1993). Interestingly, these things often are also socially constructed (Stocking & Holstein, 1993) and the pursuit of answers to them is the subject of intense scientific competition. Claims of knowledge gaps are used to support research programs and proposals, so scientists have vested interests in arguing for compelling known unknowns (Stocking & Holstein, 1993). Known unknowns, when considered to be irrelevant, are not perceived to need further inquiry or information seeking (Smithson, 1993). But when considered to be important, these things are most often the object of intense information searches. The operation of markets often depends vitally on the pursuit of known unknowns (Geertz, 1978). Many high-tech genetics firms are searching for the locations of genes that are known to exist; it's just a question of where they exist. So, the very reason for the existence of some organizations is to discover a known unknown.

Perhaps more problematic for organizations are the things we do not know we do not know, the unknown unknowns. These are the things that are most likely to result in surprises and environmental jolts. So, if we are in the airplane passenger business, and it turns out that it is ridiculously easy to develop a means of instantaneously transporting individuals from place to place inexpensively and safely, then this unknown unknown may demolish our comfortable world. As McLuhan has observed "we don't know who discovered water, [but] it was almost certainly not a fish" (quoted in Lukasiewicz, 1994, p. xx).

Error, something we think we know but do not, is most likely to be corrected through interactions with others, especially via weak ties. This is an additional benefit of widespread communication: we are more likely to come into contact with others who can correct our mistaken assumptions. If we only interact with the same others about the same topics, we are most likely to share and reinforce our mistaken assumptions.

False truths are things that are unknown, but which we think we know. As Will Rogers has observed "the trouble isn't what people don't know; it's what they don't know that isn't so" (quoted in Boulding, 1966, p. 1). False truths often form the conventional wisdom that is the basis for ongoing interactions; still, they are at times erroneous views of the world, which some fundamental questioning might overturn. But we do not question them precisely because they are accepted as truths. Treating knowledge as provisional and constantly questioning conventional wisdom may be one key to resilient, adaptive organizations, and is often recommended for effective decision making.

Denial of things that are too painful to know (so we do not) is a major barrier to information seeking within organizations. As we will see, individuals often have very powerful reasons for refusing to admit that something is true.

Perhaps even more troublesome for social systems are taboos, i.e., things that societies agree should not be known by their members because they threaten their underlying premises. Most traditional cultures throughout history have been truth preservers, rather than truth pursuers, with information seeking permitted in only very limited, often highly personal domains (Thayer, 1988). Forbidden knowledge (e.g., religious domains, shamans) is an area for which there are still significant penalties for individuals who engage in information seeking. Organizational elites and cultures, for example, may have a vested interest in protecting the basic authority relationships that are the fundamental organizing assumptions of hierarchies.

Ignorance, narrowly defined, represents the things that are known that we don't know. So, for example, we may know we don't know enough about how to work with the spreadsheet we are using in our job. We develop a search plan to address this shortcoming. We benefit greatly, however, in knowing the general parameters we need to search for. As we have seen, there are very compelling reasons for organizations to promote ignorance, to narrow the range of conscious known knowns for individuals (Smithson, 1989).

The growing interest in information seeking can be coupled with a renewed interest in ignorance (Kerwin, 1993; LaFollette, 1993; Ravetz, 1993; Smithson, 1989; 1993; Stocking & Holstein, 1993). Ignorance can occur in several major areas and is very pervasive in organizations. First, individuals may be inadequately trained for the performance of their specific job duties. While this condition is interesting, it is beyond the scope of this chapter. Second, individuals may be unaware of information, readily available elsewhere in the organization, which has a direct bearing on their job duties. Third, ignorance of employee benefits, which has a direct bearing on the employee's personal life, is also widespread (Mitchell, 1988), often in spite of government-mandated procedures for informing employees. Fourth, individuals can be unaware of the larger organization, especially its culture. Indeed, a rather common complaint in organizations is: Why doesn't anybody know anything? (Johnson, 1993a; Downs, Clampitt, & Pfeiffer, 1988).

Given the pragmatic importance of this issue, it is somewhat surprising that it has received so little research attention (Guetskow, 1965; Jablin, 1987; Smithson, 1989). Management often assumes that, if information is properly communicated, this problem will either go away or be improved (Axley, 1984). The traditional literature has tended to focus on the many dysfunctional consequences of ignorance. First, ignorance is likely to result in considerable inefficiencies in organizational operations through such impacts as misunderstandings, the duplication of effort, working at cross-purposes, time delays, etc. (Inman, Olivas, & Golen, 1986). Second, ignorance can lead to disastrous outcomes for organizations (Paisley, 1980), such as the space shuttle *Challenger* tragedy (Brody, 1986; Lewis, 1988) or the Pinto's exploding gas tank

(Strobel, 1980), where at least some organizational members knew that these outcomes were possible. Third, these inefficiencies and more dramatic outcomes are likely to have impacts on a worker's feelings of stress, tension, burnout, and frustration that, in turn, can produce low morale, increased absenteeism, and even turnover (Morrison, 1993a; 1993b). Fourth, ignorance can result in a lack of integration of the individual into the organization's cultures, thus contributing to a feeling of individual anomie. Fifth, ignorance may be associated with low levels of participation (Marshall & Stohl, 1993) and commitment to organizational change efforts (Miller, Johnson, & Grau, 1994).

Certainly ignorance is pervasive in most organizations. Two research studies eloquently speak to this point. The first study was conducted at the Library of Congress by Eugene Walton (1975). This study sought to determine the effectiveness of downward communication concerning an affirmative action program. Over a period of roughly one year, the Library of Congress used a variety of channels to increase the awareness by employees of this program: newsletters, bulletin boards, tape-slide film presentations, supervisor–subordinate face-to-face communication, and group meetings. At the conclusion of this program, almost one-half of the members of the organization responded to a ten-item quiz concerning its features. Employees responded correctly only 27 percent of the time. Interestingly, employees who perceived a self-interest in the program (e.g., they might get promoted) showed no greater level of knowledge than those employees who said they lacked self-interest.

The second study done by the Opinion Research Corporation (reported in Smith, Richetto, & Zima, 1972) also illustrates that the level of information among lower level organizational members is no better when an item of organizational interest is at stake. A metals-producing company had a problem with declining profit margins, an issue of considerable importance to the long-term health of the corporation. However, research discovered that the level of awareness of this issue declined steeply at each level of the hierarchy: top officers, 91 percent aware; upper middle management, 48 percent; lower middle management, 21 percent; and first line supervision, 5 percent. This was especially critical since the lower levels of the organization were likely to be most aware of what problems existed in production and how they might be solved, and they were the ones who were going to implement actual solutions.

These two studies illustrate a general lack of awareness by organizational members of organizational procedure and policies (Walton, 1975; Downs, Clampitt, & Pfeiffer, 1988); indeed, "organizational members display an astonishing ignorance of organizational procedures and functioning" (Brown & McMillan, 1988, p. 24). This lack of awareness has often had significant negative impacts on the implementation of organizational innovations such as word processing (Cline, 1983) and the failure of employees to assimilate information has also affected implementation of intelligent telephone systems (Levitt, 1989).

The results of ignorance are well documented, and organizations have engaged in various efforts to ameliorate it. But ignorance persists. Conventional approaches to this problem have focused on a variety of factors that lead to ignorance. For example, some have stressed the random nature of ignorance (e.g., the presence of noise or disturbances in a communication system) as a contributing factor. Others have emphasized the role of human cognitive processes (e.g., selective perception) (e.g., Kurke, Weick, & Ravlin, 1989) and psychological processes such as denial (Smithson, 1989). Still others have emphasized failures in communication as the cause for this situation. For example, surprisingly few (approximately 10 percent) pass on information they receive from the grapevine to others in the organization (Sutton & Porter, 1968).

Conventionally, given Western attitudes toward knowledge and progress, ignorance is viewed as something that needs to be overcome, in part, by increased attention to information seeking (Smithson, 1989). This belief structure is so ingrained that it is difficult for social science to come to grips with ignorance as an area of inquiry (LaFollette, 1993; Ravetz, 1993; Smithson, 1989; 1993), although interestingly, uncertainty has been legitimated as an area of study (Smithson, 1993). Yet in organizations, ignorance is sometimes planned for, and overcoming it may detract from efficiency and specialization goals, presenting organizations with a substantial dilemma. So, before considering the development of strategies for enhancing information seeking, we must consider the factors that serve to sustain high levels of ignorance in organizations, in order to contemplate the benefits of ignorance.

Our central argument will be that ignorance persists because it is useful on several levels, if not a necessity for organizations and their members (Moore & Tumin, 1949; Smithson, 1989; 1993). In fact, it has recently been suggested that instead of becoming more complex, organizations that are successful in their environmental niche strive to become more simple as a result of a number of factors—managerial, structural, cultural, and process related (Miller, 1993). The question for many organizations is whether the benefits of facilitating information seeking, and resulting complications, are worth the very real risk to the organization of any strategies that might be used to overcome ignorance. Traditionally, it has been argued that the way to improve organizations is not to produce more information, but to reduce the amount of information any one subsystem must process (March & Simon, 1958). But before we can fully articulate this argument, we will set the stage for it, by focusing on the relationship between information seeking and decision making.

DECISION MAKING

Decisions require clarity, closure, and confidence. As a result, decisive action comes more easily from the ignorant than from the wise, more easily from the short-sighted than from those who anticipate the long run. (March, 1994, p. 265)

Decision makers look for information, but they see what they expect to see and overlook unexpected things. (March, 1994, p. 11)

Traditionally, the primary impetus for information seeking in organizations has been in terms of its role in decision making. The Behavioral Decision School of organizational theory, represented primarily by Cyert, March, and Simon and Carnegie Mellon University, has cast the central issue in organizational research as decision making (Farace, Monge, & Russell, 1977). In this school, an organization can be conceived of as a system for supporting the decision-making process, and the critical issue for organizations is that well-formed decisions be made. Following these arguments, the primary purpose of "communication networks is to ensure the presence of certain types of information" (O'Reilly, Chatham, & Anderson, 1987, p. 610) to support decision making processes (March, 1994; Daft & Huber, 1987). From these perspectives, information seeking is done to support decision making.

The Behavioral Decision School has also been responsible for some central concepts for the study of communication. For example, many communication theorists have argued that the primary function of communication is the reduction of uncertainty (Berger & Calabrese, 1975; Farace, Monge, & Russell, 1977; Farace, Taylor, & Stewart, 1978; Miller & Steinberg, 1975). Uncertainty is generally seen as equivalent to lacking the appropriate information (MacCrimmon & Taylor, 1976). Information seeking is critical to uncertainty reduction, especially in the initial formation of interpersonal relationships, where each new piece of information is critical in determining the impression of the other (Berger & Calabrese, 1975; Douglas, 1985; Kellerman, 1986). Berger and his colleagues have developed an elaborate axiomatic theory of uncertainty reduction, with considerable controversy on some of its central tenets. Some research, for example, has cast doubt on the fundamental linkage between uncertainty and information seeking, with researchers suggesting that in some situations ignorance is bliss (Kellerman & Reynolds, 1990), a theme we will return to in this chapter.

Uncertainty classically has been defined as a function of the number of alternative patterns identified in a set and the probability of each alternative (Farace, Monge, & Russell, 1977). Information can remove uncertainty by helping to define relative probabilities, but it also can increase uncertainty when it leads us to recognize additional alternatives or to change the assessment of probabilities. Unfortunately, the more uncertain the information, the more subject it is to favorable distortions by those reporting it (Downs, 1967) and when information is vitally required there is a tendency to treat it as more reliable than it actually is (Adams, 1980).

While information seeking is critical to decision making and the associated process of uncertainty reduction, it is a secondary subservient process, done to support these larger objectives. As a result, information seeking research in these areas is often an afterthought, subsidiary to larger themes, although some have suggested processes related to attention and search are the most relevant to how decisions are actually made (March, 1994). A closer examination of this area can provide insights to both the underlying motivations to seek information and the outcomes of the information-seeking process.

Everyday we see the consequences of poorly made decisions, especially in our political life. For example, the term "groupthink" has come to symbolize the very human, group processes (e.g., cohesiveness, conformity) that conspire against "good," rational decision making (Janis, 1971). Janis (1971), in tracing the decision making of the U.S. foreign policy establishment in making disastrous decisions regarding Vietnam, the Cuban missile crises, and the Bay of Pigs, found one recurring theme: how group processes and the limits of human decision making restricted the range of information that was sought, and the consideration of a range of alternatives once information was obtained. Somewhat similarly, group members do not share information that does not support the position of a plurality of other group members, their preferences, or the information already in the possession of other group members (Stasser & Titus, 1985). These findings were replicated in spite of more structured discussions and instructions to focus on group process so that information would be more likely to be shared (Stasser, Taylor, & Hanna, 1989).

One insidious symptom of groupthink, directly related to information seeking, is the presence of mindguards that protect the group from adverse information after a decision is made. So, in the foreign policy decisions Janis examined, there was a tendency to ignore dissent and clear indications that things were not going well. Mindguarding acts to severely limit information seeking after a decision is reached; indeed, often organizational decision-makers will ignore the information they have available (Feldman & March, 1981). In effect, information is only sought from supportive sources, and even experts within one's organization are frozen out of the decision-making process (Janis, 1971). Several laboratory studies have also found that individuals require less information to arrive at a decision favorable to them than one against their interests (O'Reilly & Pondy, 1979).

Many of the same processes play out in organizational decision making as well, as Halberstam's (1986) case study of United States automakers' reactions to the threat of foreign competition demonstrates. Unfortunately, with increasing decision complexity, people become more conservative and apply more subjective criteria that are increasingly removed from reality (Van de Ven, 1986). Especially under conditions of threat, organizations may restrict their information seeking and fail to react to changing environmental conditions (Staw, Sandelands, & Dutton, 1981). Organizations in these circumstances rely on existing behaviors, narrow their information fields, and reduce the number of information channels consulted. Even more disturbing is the greater centralization of authority and cost cutting typically engaged in that further impedes information seeking. So, in circumstances ranging from the threat of nuclear annihilation to the demise of an entire industry, how information is gathered and then processed in reaching decisions is a critical, recurring pragmatic concern.

Information is often gathered to justify a decision already made, instead of being used to make an optimal decision (Staw, Sandelands, & Dutton, 1981). Over the last three decades, observational and research studies have repeatedly demonstrated that decision making is an irrational process. In fact, the link between decision making and the processing of information is often much weaker than we would like to believe (Feldman & March, 1981). Decision makers often ask for more information (it is after all a part of the decision-making ritual) even when they have sufficient information on hand to make a decision (Feldman & March, 1981). They know that very seldom will they be criticized for gathering additional information, but they might be blamed for failing to gather a critical piece of information (Feldman & March, 1981). Some have described this as the cynical use of information by individuals who use information solely because others see value in it and it enhances their image (Menon & Varadarajan, 1992). All too often, information is sent and processed that does not directly bear on any one particular decision (MacCrimmon & Taylor, 1976). Especially later in the decision-making process, sources are sought solely because they may say that the seeker can terminate the decision-making process (Saunders & Jones, 1990). One advantage of relying on individual information seekers in market-driven situations is that they are more likely to focus on information actually needed to support a decision, because of their greater concern for communication costs.

An interesting paradox in the literature pertains to the relationship between information load and decision making. Decision makers often seek more information than needed, even when it induces overload (O'Reilly & Pondy, 1979). While this overload of information decreases decision quality, it increases decision-maker confidence (McKinnon & Bruns, 1992; O'Reilly, Chatham, & Anderson, 1987) and satisfaction (O'Reilly, 1980). In effect, information becomes very addicting for some individuals, with a constant desire for more, even when it has harmful effects. On the other hand, information seeking can also be a form of avoidance since it could be a substitute for more direct action in confronting problems (Swinehart, 1968). To understand a problem, you have to understand the forces which cause it to persist. Often problems associated with ignorance stem from the many positive benefits members have from remaining ignorant—after all, ignorance is bliss.

Basic Distinctions in Decision Making

The key element of any definition of decision making is the selection from alternatives. If there are no true alternatives, then the decision is already made. But if there are many alternatives, all equally beneficial or problematic, then we have no basis for making distinctions and are left with a highly uncertain decision, since we do not have any basis for choosing which of the alternatives is best. So, the number of alternatives, from two to infinity, has much to do with the complexity of decision making and of information seeking in support of it. Not only do we have to gather information on each alternative relating to the various criteria that differentiate them, but we also have to gather information on how they interact and compare. For example, often in personnel decisions we have to evaluate not only the individual, but how others might react to the choice of that person. So, I may not be too disturbed if I am not promoted, but I would be very disturbed if a long-standing rival is chosen over me.

Another basic issue is how much experience I have had in making this type of decision. As we have seen earlier, the type of information-seeking situation can dictate how rational the information search might be (Johnson & Meischke, 1993; Johnson et al., 1995). Similarly, if I have settled into a routine for making a decision, the premises of the decision and the information used to support it will be well known to me. This ritualistic acquisition of information is often troublesome, since organizations often do not recognize the costs of gathering information, especially in terms of opportunity costs or benefits foregone (Feldman & March, 1991).

Programmed decisions are routine, repetitive ones for which the organization has developed a specific process, often computerized and quantitative (MacCrimmon & Taylor, 1976; Simon, 1960). Programmed decisions are often highly formalized, with set rules to follow and penalties associated with the breaking of the rules. So, for example, government procurement is based on some means of selecting from the lowest bidder. On the surface, this is a rational, cost-effective means of making a purchasing decision. But, as the old joke goes, how comfortable would you feel if you were an astronaut, on top of a rocket launcher containing thousands of parts, all selected on the basis that they were the cheapest available.

Decisions are nonprogrammed to the extent they are novel, unstructured, and important, and to which only very general models of decision making can be applied (Cyert, Simon, & Trow, 1956; Simon, 1960). In their classic case study of an early business decision focusing on the adoption of an information processing technology, Cyert, Simon, & Trow (1956) point out how tortuous and cumbersome nonprogrammed decisions can be for organizations. In effect, the organization has to decide how to decide. The decision-making process involves at least two major decisions, the first of which can contain many surprises. It may be the case that you discover that a major issue, that you hadn't included at first, needs to be included in the decision-making process. So, the whole decision has to be put on hold until you go back to square one on this aspect of the decision. When you gather information on it, you discover it interacts in unexpected ways with things you already thought you knew, which then forces you to rethink some already settled aspects of the decision. For some highly complex, novel, important decisions, organizations can literally go round and round for months, if not years, before they can reach the final stages of making a decision. One basic problem with most technologically driven support structures for decision making is that they are grounded in rational decision-making processes, whereas the actual decision making of upper level managers often focuses on nonprogrammed decisions. As a result, it is often irrational (Mintzberg, 1975a, 1975b) and/or intuitive (Simon, 1987).

Relatedly, since information seeking operates in the support of making a decision, you also can be faced with decisions on how to gather information. So, this is also a critical distinction for information seeking in organizations, with some individuals arguing that organizations make two classes of decisions: one set on the substance of the matter and another on how to search for information (O'Reilly, Chatham, & Anderson, 1987).

As we have seen, the role of information seeking, and more generally communication, comes primarily in supporting the decision-making process by determining alternatives and gathering information related to them. The primary issue here is that a complete range of alternatives be selected and that the pertinent information related to each of them is gathered. One key factor that distinguishes organizational as opposed to purely individual decision making is the central role of communication, especially in the selection of information sources and how they inevitably "filter" information (Cyert, Simon, & Trow, 1956). Communication processes also play a critical role in how the alternatives are discussed and eventually how decisions are implemented.

While the selection of an exhaustive list of alternatives seems to be a straightforward process, any casual review of case studies of decision making would suggest that often organizations, especially United States decision makers, seize on a limited range of alternatives and then tend to gather information to support these early choices. American organizations appear to be so focused on developing solutions to problems that they do not pay enough attention to the earlier aspects of decision making (Jablin & Sussman, 1983; Nutt, 1984). In fact, it appears that executives "prefer to copy the ideas of others or search for ready made solutions instead of seeking innovation" (Nutt, 1984, p. 445). This occurs partly because being the first to experiment or use new ideas increases the probability of failure that is often more costly to the individual than would be any rewards from a successful innovation (Nutt, 1984).

To a certain extent, we are all prisoners of our pasts and of our ideologies. Some have argued that the first stage of decision making really rests on the frame, or knowledge base, which an individual has developed because of their preexisting information fields and positioning within communication structures (Carley, 1986). The communication structure an individual is embedded in is a critical part of the decision-making process (Connolly, 1977), influencing the volume of information and the diversity of information sources (Johnson, 1993a). So we, in effect, are doubly vexed—the support structures we rely on for determining alternatives may have already formed the alternatives we are likely to identify. Thus, the essential insight of a strength of weak ties arguments also can be applied to decision-making approaches, especially for non-programmed decisions, we need to expand the range of communication sources to which we attend if we are to optimize our decision making.

Once the major alternatives have been identified, then information needs to be gathered on the crucial dimensions of each of them and their consequences (Cyert, Simon, & Trow, 1956). In many ways, this area, although it has been understudied when compared to the psychological processes associated with decision making (O'Reilly, Chatham, & Anderson, 1987; Saunders & Jones, 1990), represents some of the most intriguing findings related to decision-making research. Particularly so for the oft-repeated finding, across several contexts, that people will knowingly use lower quality, accessible information sources, which also directly relates to a manager's strong preferences for oral/interpersonal sources of information (Mintzberg, 1975a, 1975b; O'Reilly, Chatham, & Anderson, 1987).

In reviewing 78 case studies, Nutt (1984) describes two basic search strategies employed by organizations in decision making. A sequestered search, used in 60 percent of the cases, was carried out when a manager felt a need was ill-defined and threatening, precisely the case for most nonprogrammed decisions. In this situation, passive and defensive strategies were often employed, with only a few others involved in the search, and often with managers awaiting the serendipitous discovery of information. An open search, seemingly the kind most frequently promoted in the academic literature, was used when needs were seen as trivial and/or vague, and only then were subordinates brought in to help.

Advanced technology has often been cited as a boon to decision-making processes since it is said to lead to: more individuals, representing greater variety, participating as information sources; fewer people composing the actual decision unit; fewer organizational levels involved; greater spread of relevant information across the organization; less time devoted to meetings and other related activities; higher quality decisions; and more timely decisions (Fulk & Boyd, 1991; Huber, 1990). In the professional strategies section, we will discuss specifically how various groupware products are designed to overcome the problems discussed in this section.

Increasingly, organizations must structure themselves to promote the gathering and sharing of information. There is a constant dilemma for organizations: the imperative, in part stemming from efficiency needs, to limit the availability of information; and the recognition that structural designs are flawed and circumstances change, requiring individuals to seek information normally unavailable to them. Still, the design of the formal structure, and the rewards associated with it (e.g., promotion) often are designed specifically to discourage the sharing of information (Powell, 1990). Not only are there structural limits on the amount and kinds of information that any individual is likely to be exposed to, but there are also real limits to the amount of information that individuals can process given their limits (Guetskow, 1965) and the constraints of their formal roles. How they resolve these conflicting imperatives is a critical question for the modern organization.

The most basic limit on most organizational members is time. Even the most trivial organizational tasks could theoretically consume a lifetime, if all the information needed to understand them was gathered. Suppose one day I become concerned that the walkway to my office building does not convey the image I want to present of my organization. So, I decide to investigate the possibility of upgrading the landscaping. I quickly become immersed in various gardening books and am confronted with aesthetic decisions (What colors do I choose?), medical decisions (Which plants might I or potential customers be allergic to?), long-term maintenance decisions (perennials or annuals?), staffing decisions (Do I do this for a hobby, do I delegate it to an existing organizational member, do I contract it out?), ecological decisions (Am I going to use pesticides or do I decide on organic gardening?), and so on. Starting with one momentary, passing thought, I could quickly fill every waking moment with more and more information on an ever expanding problem. But I have the even more pressing problems of keeping my original business afloat, dealing with the strains on my marriage brought on by the time I have spent on this diversion, consulting my physician on the eye strain I have developed from all this late night reading, etc.

The problem is often not in deciding to seek information, but on deciding when to stop. Adept decision makers know intuitively when they have gathered enough information for any particular purpose. They "satisfice" (Mac-Crimmon & Taylor, 1976). They develop their own formula on when they have spent as much energy as they can in deciding what they should do about any particular problem that confronts them and searching for information related to it (March, 1994). They also learn to approximate, or to reach a judgment on when they can make a high enough quality decision for any particular event (Farace, Monge, & Russell, 1977). Thus, decision makers search for an appropriate solution, not *the* optimal solution (Hickson, 1987). They reach these judgments because they have developed an appreciation for what their limits are; they can mentally weigh only so much information at any given time.

The pace of managers' activities and the variety of tasks they are engaged in heighten the problems associated with any one decision, since their optimal level of performance is degraded to the extent that their energies are focused on other problems. So, the more decisions they are engaged in, the less they can really engage in concentrated information seeking on any one of them. When this is coupled with the vast amounts of information available on most business-related topics, the manager is faced with a daunting set of judgments.

Beyond these factors is the even more depressing fact that some critical information related to a decision may be unavailable. One of the ironies of the age of information, and the constant cliched arguments that we all are overloaded with information, is that there never seems to be enough information to answer very specific operational questions that we might have. Most importantly, we never know how the future may hold untold events that will alter even the most carefully laid plans. Suppose that I have spent the requisite time needed to construct the perfect walkway to my office. It is beautifully landscaped and gardened. In the following year, global warming finally kicks in, and while I had planned for a temperate climate, my garden will not withstand the desert environment it is soon to occupy.

How do I decide to go ahead and make a decision although I am missing some information? First, I need to decide how useful and available the information really is. If the missing information (e.g., what is my competitor planning) is easily available from trade sources and is critical to what I will do, I may decide to wait until I have spent the extra time and energy needed to gather it. If it is unavailable, in spite of my best efforts, and only of tangential relevance, I may decide to press ahead and make a decision, realizing that at least I will have learned that this alternative does not work. (Postponing a decision is always a decision for the *status quo ante*.) The best managers have an intuitive feel for when they have reached the optimal balance of these factors; they have reached a subjective level of confidence of when they know enough to make the best decision they can make in their current circumstances. Managers also can take some comfort in knowing that they often control how things turn out (e.g., they can provide more resources if they are needed to make something work) and they control, to a certain degree, how outcomes are interpreted (Thayer, 1988).

STRUCTURAL BARRIERS

[E]verybody is ignorant, only on different subjects. (Will Rogers, quoted in Smithson, 1989, p. 92)

Specific information about the way the company and each division are organized is carefully controlled so that employees in one division may not have a clear picture of other divisions or the company in its entirety. Official communication is handled hierarchically. Negotiations between divisions are made "from the top down." The mid- and upper-level managers are usually the most skilled communicators in the organization; they are in charge of executing cross-divisional work. In general, management of communication is an important aspect of the job. There are periodic warnings about only sharing information on a "need-to-know basis." (Zuboff, 1988, pp. 366-367, quoting an internal corporate report)

We take it as a given that some of the information that is important for the organization to make good decisions is not directly available to those charged with making the decisions. Instead, it is lodged with or producible only by other individuals or groups that are not empowered to make the decisions but may have a direct interest in the resulting outcomes. . . . In such situations, the members of the organization may have an incentive to try to manipulate the information they develop and provide in order to influence decisions to their benefits. (Milgrom & Roberts, 1988, p. 156)

Because of individual and system overloads, organizations must achieve efficiencies in their internal communication systems by message routing and message summarizing (Daft & Huber, 1987; O'Reilly & Pondy, 1979) or condensing (Downs, 1967). Underload situations and organizational slack increase the opportunities of individuals for information seeking, but it may not be clearly related to organizational objectives. Overload situations may increase the stimulation to seek information, with information junkies likely to seek more, especially for information related to enhanced performance.

One impetus behind the development of constrained communication structures is their role as information processing tools, with some even casting formal organizations as the first primitive computer (Beninger, 1990). Hierarchical systems require less information transmission than other systems, with individuals only requiring detailed information about their unit, while relying on a summary of the activities of others in the organization (Simon, 1960). Whether or not information reaches a decision maker has been said to be influenced by three factors: hierarchy, specialization, and centralization (O'Reilly, 1978).

One special type of centralization of formal communication of direct relevance to decision makers is Management Information Systems (MIS) that are designed to provide systematic information on the performance of organizational units. Considerable controversy exists over whose needs these systems really serve, in part because most managers traditionally have not found them very useful. Mintzberg (1975a) in his classic study of MIS found four basic weaknesses: (1) they are too limited in the scope of information gathered (e.g., gossip and guesses are excluded); (2) the aggregated data they produce are too general for most managers; (3) they are not timely; and (4) the information they contain is often unreliable. These problems are often exacerbated by rigid, limited organizational goals (e.g., profit maximization), the political nature of formal hierarchies, the lack of information from the organization's environment, and managers clear preferences for verbal, face-to-face channels. These weaknesses act to increase managers' reliance on informal sources of information.

As we have seen, the central impetus underlying the development of communication structures is the formal differentiation of entities into specialized subtasks who depend on each other and thus require communication to integrate their activities. "Some exclusion of organization members from organizational activities is implied in any structure of roles" (Katz & Kahn, 1978, p. 767). However, breaking up a decision-making problem into subproblems is only advantageous if there are not too many interrelationships, otherwise the coordination problems clearly outweigh the advantages of decomposition (MacCrimmon & Taylor, 1976).

The ignorance resulting from compartmentalization has the benefit of maintaining security (Moore & Tumin, 1949), and the ignorance of certain participants is essential to the maintenance of system equilibrium (Schneider, 1962;

Smithson, 1989). In fact, planned ignorance is essential to organizational efficiency. Decentralization in classic formal structures can lead to critical information being available in one unit but not in another. It also can lead to a lack of clear guidelines concerning what information is needed (Menon & Varadarajan, 1992). Imbalances in the distribution of information in organizations are a key consequence of differentiation that often benefit the interests of particular individuals, especially those in privileged or specialist positions (Moore & Tumin, 1949).

By definition, a specialist focuses on a limited domain of knowledge. The broader the domain, the less sophisticated the specialist. One way to increase the efficiency of communication is to minimize the need for it by such strategies as coordination by plan, where specialized units concentrate on fulfilling formally assigned tasks that fit into the larger whole (March & Simon, 1958). This organizational design strategy purposively encourages ignorance of the operation of other subunits, often sacrificing consistency of action of the whole for internal group consistency (March, 1994). The classic antidote to a monopoly on information is competition, often accomplished by establishing more than one channel for reporting the same information (Downs, 1967).

Kanter (1983) has offered compelling arguments that organizations that are segmented into different functional groups with strong barriers between them, especially with informal rule structures, are not going to be capable of generating or diffusing innovations. Differentiation is necessary for the synergy essential to the creation of ideas, but it also makes it difficult to ensure the consensus necessary for their implementation. Coordination relationships are critical to innovation because they are the vehicle by which information and perspectives are shared. The diverse nature of this information often is crucial to the development of unique ideas and approaches that are holistic and concerned with the overall organization and new directions for it. Segmentation inevitably leads to ignorance; structure enables and even encourages ignorance. It also leads to power imbalances, with units paradoxically becoming more powerful by avoiding dependence on others in loosely coupled organizations (Astley & Zajac, 1991); yet, in organizations of any size, "no manager will ever be knowledgeable enough to be independent of others expertise" (O'Reilly & Pondy, 1979, p. 133).

A balance must be reached between efficiency, which results from highly constrained systems, and effectiveness. While it is important to reduce information load, for example, it is also important to allow some leakage between units, so that new ideas and perspectives can be brought to problems (Peters & Waterman, 1982). Total segmentation of an organization into isolated work groups may be just as harmful as no segmentation (Kanter, 1983). Zaltman, Duncan, & Holbek (1973) have argued that low formalization, decentralization, and high complexity lead to idea generation which reflects the market-driven forces necessary for informally generated innovations. Networks may be especially useful for more qualitative information exchanges based on expert knowledge or ideas; they also create incentives for learning and the dissemination of information that promotes the quick translation of ideas into action (Powell, 1990). This is also reflected in the work of Aiken and Hage (1971) who suggest that organic organizations, with decentralized decision making, many occupations, slack resources, and a history of innovation are more likely to be innovative. Still, implementation requires high formalization, centralization, and low complexity.

One strategy which organizations adopt is to compartmentalize these processes with very rigid structures in production processes (and more flexible ones in R & D labs). However, although there is no research evidence to speak to this point, the most effective strategy in the long term may be to try to adopt a dynamic synergism between two differing structures, which sometimes overlap in messy and troublesome ways. In this regard, organizational incongruence may be related to organizational effectiveness, since it may establish the creative tension necessary to move to more productive organizational systems (Fry & Smith, 1987); this is an argument that is borne out by the research evidence that suggests individuals in liaison positions in informal networks are more productive (Downs, Clampitt, & Pfeiffer, 1988) and also more innovative (Reynolds & Johnson, 1982). Somehow organizations must achieve a balance between stability and flexibility (Weick, 1969); how to strike that balance is still very much open to question, with the answer often dependent on the nature of the culture of the organization.

CULTURAL FACTORS

Strong cultures can severely restrict the content and interactants available to individuals in their information searches; but interestingly, because of the increased sophistication of shared understandings, they can enhance the effectiveness of information seeking. They also can improve efficiency by clearly delineating roles, relationships, and contexts within which individuals seek information. In the interpretive perspective of organizational learning, the organization is viewed as a system for giving meaning to data. These meanings are determined by participants in socially constructed processes, hence, actions lead to understanding (Daft & Huber, 1987). Broadly speaking, then, culture enriches our understanding of any information we gather, while it restricts the range of answers we can seek, most obviously by specific rules structures governing the search process (March, 1994).

All cultures develop rules which limit the sharing of information. Natural language is well suited for ambiguity and deception, and often concerns for politeness lead us to equivocate, dissemble, and to tell others "white lies." We also may be limited in polite discourse to the extent to which we can self-disclose personal information. Conversely, others may be limited in the questions they feel they can ask us and the strategies they can pursue in seeking information. The line between natural curiosity and intrusiveness may be narrow. In fact, the Latin root for nice means ignorant, which also may explain why, at a societal level, good news tends to be more frequently, quickly, fully, and spontaneously communicated (Smithson, 1989).

It has been assumed for too long that overcoming organizational ignorance is simply a matter of improving communication systems and processes. It is not that organizations do not gather information or learn things, but often they gather the wrong information for the wrong reasons from the wrong sources. So, many organizations will discount external information sources because of the not-invented-here syndrome, which can result in substantial declines in performance in R & D groups when membership is stable for an extended period (Katz & Allen, 1982). Organizations also gather more information than they need to make decisions because of social norms (Feldman & March, 1981). "People seem to seek not certainty of knowledge but social validity" (March, 1994, p. 40).

Decision making and its associated formal rules can be taken to be the ultimate expression of general societal norms and specific organizational norms related to the penultimate value of rationality (March, 1994). The gathering of information often provides ritualistic assurance that the appropriate norms are being followed (Feldman & March, 1981) and someone acting as an effective decision maker is fulfilling his/her role in the organization's culture (March, 1994). Ritualistic, repetitive information gathering is commonplace with individuals in interpersonal situations; we continue to go over the same ground with individuals we like (Kellerman & Reynolds, 1990). In group contexts, members are more likely to share information they have already discussed, than to share unique information in their possession with the group (Stasser, Taylor, & Hanna, 1989). It appears that much repetitive information seeking is really aimed at increasing the confidence of decision makers in a choice they have already made (March, 1994). Information seeking often becomes a ritual which supports the appearance of rational decision making.

An example of how culture limits organizational choices is often found in innovation processes related to new technologies (Contractor & Eisenberg, 1990). Culture plays a significant role in innovation processes. Organizations often adopt information technologies not for their technical capabilities, but for their symbolic value, to demonstrate they are on the cutting edge (Nass & Mason, 1990). Cultural factors, and how groups socially construct the use of new technologies, can often limit the effectiveness of group decision-making technologies in organizations (Fulk & Boyd, 1991). Informal rules also can significantly restrict the full usage of other technologies designed to enhance information sharing (Zuboff, 1988).

At a formal level, management can effect innovation by setting goals and priorities (Daft, 1978) and a cultural emphasis on the diffusion of innovations helps (Hoffman & Roman, 1984). Perhaps the most direct assessment of the role that organizational culture plays is in issues related to the compatibility of the innovation with existing values, past experience, and the needs of adopters (Rogers, 1983). The more compatible an innovation is along these dimensions, the more likely it is to be adopted. For example, innovations such as word processing are "sold" to organizations as more efficient replacements for current practice or technology (Johnson & Rice, 1987). It is only later that an organization discovers the truly innovative features of such technologies.

Rule-Governed Relationships as Constraints on Information Seeking

Rules for gathering, storing, communicating, and using information are essential elements of organizational operating procedures. (Feldman & March, 1981, p. 171)

Rules do many things in organizations: they protect as well as restrict; coordinate as well as block; channel effort as well as limit it; permit universalism as well as provide sanctuary for the inept; maintain stability as well as retard change; permit diversity as well as restrict it. (Perrow, 1972, p. 32)

The major advantage of rules is that they provide predictability. They specify who is to do what, when, where, and sometimes how. (Hage & Aiken, 1970, p. 21)

The notion of rule has always been central to theorizing about organizations (March, 1994; Perrow, 1972; Porter, Allen, & Angle, 1981). The earliest thinking about bureaucracy noted the importance of rules for determining the actions of organizational members, and every bureaucratic organization has an elaborate set of formal rules (Rogers & Agarwala-Rogers, 1976).

Formal rules have also been seen as one primary means used by organizations to control the activities of their members, and the extent of this formalization has traditionally been considered an important element of organizational structure (Hage & Aiken, 1970; Pfeffer, 1978). Rules have also been viewed as a means of minimizing communication activities and therefore costs, since it can be presumed that rules will be followed most of the time therefore minimizing the need for direct intervention through communication to control the actions of organizational members (Pfeffer, 1978).

While rules constrain behavior, they also can be enabling. They limit the raw exercise of power in the organization and thus protect lower level organizational members (Pfeffer, 1978), partially because rules also mean workers know what is not expected of them (Morgan, 1986). Since rules often require some creativity in their application and interpretation (McPhee, 1985) they also can preserve the autonomy of organizational members (Perrow, 1972).

"To the extent that regular, habitual patterns of behavior are noted in communication activities . . . we say that certain 'rules' . . . are in effect" (Farace, Monge, & Russell, 1977, p. 132). Many deeper elements of cultural value systems become embedded and reflected in the rules governing organizational member behavior (Poole & McPhee, 1983); thus "at the heart of an organization's rule system is its culture" (Cushman, King, & Smith, 1988, p. 78).

These emergent rules are what communication scholars have focused on most in recent years. For our purposes, *rules* will be considered to be followable, prescriptive, contextual, and they pertain to behavior (Shimanoff, 1980). Thus, rules provide clear guidelines for action, including those related to information seeking, which are embedded in an organization's culture. They are prescriptive in the sense that if they are not followed, the organization may punish the violator in some manner. Rules also may function to regulate, evaluate, justify, correct, and predict behavior (Shimanoff, 1980). Indeed, a high level of coorientation, or agreement, about rules is a necessary condition for coordination in organizational settings (March, 1994; Schall, 1983).

Cushman and Whiting (1972) distinguish between two general types of rules that are critical to our understanding of organizational communication structure: content and procedural. Content rules govern how symbols (e.g., words) are used in organizations. They also can refer to such issues as what topics it is permissible to seek additional information about. For example, many organizations regard salaries of their members as confidential information, so there are rules against information seeking concerning them. On the other hand, organizational members may be encouraged to seek out information which enhances their technical performance on the job.

Procedural rules are perhaps the most central to the patterning of communication relationships in an organization. They govern such things as when an interaction will take place, how long it will last, where it will take place, etc. Most important in this context are interactant selection rules and transmission rules. Interactant selection rules govern things like whom I can solicit information from. These rules will ultimately have a major influence on the form and shape of a communication network. If I cannot seek information from people more than one level below or above me in the hierarchy, then my level of vertical communication is severely restricted. Transmission rules govern what I can do to a message that I am sending to someone else in the organization. If I am permitted to modify the content of the message, then it is more likely that the sort of problems in vertical communication discussed earlier will emerge.

Practical force determines the strength of an organization's rule system and the degree to which it can predict individual interactions. There are several factors that determine the degree of practical force in a rule system. First, the degree of coorientation of the interactants determines their level of intersubjectivity. If two parties have a consensus on the nature of a rule and its importance for various goal states, then there is more practical force. Second, the specificity of rules can affect their level of ambiguity. Third, the degree to which rule systems allow multiple paths can affect the pursuit of goals; for example, are there multiple potential sources for information? Fourth, the strength of the sanctions imposed when rules are violated can be a determinant (Poole & McPhee, 1983).

All this implies, of course, that there are interactions not governed by organizational rule systems, and that there can be conflicts between multiple rule systems (e.g., management and workers), where interactants have some discretion in negotiating their rule systems. Still, a certain minimum level of rules (and relatedly intersubjectivity) is a necessary ingredient for successful communication, and serves to structure information seeking in organizations.

INDIVIDUAL IMPEDIMENTS

[T]here is something about the uninformed which makes them harder to reach, no matter what the level or the nature of information. (Hyman & Sheatsley, 1947, p. 414)

[B]rains have difficulty processing all the relevant information—there is too much, it may not fit with expectations and previous patterns, and some of it may simply be too threatening to accept. (Mintzberg, 1975a, p. 17)

In public communication campaigns, Hyman and Sheatsley (1947) found some members of the public to be Chronic Know Nothings who appeared to have something in their psychological makeup that made them impossible to reach. Similarly, in organizational settings, there appear to be several psychological factors which make it very difficult to reach certain groups of individuals. These psychological processes are directly related to the often irrational search processes that organizational members engage in (Huber & Daft, 1987). It is in these areas especially that ignoring is not necessarily the same thing as ignorance.

Smithson (1989) has identified three normative roles underlying psychological perspectives on ignorance. The first is the "Certainty Maximizer" who tries to attain as much control and predictability as possible by learning and responding appropriately to the environment. As we have seen, this is also a very popular approach to uncertainty reduction in interpersonal communication. The second is the "statistician" approach, popular among managers, of treating uncertainty probabilistically when confronted with the unknown, ignoring ignorance where it cannot be overcome or absorbed, and selecting alternatives that maximize utility in the long run. Finally, there is the "Knowledge Seeker" thesis that argues that individuals strive to gain full information and understanding, ignoring nothing that is relevant. When we discuss information and ignorance, the image that is often fixed in our minds is that of the scientist valiantly struggling with some known unknown, or of a fictional detective trying to solve a particularly perplexing puzzle. However, beyond obsessions, curiosity, and creativity, lie a host of motivations not to seek information.

First, it is not uncommon for managers to avoid information that would force them to make a decision to overcome some problem. One can always claim that a decision was flawed because s/he was ignorant of a crucial factor in the initial decision-making process (Smithson, 1993). If they refuse to confront it, at least they won't be involved (MacCrimmon & Taylor, 1976) and they can avoid culpability and accountability (O'Reilly & Pondy, 1979; Smithson, 1989).

Second, ignorance can be used as a justification for inaction (Smithson, 1989), as represented by the classic rationalization that: "I cannot do anything until I know more about the problem." Ignorance is often used as a justification for maintaining the status quo (Smithson, 1993). Somewhat relatedly, an individual's perception of the extent to which they can shape or control events also will have an impact on their level of awareness. For many individuals, it does not make much sense to learn more about things over which they have no control, so the powerless tend not to seek information (Katz, 1968). This is true even in areas that directly bear on their well-being. For example, DeVito, Bogdanowicz, and Reznikoff (1982) have found that perceived internal locus of control was positively related to health-related information seeking.

Third, the specialist might argue that you should be ignorant of my actions, otherwise you are suggesting that you do not trust me (Smithson, 1989). Somewhat relatedly, trust is a major mediator of the open exchange of information (D'Aprix, 1988) and of cooperative relationships in organizations (Smith, Carroll, & Ashford, 1995), especially in politically charged atmospheres, it is more rewarding to be closed (Eisenberg & Whetten, 1987). In these contexts, seeking information in proscribed, taboo areas could result in sanctions that make ignorance a preferable alternative.

Fourth, often ignorance is a way of avoiding conflict. I can tacitly assume that someone agrees with me, when real knowledge of their position would lead to disputes (Smithson, 1989). This is directly related to the strategic use of ambiguity in organizations—the purposive clouding of one's true meaning (Eisenberg, 1984; Smithson, 1993).

Fifth, ignorance can often be reassuring of a comfortable inertial state, whereas knowledge might lead to arousal to take action (Smithson, 1989) or to fear. Adult learners have become highly skilled at protecting themselves from the pain and threat posed by learning situations (Senge, 1990). Often, information seekers who are conducting an unfamiliar search process, even one as simple as going to the library, experience considerable anxiety and frustration because of the unfamiliarity of the situation (Kuhlthau, 1991; Taylor, 1968).

Information carriers may be avoided because they increase uncertainty and thereby stimulate fear (Swinehart, 1968; Donohew et al., 1987). Fear can play a major role in impeding information seeking (Atkin, 1979). Fear may be so debilitating that it renders a person incapable of thinking rationally about a problem (Rosenstock, 1974). Still, in some situations, a continued state of anxiety may be preferable to the possibility of having the validity of fears confirmed (McIntosh, 1974). Acquiring more information and enhancing awareness can increase a person's uncertainty and relatedly their stress levels.

As a result, individuals and organizations often choose to reduce this uncomfortable state through processes associated with denial and apathy.

Organizations, and the individuals within them, often deny the presence of disturbing information rather than confronting it, choosing instead to smooth over differences between units (Lawrence & Lorsch, 1967). They do not want to know certain things or they hope problems will just go away. More generally, it has been argued that information seeking may not resolve ambiguity, it may create more, as it forces us to confront an often mysterious and unknowable universe (Babrow, 1992).

Sixth, while sometimes admissions of ignorance can enhance one's credibility (Smithson, 1993) and might even justify action, at least in terms of delving into the known unknown, the very act of seeking information involves admitting one's ignorance (Conrad, 1985). However, if it is an area in which they are supposed to be competent, then it may have untold consequences. Often claims of ignorance against others can be used to one's competitive advantage (Smithson, 1993). Admissions of ignorance come at substantial costs to one's own ego. Some individuals just don't have the interpersonal skills necessary to form the informal network relationships necessary to acquire information (Wilson & Malik, 1995). Others have such low self-esteem they are afraid that any information they get will confirm their already low self-concept. As a result, individuals will only admit ignorance in certain limited situations.

Allen (1977) found that a significant barrier to face-to-face interaction in which advice is sought is the ego cost to the initiator of the interaction. Engineers would prefer not to lose self-esteem in the eyes of a colleague by seeking information from them. They would seek advice, however, in situations where they knew the other engineer socially, presumably because these more multiplex relationships have more complex exchange arrangements. So, I may trade my professional expertise with a colleague in exchange for a lesson on how to play shortstop on the company softball team.

Similarly, in his classic study of a government bureaucracy, Blau (1954) found that advice seeking was related to perceived status within organizational groups. A member's status would be lowered by the constant seeking of information from higher status members, especially when the other member did not in turn ask them for information. Members preferred exchange relationships where ties were more multiplex or where there was a two-way flow of advice. Sometimes members preferred to share ignorance, even when this was explicitly proscribed behavior, rather than seeking out more authoritative information from a higher status organizational member.

Finally, and fundamentally, as we have detailed, there are cognitive limits on the amount of information individuals can process, especially in short-term memory. Miller's classic observation that we can only viably keep seven things in mind at any one time establishes an absolute barrier to information processing. Beyond this absolute limit, the presence of additional information, especially in overload conditions, lowers even this limited capacity (Mintzberg, 1975a). While it has become a truism that knowing how to search for information should be a major focus of our educational systems, rather than imparting perishable knowledge, the limits on short-term memory suggest having a sound and deep knowledge base is critical to management decision making (Lord & Maher, 1990; Mintzberg, 1975a).

There is evidence that individual information processing can be substantially enhanced by holding positions that demand higher levels of processing (Zajonc & Wolfe, 1966) and by long experience in managerial roles. So, somewhat akin to chess masters who can instantly react to complex patterns based on experience, upper level managers develop an intuitive feel for how to react to complex information patterns in organizations (Simon, 1987).

Beyond the limits of memory, humans have a limited ability to process and interpret information. They tend to exaggerate information they do register (Wales, Rarick, & Davis, 1963). They consistently tend to a confirmation bias, ignoring or discounting disconfirming evidence. They often ignore their existing base of information (the base-rate fallacy) and will focus on compelling new information. So, for example, a prodigal employee, who has been a consistently low performer, may still be viewed favorably if there is one recent positive experience. Humans also engage in the sample size fallacy, generalizing from very limited experience. So, if one recent product has met with success in a new market, they may assume other products will meet with similar success. At best, humans are limited in their capacity to seek, to process, and to correctly interpret information (Smithson, 1989).

In sum, ignorance is only one of many problems an organizational member has to confront. At times, it is better to rely on easily obtained information than to spend the effort necessary to seek complete information. In short, the costs of overcoming ignorance at times outweigh the gains. (And what is amazing is how low the costs are that establish absolute barriers to information seeking.) It is even possible, at least for particular topics, to be sated, to have acquired enough information. In the end, there may be as many, if not more, reasons for not seeking as for seeking information.

TECHNICAL ACCESS BARRIERS

Glorification of exploration obscures the fact that most new ideas are bad ones, most changes are detrimental, and most original inventions are not worth the effort devoted to producing them. (March, 1994, p. 238)

The weak link in the information chain is the increasingly inadequate absorption capacity of individuals and organizations. Computer technology does not help much—unless underlying information is quantitative and structured, and questions are well defined. (Noam, 1993, p. 203)

Organizations may be unable, because of organizational or human limitations, to process the information they have. (Feldman & March, 1981, p. 875)

"[A]ll men by nature desire to know": these familiar opening words of Aristotle's *Metaphysics* (which, over the centuries, teachers of the young have repeatedly had reason to question) continue to state the underlying rationale of university education. (Pelikan, 1992, p. 32)

As we have seen, there are deep-seated barriers to information seeking— structural, cultural, the limits of individual decision makers, and so forth. Unfortunately, many of these barriers present insurmountable dilemmas for anyone interested in facilitating information seeking, partly because maximizing information seeking means minimizing an often more important organizational process (e.g., preserving existing power bases, maintaining an organizational culture). Technical access barriers primarily involve lack of familiarity with or access to information sources, and so would appear on the surface to be much more amenable to rational solutions. Regrettably, and somewhat disconcertingly, the threshold where these issues become absolute barriers to information seeking is low.

Search Problems

Barriers related to technical search problems primarily relate to awareness of and access to information sources. A large part of technical education consists of defining for individuals what is an appropriate source of information and how one can gain access to these sources. As we have seen in Chapter 4, when the CMIS was discussed, an individual's education level probably has the most important consequence for their subsequent information seeking (Chen & Hernon, 1982). Another factor that affects information seeking in the CMIS is an individual's degree of direct experience. Unfortunately, while our knowledge of how to seek information improves with age, our ability to use the resulting information does not (Rouse & Rouse, 1984).

Direct experience has somewhat of an insidious side effect, since once someone is familiar with a source they tend to continue to use it (Culnan, 1983). This leads to a certain amount of inertia in the use of information sources. Individuals are reluctant to move from the old tried-and-true sources, partly because they hold off evaluating a source until they have some experience using it (Culnan, 1983). Interestingly, almost two-thirds of respondents in a regional survey said they would return to a source even when they had characterized it in the least helpful category (Chen & Hernon, 1982).

The problem of inertia is exacerbated by the number of competing sources of information available on any one subject. Most individuals find, partly because of time pressures, that they cannot engage in a comprehensive search for information. Given that there may be ten sources of information available and they are familiar with two, and they trust them based on prior experience, there may be little perceived benefit to consulting any one of the remaining eight. Most often, "the search for alternatives terminates when a satisfactory solution has been discovered even though the field of possibilities has not been exhausted" (Cyert, Simon, & Trow, 1956, p. 246). This happens, in part, because each additional piece of information makes it more difficult to determine what might be relevant to a particular problem (O'Reilly & Pondy, 1979). Individuals also fall into competency traps—they will not learn new, often superior techniques, because they are performing well with the old ones (March, 1994).

Of course, each additional source of information adds confidence in a course of action if they corroborate each other. But if the sources do not provide consistent answers, a not unlikely circumstance, then someone has complicated their decision making. In fact, more communication can result in greater ambiguity and uncertainty, not improved decision making (Rice & Shook, 1990). While inconsistent information may often be a spur for additional information seeking to find a "tie breaking" source of information, there is no guarantee that this additional source of information will not present yet another major alternative. So it becomes easier to understand why there might be real benefits, at least in terms of the amount of effort expended, to consulting only a limited range of familiar sources.

Access

In many ways, the findings related to the importance of access are some of the most compelling in the social science literature. What is fascinating, if not downright amazing, is the consistent set of findings suggesting that the threshold point where a source is considered inaccessible is amazingly low. For example, Allen (1977) describes information access in research and development laboratories as determined by gradually diminishing communication up to 50 feet away from an interactant, with communication beyond that characterized by a dramatic dropoff. So an engineer who is seeking an answer to a technical problem (e.g., what is the best material to use for constructing a safe bridge) is usually unwilling to walk more than 50 feet away from his/her desk to get this information. Somewhat similarly, organizational members will not invest more than 30 minutes of their time to learn an online catalog information system; and when they did use computerized retrieval systems, they would typically rely on a very limited number of commands (Borgman, 1986).

Even more disturbing is that access also may be the single most important criterion in evaluation by users of an information system (Rice & Shook, 1990). So accessibility outweighs quality to determine usage of information from particular sources (Choo & Auster, 1993; Culnan, 1983; Gerstberger & Allen, 1968; O'Reilly, 1982; Taylor, 1968). If our engineer is walking to the optimal source of information 45 feet away, and happens to run into another, albeit less reliable, source of information in a 20-foot radius, then his/her search is likely to stop there.

In fact, it is a common finding that individuals will knowingly rely on inferior information sources for answers to their problems, because it would take too much effort to get authoritative information (Pinelli, 1991). A number of studies document cases where organizational members will seek out information from inferior sources because of the reduced costs involved (Blau, 1954; Allen, 1977). Allen (1977), in his research stream involving communication in research and development laboratories, has consistently found that professionals will seek the most readily accessible source of information, both in terms of physical distance and comprehensibility, rather than the "best" sources, which offer more professionally authoritative information. Somewhat relatedly, less than 20 percent of the general populace followed up on referrals by information specialists to professionals or institutions for answers to their questions (Chen & Hernon, 1982). Beyond accessibility, the relevance of the information also is more important than its quality to managers (Menon & Varadarajan, 1992) and respondents are not very concerned with how up-to-date information is (Chen & Hernon, 1982).

Even when individuals need information, they often do not actively, comprehensively search for it; rather they will wait until they accidentally stumble across the information, often in interpersonal encounters (Scott, 1991). "Many respondents reported that they made use of an information provider only as an afterthought in relation to another need" (Chen & Hernon, 1982, p. 57). Often people have pending questions, but they will only pose them if they are running out of other options of what to do with their time. (For instance, there is the classic medical example of a person with a lump s/he is concerned about, but does not do anything about until s/he is running out of topics for conversation with the doctor s/he has just met at a party. Even more disconcerting is that s/he is likely to accept an answer from a nurse's aide or even a car mechanic rather than a physician [Chen & Hernon, 1982].)

Costs

These technical access problems all are related to the "costs" of information seeking compared to the value or benefit of the information sought, particularly in relation to decision making (March, 1994). The costs of information acquisition are many—psychological, temporal, and material. Most seekers appear to assume it is better to rely on easily obtained information, they have an answer after all, no matter how dubious, than to spend the effort necessary to get complete information. The "costs" in terms of extra time and effort for a complete information search, which also may result in delaying opportunities, complicating decision making, and increasing information overload, are real. There are also additional psychological costs, such as the loss of self-

Table 5.2
Costs and Benefits of Differing Levels of Ignorance

Level of Ignorance	Costs		Benefits

High	(1)	Don't Confront Problems
		Lack of Coordination
		Lower Integration
		Opportunities Foregone
			(2) Comfort of Denial
			Easier Control
			More Anomie/
			   Easier to
			   Manipulate
			Lower Information
			   Processing Costs

Low	(3)	Increased Conflict
		Alienation
		More Difficult to Control
		Higher Information
		   Processing Costs
			(4) More Likely to
			   Confront Problems
			Greater Coordination
			Higher Integration
			Opportunities
			   Addressed

esteem and frustration, that result from an unsuccessful search (Hudson & Danish, 1980).

These consistent patterns of findings have been articulated in various "laws" of information-seeking behavior. The classic law of "least effort" has been evoked to articulate why channels are chosen first that involve the least effort (Broadbent & Koenig, 1988; Doctor, 1992; Hudson & Danish, 1980; Krikelas, 1983; Pinelli, 1991; Saunders & Jones, 1990). Mooer's Law suggests an information source or system will tend not to be used whenever it is more painful and troublesome to have the information than it is not to have it (Culnan, 1983).

Beyond these generalizations lies the basic assumption that people desire to know. In user needs studies of the public, done for libraries, from 10 to 20 percent of respondents report that they have *no* question or problem for which they need answers (Krikelas, 1983). In sum, in many instances, the costs of obtaining information make ignorance, or at least less than complete information, a preferable state.

SUMMARY

As a way of summarizing this chapter, we will organize our discussion around the dimensions presented in Table 5.2. The cells in this table are classified by levels of ignorance (awareness of things known to others in the organization), and the costs and benefits of ignorance for organizational members. Typically, research and thought in organizational theory has dwelled on Cells 1 and 4 to the exclusion of Cells 2 and 3. It is by analyzing these cells for the inherent dilemmas information seeking presents for an organization that a greater understanding of the persistence of ignorance will result.

Cell 1 is the straw man to which Cell 4 is often compared, the worst case scenario of high levels of ignorance and high costs to the organization. In this situation, the organization does not confront problems and therefore does not correct them in a timely fashion. It also does not seize opportunities that can result from successful problem solution. As in the case of the classic segmented organization discussed earlier, there is a general lack of coordination and integrative efforts toward common organizational goals. As a result, at the very least, there is a lot of wasted energy; at the worst, often members of this type of organization work at cross purposes to each other

However, as we have seen, there are also benefits to high levels of ignorance in organizations. This is the set of conditions that serve to maintain ignorance that are often overlooked by management theorists and that have been neglected in the research arena. Managers in traditional hierarchical organizations can use these segmented organizations to divide and conquer. They can always maintain to any employee pressing for change "if only you knew what I know then you would act in the same way that I do." So control in this type of organization is easier to achieve. In addition, there are lower levels of information load and therefore lower information processing costs. Individuals also have the comfort of denying the existence of problems that they would have to work to overcome. Particularly for individuals, then, the benefits of high levels of ignorance may offset the costs, which are largely borne by future organizational members.

The costs of achieving low levels of ignorance are substantial, especially for effective information processing systems (Hoffman, 1994). Curiously, more detailed knowledge of how the system really works can sometimes result in higher levels of cynicism (Bellah et al., 1991; Greider, 1992). Some have suggested that since coordinated action is what is important in an organization, sharing information about values and beliefs may be dysfunctional because of the possibility for increasing conflict (Eisenberg & Riley, 1988). Since traditional behaviors and value maintenance often depend in part on ignorance of alternatives (Moore & Tumin, 1949), ignorance often serves to reinforce ultimate values and heighten a sense of community (Smithson, 1989).

In many ways, Cell 4, characterized by low levels of ignorance and many benefits, is the optimal cell, since this is the set of conditions many management theorists and popularizers of management issues seem to suggest we should be striving toward (Peters & Waterman, 1982; Dean & Bowen, 1994; Galbraith, 1995). In this utopian world, we have high levels of coordination and integration. We have knowledgeable organizational members confronting and then solving problems, thus not letting opportunities slip through their grasp. Indeed, Blau (1955) found that information seeking related to novel, unique cases was educational to other agents, stimulating useful work-related discussions.

Still, this, as the other cells demonstrate, can be a costly world for organizations and their members. What tips the balance toward this cell in today's environment is that organizations may have no other choice; if they are to survive in the long term, they must pay the price of adopting the strategies we discuss in the next two chapters.

SIX

STRATEGIES FOR SEEKERS
(AND NONSEEKERS)

Yet it seems that information-seeking must be one of our most fundamental methods for coping with our environment. The strategies we learn to use in gathering information may turn out to be far more important in the long run than specific pieces of knowledge we may pick up in our formal education and then soon forget as we go about wrestling with our day-to-day problems. (Donohew, Tipton, & Haney, 1978, p. 389)

Those who do not become learners again, regardless of age or rank, will find themselves at an increasing disadvantage as the information economy takes root. (Marchand & Horton, 1986, p. 21)

As we have seen, information seeking in organizations is a complex phenomenon and there are many barriers to it that seekers must overcome. Individuals are faced with three fundamental information-seeking problems: (1) they have more choices; (2) they have more sources of information regarding these choices; and (3) more information is targeted at influencing their behavior (Marchionini, 1992).

The previous chapters have been devoted to understanding information seeking. In this and the following chapter, we turn to strategies that might be employed by seekers and by management to facilitate and enhance information seeking. Before we turn to that task, a summary of some common findings in the information-seeking literature is in order, since they can serve as useful benchmarks for evaluating the comprehensiveness and efficacy of any strategies we recommend.

First, people seek out information that is the most accessible. Accessibility may be *the* most critical issue in designing information systems. What is most surprising is how little it takes for a source to be deemed inaccessible. Similarly, and somewhat disconcertingly, accessibility overrides such issues as the credibility and authoritativeness of a source. So, individuals will knowingly seek out inferior information from a more accessible source. Hanser and Muchinsky (1978) found interpersonal sources like supervisors were seen as more reliable, and respondents gave more weight to characteristics of the source than to types of information provided in selecting sources of information. Yet, having access to information means very little if an individual does not have the proper information-seeking skills and training to retrieve it (Doctor, 1992).

Second, seekers are often unaware of sources and how to use them (Doctor, 1992; Varlejs, 1986). Caldwell and O'Reilly (1985) found that individuals who sought the most information from differing sources related to a job change, and who were later concerned about the usefulness of the information they gathered, were most likely to leave after a period of six months. In other words, unsuccessful searches led to poor job choices. Especially at the beginning of a search, users are often in a state of flux, without clear criteria, and with the search proceeding in a dynamic fashion with values of information and sources changing as it proceeds (Chang & Rice, 1993). In their early stages, searches can be characterized by the gathering of bits and pieces that an individual can fit into a coherent whole (Bates, 1989). This implies that one viable strategy for organizations may be to conduct information campaigns and training programs that increase an individual's awareness of sources and how to use them, and that help them determine what they are appropriate for. Interestingly, the more experience someone has with a channel, the more accessible they also perceive it to be (Gerstberger & Allen, 1968). This also leads to the expert's paradox: the greater one's subject matter expertise, the greater the likelihood they will find information, but the less likely that it will be informative (at least in its novelty) (Buckland, 1991a).

Third, people follow habitual patterns in their information seeking (Chen & Hernon, 1982; Varlejs, 1986). They fall into a pattern of information seeking on particular topics. The information they have previously acquired facilitates any efforts to acquire additional information (Chaffee & McCleod, 1973), which suggests that the critical first step in facilitating information seeking is encouraging a habit for it. Unfortunately, most people have bad information-seeking habits, and there is considerable inertia that must be overcome in changing their existing behaviors. For example, for the general populace, regardless of the type of information needed (e.g., health information), the first source they will consult is a friend or family member (Beal, 1979).

Fourth, face-to-face interpersonal communication is *the* preferred mode of communication for information seeking. As we have seen, face-to-face communication offers many compelling advantages, including flexibility, feedback and subsequent message modification, greater relevance, and a greater variety of rewards (Brittain, 1970) and timeliness (Katzer & Fletcher, 1992). It also is specific, vivid, and concrete, which generally is the kind of information organizational decision makers prefer (March, 1994). It is the type of information managers prefer for environmental scanning as well, especially for information on markets and competitors (Choo & Auster, 1993).

Some have argued that the heavily interpersonal nature of managerial work places a real upper bound on the use of information technologies (McGee & Prusak, 1993), with users especially resistant to technologies that they see as barriers to interpersonal contact (Paisley, 1993). Even factual, quantitative data like sales figures is often distributed in a manner similar to classic diffusion of innovation patterns (i.e., verbally through the grapevine) before it is released officially in written documents (McKinnon & Bruns, 1992).

Yet, face-to-face communication also has its liabilities, especially in terms of completeness, since most organizational members either do not get needed information or are information sinks who do not pass it on.

Individuals would prefer to turn to an individual that they know and trust for information (Burke & Bolf, 1986; Doctor, 1992; Hudson & Danish, 1980), so they are more likely to seek sources of information from inside rather than outside the organization (Dewhirst, 1971). Most especially, people want to consult others who have digested and evaluated an array of written information (McGee & Prusak, 1993). Thus, information seeking is very similar to the traditional findings of opinion leadership. In our interpersonal networks we know who has expertise in particular areas. These people are likely to be the first objects of information seeking when we have a problem in their domain. Interestingly, this preference also preserves the power and authority of senior managers, who may be the only ones who can consistently demand face-to-face access to a wide range of others in organizations (McKinnon & Bruns, 1992).

Fifth, different types of persons use different sources of information (Varlejs, 1986). Usually the more experienced, educated, and knowledgeable the individual, the wider the array of information sources consulted, and the greater his/her access to professionals and organizations (Doctor, 1992). Creative scientists and engineers are more likely to consult a wide range of information sources, especially sources outside their disciplines (Kasperson, 1978).

Beyond such broad generalizations, however, are the different patterns of searches that have become accepted as "standard practice" in various disciplines. Gould and Pearce (1991) have detailed the differences in a wide range of natural sciences in what are considered to be authoritative sources of information likely to be consulted by researchers. So, while we will cover general strategies of information seeking, the reader needs to understand that the particular "profile" of any one individual also may reflect the unique informal norms and socialization practices of a particular profession. (What is "truth" for an accountant may be considerably different from what is "truth" for a personnel officer.)

In this and the following chapter, we develop general approaches targeted at seekers and managers for facilitating and encouraging information seeking. If for no other reason than that individuals are driven to make sense of their environment, it would be to management's benefit to at least be aware of the sources they are likely to consult for this purpose. In turn, the information they actively seek is more likely to have an impact on their attitudes and behaviors than information that has been provided to them.

MOTIVATED SEEKING

In general, the focus of the literature has been on how we can provide information to organizational members, rather than what motivates them to seek answers to questions they pose for themselves. We do not know much about what motivates an individual to seek information, especially in terms of more prosocial seeking associated with personal growth, creativity, curiosity, or sharing information with co-workers (Burke & Bolf, 1986). One consistent argument found in the literature is that people with high growth needs are more likely to consult a wide range of information sources (Varlejs, 1986). Organizations should nurture these individuals by providing them with the autonomy to pursue their searches. In short, organizations must provide an environment that values and encourages learning (McGee & Prusak, 1993).

A condition that organization's may wish to encourage is one where individuals feel that they are in the "groove," i.e., that they are jamming with the information environment around them (Eisenberg, 1990). People want to maximize their cognitive load, as well as their enjoyment (Marchionini, 1992); they do not like tasks or information systems that add to their frustration or interrupt their task performance. They prefer systems that are intrinsically gratifying and that have an intuitive game-like feel (Paisley, 1993).

So, for example, people do not like "two-step" information systems that cite sources of information that they must later look up. The concept of flow, which captures playfulness and exploratory experience, has been said to encourage people to use new and unfamiliar information technologies (Trevino & Webster, 1992). Flow theory, most associated with the work of Csikszentmihalyi, suggests that involvement in a flow state is self-motivating because it is pleasurable and encourages repetition (Trevino & Webster, 1992). A flow state exists when an individual feels in control (e.g., feedback, selecting from options) of the technology, his/her attention is focused, curiosity is aroused, and the activity they are engaged in is intrinsically interesting. Increasingly, the best computer software, especially that with multimedia capability, captures the conditions of a flow state.

As we have seen, there is a major discrepancy between optimal information-seeking behaviors and the typical pattern of information seeking one finds in organizations. One way organizations can address this problem is to be very careful in their recruitment and hiring practices to ensure that they are getting self-sufficient seekers. It must be recognized that information acquisition is an important life skill that should be central to our educational efforts to produce life-long learning, as well as training for particular professions. Most of our major life problems are associated with lack of knowledge, skills, or ability to assess risks. Information and the skills to acquire it are critical to surmounting these problems (Hudson & Danish, 1980).

Another strategy is to increase the salience of these issues through better training programs that address optimal search behaviors (e.g., appropriate key word selection) and acquaint individuals with unfamiliar sources of information, such as the search engines we will discuss in the next chapter. In general, organizations do not give their workers sufficient guidance on what the optimal sources of information are (Burke & Bolf, 1986). Acquainting individuals with sources that are relevant (Saracevic, 1975) and useful in their immediate work is the critical first step to developing better information-seeking habits.

In looking at the individual, we must recognize that communication events in organizations are characterized by a complex of goals, with multiple motives. Strategies that individuals pursue also can be complex; an information-seeking attempt may be masked as a persuasive message on another matter (Contractor & Eisenberg, 1990). So, I may go into my boss with a suggestion for improving work in the office, but the answer I am really seeking is whether s/he still values me enough to give me material support. In this section, we will look at two issues: the information requirements of individual roles in organizations, and feedback-seeking strategies related to individual work performance.

Information Requirements of Positions

In general, task characteristics have been argued to be the most influential factor in determining interpersonal and group communication patterns in organizations (Jablin, 1987; Penley, 1977). For example, Simpson (1952) found that mechanization reduced the need for close supervision and vertical communication, since machines dictated the work pace for subordinates. Mechanization correspondingly increased the need for horizontal communication among first-line supervisors related to joint problem solving and coordinating the work. A worker's need for information differs by the requirements of the positions they occupy. Often, jobs are reengineered to minimize the need for someone to seek information, which is an approach that has been labeled by its critics as deskilling. Thus, the institution of plans in bureaucratic organizations are designed to reduce the amount of information processed (Galbraith, 1973).

Technological imperatives heavily influence the content of communication that flows within a role set, although the amount of this communication can be mediated by spatial factors as well (Katz & Kahn, 1978). Role set communication is one of the most direct indications of interdependencies and coordination requirements existing within an organization. In fact, as Katz and Kahn (1978) note, occupants of the offices to which roles are tied are usually associated with a few others who are adjacent to them in the work flow structure or the hierarchy of authority of an organization. Thus, "Generally, role behavior refers to the recurring actions of an individual, appropriately inter-related with the repetitive activities of others so as to yield a predictable outcome" (Katz & Kahn, 1978, p. 189).

Katz and Kahn's (1978) role episode model provides a good framework, then, within which to examine the impacts of information seeking on task performance. A role is defined as the total requirements with which the or-ganizational system faces the employee. A role set might be composed of the focal person's supervisor, subordinates, and those others with whom the mem-ber must work. In other words, the role set is a focal network of relationships emanating from the individual. Each member of the role set has expectations about the focal person's behavior; role sending occurs when these expectations are communicated to the focal person. Thus, members of a role set are likely to be the immediate, local source of information-seeking attempts.

Managing interdependence between units by coordinating and controlling their activities is critical to organizational design (Pfeffer, 1978). The greater the interdependence among work units, the greater their need for coordination (Cheng, 1983) and, somewhat relatedly, information seeking. In turn, the higher the levels of coordination required, especially by more personal mech-anisms, the greater the volume of communication (Hage, Aiken, & Marrett, 1971). These processes are also crucial because of the many communication problems associated with hierarchies, such as blockage of information and slowing of message flow, as well as the natural tendency for rivalries to develop between functionally separated units (Lee, 1970).

A variety of means (e.g., matrix, human relations, and formal integrating mechanisms) have been used to encourage interaction between entities of the formal organization, which the organizational chart in effect serves to isolate (O'Neill, 1984). There is a rich literature on various levels of coordination reflected in such notions as loose coupling and the strength of weak ties. Perhaps the most comprehensive, systematic discussion of this issue, espe-cially in the context of formal structural approaches to design related to in-formation processing, is found in the early work of Galbraith (1973, 1974).

Galbraith's central assumption is that the greater the uncertainty faced by the organization, the more it must concentrate its efforts on communication, particularly integrating mechanisms designed to increase the levels of coor-dination between work units (Galbraith, 1973, 1974). These integrating mech-anisms, especially the more personal ones (e.g., liaisons), also overcome some inherent communication problems (e.g., failures to report critical information) of the hierarchy (Lee, 1970). The organization's capacity for handling com-munication related to coordination will determine how much interdepen-dence, and relatedly differentiation, it can handle (March & Simon, 1958). One way to increase the efficiency of communication is to minimize the need for it by such strategies as coordination by plan, where units concentrate on fulfilling formally assigned tasks that fit into the larger whole (March & Simon, 1958).

At low levels of uncertainty, an organization can rely on rules and programs, the hierarchy, and goal setting to accomplish integration. These strategies constitute the traditional formal managerial structure of an organization, and they will be used in sequence as uncertainty increases within an organization. Rules and programs refer to procedures established in advance for predictable organizational behaviors. Each unit contributes its part of the larger project without much need for communication between units. For example, a plan may be in place that specifies in great detail the contribution of each unit in a production process. Still, even the most detailed plan often runs into difficulties in implementation. Exceptional circumstances may arise that require coordination by management to ensure that proper levels of relationships are maintained between units. This intervention by the hierarchy ensures completion of the project. As uncertainty increases, management may decide that it is more efficient to coordinate units by establishing targets for them. Management lets the units themselves decide how the targets will be achieved. Coordination is achieved by each unit reaching the goal set by management.

However, as uncertainty reaches even higher levels, the traditional hierarchical approach runs into difficulty and the organization is confronted with strategies that involve a departure from traditional perspectives of coordination. Essentially, the major choice an organization faces is whether to reduce the need for information processing or increase its capacity to process information. Reduction in need depends primarily on the strategies of creating slack resources and self-contained tasks, which are both aimed at reducing the need for communication between units. Increasing the capacity requires investments in vertical information systems, such as computer-based management information systems that we will discuss in the next chapter, and the creation of lateral relations that require a heavy investment in human resources. The creation of lateral resources involves much more personalized integrating mechanisms such as liaisons, task forces, and teams. In these groups, often individuals are charged with specialized information seeking relating to a more holistic organizational goal. Thus, the group defines the problem set for individuals within it. As we will see shortly, groups are an important moderator of individual information seeking in organizations.

Feedback Seeking

The area related to information seeking that has probably received the most research attention over the last decade is feedback seeking related to individual performance (Ashford & Tsui, 1991), especially during organizational entry or job changing (e.g., Feldman & Brett, 1983; Brett, Feldman, & Weingart, 1990; Comer, 1991; Morrison & Bies, 1991; Morrison, 1993a, 1993b). Of particular interest has been the strategies that individuals use to uncover information about task, cultural, and other expectations an organization might have related to their performance (Miller & Jablin, 1991). The information that newcomers acquire is critical for determining their adjustment to the organization and their performance within it. Information seeking thus becomes a significant coping mechanism for individuals (Brett et al., 1990). Typically feedback seeking about performance is associated with positive adjustment of newcomers and poor adjustment for job changers (Brett, Feldman, & Weingart, 1990), who perhaps thought they knew more about a job from their past experiences than they really did.

A newcomer in the organization is often confronted with a vast array of information that s/he must make sense of in order to determine appropriate behaviors. Formally, his/her supervisor may lay out a set of expectations, which are then reinforced by a job description sheet. Informally, s/he may be told that job performance is not the critical issue: how well you perform on the company softball team is. Feedback seeking often complements formal organizational socialization efforts, filling in the gaps and interpreting seeming discrepancies in the information provided to employees (Miller & Jablin, 1991). Active information seeking is often necessary because organizations withhold information inadvertently or purposively (Miller & Jablin, 1991). Organizations may not want to share all their secrets until someone has passed an initiation period and can be trusted. They also may want to "protect" employees during the initial "honeymoon" period. At times, they also may try to keep employees from coming into contact with dissidents who may impede socialization efforts. They also may want to keep employees "on edge" because they assume that withholding positive feedback will heighten employee effort. Whatever information is acquired must be assimilated quickly because typically, especially in American companies, impressions are formed very rapidly about an organizational member's capabilities.

The vast array of information that newcomers are exposed to, and the gaps in the information they are provided, often result in high levels of uncertainty. This uncertainty affects people's perceptions of role ambiguity and can impede an employee's job satisfaction, productivity, and ultimately affect his/her tenure. With such uncomfortable feelings, employees are driven to seek information that would reduce the uncertainty they are experiencing (Miller & Jablin, 1991). But here they may be doubly vexed because they may be inexperienced information seekers who don't know what strategies are appropriate or useful in this organization. So, often a naive employee will think that question-asking is the only available information strategy they have, little realizing that asking direct questions about sensitive areas may be taboo. Counterbalancing the uncertainty newcomers are experiencing are the social costs of seeking information (Miller & Jablin, 1991) and a desire to manage the impression they give others (Morrison & Bies, 1991). However, impression management is often a subtle process, with actively seeking negative information more associated with positive impressions of supervisors (Ashford & Tsui, 1991), since it appears to be motivated by a desire to improve.

Costs, as we have seen, are real and numerous, and may impede information-seeking behaviors. Individuals may be afraid of going to the well once too often and being cut off from information from a particular source. They may assume that someone will think they are dumb for asking a particular question. They may think that information seeking reflects poorly on their competence and their training to perform a particular job (Ashford, 1986). These factors may result in individuals pursuing less direct, overt means of acquiring information (Miller & Jablin, 1991).

Information seeking for newcomers differs in several ways from that of established organizational members. As we have seen, it may involve much more uncertainty and urgency. It also may be more thoughtful, with newcomers consciously weighing the efficacies of various strategies they might employ, since they have not yet established the habits of information seeking particular to their profession and a specific organizational context (Miller & Jablin, 1991). Newcomers also focus on three primary types of information: referent (what are my job requirements?), appraisal (how well am I doing?), and relational (do other people like me?) (Miller & Jablin, 1991).

Strategies for Individual Information Seeking

While we will primarily focus on strategies that have been identified for newcomers in this section, we also will try to develop a comprehensive list of strategies that are more generally used by individuals in organizations. As always, we are most concerned with how individuals gather information for their purposes. Thus, information seeking can be directly related to self-performance assessment, where individuals determine if they are meeting personal standards and goals (Ashford, 1986, 1989; Ashford & Cummings, 1985; Ashford & Tsui, 1991).

The most obvious strategy, and seemingly the most efficient (Comer, 1991), is to ask *overt questions* on the topic of interest. So, if I am a new secretary, I may ask if I am expected to make coffee every morning. Asking overt questions may be expected and encouraged early in someone's tenure in an organization. This strategy is more likely to be used when an individual feels comfortable with a situation—when they want a direct, immediate, and authoritative reply. Individuals may feel uncomfortable asking direct questions if they perceive others will view them as constantly pestering them for information, or if the question reveals (e.g., I do not know how to perform my job) more about themselves than they want others to know (Miller & Jablin, 1991). Use of questioning also involves a choice for the target of the question (Ashford, 1986), which in itself may be a difficult choice (Morrison, 1993b). Similarly, there is also the risk that a question (e.g., How well am I doing?) will result in a negative answer (Brett, Feldman, & Weingart, 1990) that both supervisor and employee would like to avoid (Ashford, 1986; Larson, 1989).

Indirect questions are often employed in cases where someone is uncomfortable (Miller & Jablin, 1991). They usually take the form of a simple declarative sentence or observation that is meant to solicit information, often disguised within an apparently casual conversation. Blau (1955) observed workers establishing occasions for information seeking by hanging out with others (i.e., merely being present at informal events). So at lunch, I might say to a co-worker: "You know the boss was really nice when I talked to her. She encouraged me to come and see her whenever I had a question." The co-worker, if they are concerned about my well-being, and this observation is inaccurate, might then tell me: "Well, she means well, but she is really busy, and might not like it if you interrupt her too often."

Yet another strategy is to use a *third party* as an intermediary to gather information. Thus, rather than asking your supervisor, who serves as a primary source, you might ask his/her assistant as a secondary source of information (Miller & Jablin, 1991). This strategy would be used most often when a primary source is unavailable or the seeker feels uncomfortable approaching him/her directly. The downside to this strategy is that the secondary source must be trustworthy and a true surrogate for the primary source. At times, the most approachable individuals to a newcomer are those individuals who are most likely to lead them astray, who may have their own motivations for undermining a supervisor or giving an alternative version of an organization's culture.

Another, more dangerous, strategy that individuals might engage in is *testing limits* (Miller & Jablin, 1991). So, if an individual really wants to find out how his/her supervisor will react to tardiness, s/he might try getting to work progressively later each day. Obviously this strategy is potentially confrontational and the employee runs the risk of the supervisor generalizing from the specific behavior to more global assessments (e.g., this employee is untrustworthy). Still, individuals might use this as a last resort, especially when the issue is of paramount personal importance to them.

A less direct strategy is that of *observing* (Miller & Jablin, 1991). Employees can watch the actual behaviors of their supervisors and co-workers and weigh them against their words. Managers, too, are likely to give special credence to what they observe (McKinnon & Bruns, 1992). Employees can often learn how to handle critical situations from just being with an experienced coworker. Thus, an individual can inconspicuously imitate another's behavior. There are limits, however, to what a new employee can directly observe, especially concerning the thought processes that may underlie particular actions.

Beyond the newcomers information-seeking strategies identified traditionally in the literature, there are other strategies [e.g., skimming, berrypicking (Bates, 1989), chaining, monitoring key sources for developments (Ellis, 1989)] that have been identified in the information science literature, that also might pertain to this problem, and, more generally, to other information-seeking situations as well. Probably the most interesting of these is browsing, because of its random, nonrational surface appearance.

Browsing essentially involves scanning the contents of a resource base. It is often used as a strategy early in a search process or when someone is scanning his/her environment (O'Connor, 1993). A key element of browsing is preparedness to be surprised and to follow up (Chang & Rice, 1993). Thus, in researching this book, I would look at book titles surrounding those identified by more formal, rational computerized searches. In doing this, I often found works that were more interesting to me than the immediate objects of my search. Inadequate browsing capacity has been traditionally a major short-coming of most computerized search software (Chang & Rice, 1993). Browsing in social contexts often takes the form of informal networking. Casual conversations (e.g., gossip) in a group may take on elements of browsing, with more intensive followups on topics that interest an individual. Even the classic principle of management by walking around (e.g., touring a plant) has been identified as a type of browsing (Chang & Rice, 1993). Browsing is facilitated by accessibility, flexibility, and interactivity (Chang & Rice, 1993).

In sum, while many tactics have been identified, we know less about which factors will trigger the use of any one tactic. We also do not know answers to such fundamental questions as how many tactics individuals are aware of and actually use in their behavioral repertoire. We also know very little about the sequencing of tactics and how individuals might use them in combination for particular effects (Miller & Jablin, 1991). We do know that newcomers use a variety of channels and obtain information on a range of contents (Comer, 1991), with particular channels and sources associated with each other. So, for example, accountants are more likely to use a questioning strategy for technical problems and are more likely to consult co-workers for normative and social information (Morrison, 1993b).

BROKERS OF INFORMATION

As much of this book details, information seeking is often a great challenge to individuals. They have to overcome their tendency to deny the possibility of bad news, and perhaps some of the distasteful problems associated with organizational life. They also have to be willing to believe that their individual actions can make a difference, that by seeking information they gain some control and mastery over their tasks. They also have to overcome the limits of their education and knowledge base. They have to possess: skills as information seekers, a knowledge of databases, familiarity with the Internet, and an ability to weigh conflicting sources of information and to make judgments about their credibility. In short, any one of the factors on this rather long linked chain could severely impede, if not halt, the information-seeking process.

Recognizing this, individuals are increasingly relying on intermediaries to conduct searches for them. Here we are not discussing organizations, such as the Commerce Department or various technological competitiveness incubators (as we will detail in the next chapter), which are very useful repositories of information for organizations. Nor will we focus on traditional organizational boundary spanners, such as customer service representatives, whose primary function is to help a customer locate information they need within the boundary spanner's organization (Gurbaxani & Whang, 1991). Rather, we will focus on a growing trend for individuals to seek out representatives charged to act for them in acquiring the information that they need.

Perhaps the most interesting recent development in the area of individual intermediaries/advocates is the emergence of individual entrepreneurs who take over the information-seeking tasks of individuals for them. In addition to more efficiently linking buyers and sellers of information, the traditional role of brokers (Malone, Yates, & Benjamin, 1987b), electronic brokers serve direct information-seeking functions. These individuals are most useful when an individual is willing to engage in a proactive search but does not possess the technical skills to do so. This is especially the case for individuals who want to surf the amazing array of databases available on the Internet, but who do not have the technical skills, knowledge, or experience to get the information they need in an acceptable time frame.

Individual entrepreneurs, recognizing the significant barriers to entry for novices in the Internet, with its search engines and specialized databases, will engage in a search for individuals and provide them with timely information (Corman, in press). Perhaps most importantly, these individuals also can weigh the relative value and credibility of the information they acquire. While the Internet makes a wealth of information available for particular purposes, it is often difficult for the novitiate to weigh the credibility of the information—a critical service that the information broker can provide. Managers, in general, should cultivate brokers for highly technical information beyond their expertise (Mintzberg, 1975a). For some, hiring a broker skilled in these abilities is an excellent choice.

One example of such a service, which acts as a "quasi-agent," is First!tm. A quasi-agent is a discrete entity, often in the form of specialized computer service and/or software, which acts autonomously, communicates with human and other agents, and substitutes for human action (Corman, in press). These quasi-agents can serve as powerful new tools for individuals within organizations in their information seeking, acting to promote access and overcome the inertia that serves as a significant barrier to information seeking.

Users of First!tm tell the individual firm what they need to know in plain English. This results in an interest profile for the individual that is then used to analyze 12,000 stories a day from hundreds of different sources (e.g., newspapers, technical reports). The software then selects the most critical items to develop a daily report and sends it to the client by e-mail or various other methods. This service may consult sources unfamiliar to the client and it provides the information in a very timely manner. The user also can give feedback to the system, informing it of items not relevant to their needs. This information is then used to update the individual's unique interest profile (Corman, in press). This last feature recognizes that the most useful brokers are those who know us and who can provide us with tailored information (Marchionini, 1992).

Increasing the use of secondary information disseminators is really a variant on classic notions of opinion leadership (Katz, 1957; Katz & Lazarsfeld, 1955; Rogers, 1983) and gatekeepers (Metoyer-Duran, 1993). Opinion leadership suggests ideas flow from the media to opinion leaders to those less active segments of the population (Katz, 1957). Opinion leaders not only serve a relay function, they also provide social support information to individuals (Katz, 1957) and reinforce messages by their social influence over the individual (Katz & Lazarsfeld, 1955). So, not only do opinion leaders serve to disseminate ideas, but they also, because of the interpersonal nature of their ties, provide additional pressure to conform as well (Katz, 1957).

How one person influences another is often determined by their structural positioning within groups (Katz & Lazarsfeld, 1955). One classic finding of research into the relationship between interpersonal and mass media channels is that individuals tend ". . . to select media materials which will in some way be immediately useful for group living" (Riley & Riley, 1951, p. 456). Some have gone as far as to suggest that group membership can be predicted based on an individual's information-seeking preferences (Kasperson, 1978). As we have seen, several studies have also demonstrated that one reason individuals seek out information is so they later can talk about it in peer groups.

Increasingly more formal groups are serving as opinion leaders and information seekers for individuals. For example, there are many self-help groups for various diseases, with estimates as high as 500,000 groups with over 20 million members (Pettigrew & Logan, 1987). It is important for organizations to respond to these groups, especially environmental and customer groups, which can directly impact an organization's well-being. Organizations should support/facilitate these groups because of the information dissemination role they can perform. It may be in an automobile manufacturer's best interest to support car clubs, like those that exist for Corvettes, because they can serve as useful intermediaries to their customers. Targeting messages to support networks surrounding individuals may be very effective in achieving change (Freimuth, Stein, & Kean, 1989). These audience members can be (and probably are) opinion leaders in the old sense, who are influential with the very audience members that organizations most want to reach.

Advocacy groups for organizations (e.g., Chambers of Commerce, trade associations, etc.) serve as increasingly important lobbyists for the provision of information to organizations. They actively seek more money for research that leads to information for databases, for enhanced access and availability of information, and so on. In short, they lobby for an information infrastructure. At times, these groups will have agendas that do not necessarily coincide with an individual's need for information. While the entrepreneurial broker is an individual's agent, an advocacy group needs members to advance the group's agenda. So, at times, individual and group interests coincide, and, at times (of course), they don't. This is something to remember when we turn to the next chapter that focuses on the role that management can play in facilitating information seeking.

SUMMARY

This chapter started with a recapitulation of several recurring findings in the information-seeking literature that must be addressed by any individual or managerial strategies. Many of these traditional barriers to information seeking can be addressed. Training programs and support structures can be designed to overcome individual lack of skills and awareness of information sources. They also can increase the salience of information seeking as an important life/career skill. Perhaps most importantly, new technologies, which will be explored in detail in the next chapter, offer the possibility of overcoming and/or substituting for the traditional problems of accessibility, inertia, and the limitations of humans as information processors. But, as Paisley (1993) details, knowledge dissemination research has gone through similar cycles of the excitement of promising new technologies that have fallen by the wayside. Perhaps the most serious limit on these technologies is the recurring preference of individuals for interpersonal information sources who can digest and summarize vast quantities of information for individual seekers.

SEVEN

STRATEGIES FOR MANAGERS

[S]uccessful managers develop the ability to collect and use diverse, ambiguous, and sometimes contradictory information effectively and efficiently. (McKinnon & Bruns, 1992, p. 15)

The challenge faced by managers is how to restrict great amounts of upward communication that may result in overload, and at the same time ensure that relevant and accurate information is transmitted up the hierarchy. (Glauser, 1984, p. 615)

The dilemma is clear: on the one hand, managers receive too much information, while on the other hand, they don't get enough of the right information. (Katzer & Fletcher, 1992, p. 227)

Managers face a daunting task in today's information environment that has been variously described with phrases ranging from a mosaic (McKinnon & Bruns, 1992) to a jungle (Holsapple & Whinston, 1988). They must come to intelligent judgments based on the welter of facts, forecasts, gossip, and intuition which make up their information environment. Perhaps most importantly, however, managers are not only responsible for themselves, but they also must nurture and enhance the information capabilities of their subordinates.

It seems like almost every issue in organizational behavior can be examined on two levels: its impact on individuals, and its impact on the organization as an institution. In this chapter we will describe traditional search strategies used by managers to get information from often recalcitrant bureaucracies; we will then turn to what managers can do to facilitate information seeking by others in their organization. As we have seen when we discussed formal structures, the central problem for management is condensing a wealth of information in such a way as to obtain an accurate picture of the organization, an area where new technologies have been of considerable assistance (Porter & Millar, 1985). Yet, this imperative often provides the opportunity for subordinates to actively distort and withhold needed information from managers.

Bureaucracies encourage managers to think of a one-way top-down flow of communication. Historically, managers have relied on the mass media, especially written channels, to efficiently reach large numbers of workers in their campaigns (e.g., improving safety and quality). These authoritative dicta and the lack of interactivity in the communication mode were meant more to discourage information seeking than to stimulate it. Many approaches and assumptions of traditional media research were often implicit in this approach.

Somewhat akin to mass media's historical bullet theory, workers were thought to be a relatively passive, defenseless audience. Communication in effect could be shot into them (Schramm, 1973). This view of communication was embedded in the more general stimulus-response notions popular in psychological research in this time period (Rogers & Storey, 1987). However, it soon became apparent that, while there were some notable successes, audiences could be remarkably resistant to campaigns, especially when they did not correspond to the views of their immediate social network (Katz & Lazarsfeld, 1955; Rogers & Storey, 1987).

There developed a tendency among theorists of communication campaigns to cast "the audience as 'bad guys' who are hard to reach, obstinate, and recalcitrant" (Dervin, 1989, p. 73). The term "obstinate audience" was coined by Bauer in his classic research article detailing the active role audience members play in the processing of communication messages (Bauer, 1972). In natural situations, Bauer contends, the audience selects what it will attend to. These selections often depend on interests, and the interests of audience members are reflected in their level of knowledge and the strength of their convictions. While exposure is the first step to persuasion (McGuire, 1989), the audience members most likely to attend to messages related to management's interests are those organizational members already committed to them. Dervin (1989), in this connection, has suggested that the most appropriate strategy might be to change the institutions delivering the message, rather than to expect the audience to change deeply seated behavior patterns. In effect, management campaigns may be reaching the already converted. While this might have a beneficial effect of further reinforcing beliefs, the organizational members who are most in need of being reached are precisely those members who are least likely to attend to management's message.

Management campaigns often fail because their recommended beneficial effects are not apparent to employees, and they do not identify market segments within the total audience who require different communication approaches in line with their specific needs (Robertson & Wortzel, 1977). The bottom-line issue is that interested people acquire on their own most of the information available on any subject (Hyman & Sheatsley, 1947).

One essential pragmatic benefit of the perspective adopted in this book is to increase the "match" between management communication efforts and their audiences. A focus on individuals is necessary since their perceptions of the information environment will determine their usage irrespective of the "objective" nature of this environment. Individuals are active information seekers, not just passive recipients; the dynamic nature of their information-seeking patterns has proven to be a more powerful predictor of their information acquisition than a focus on such traditional areas as demographics or past media exposure (Dervin, Jacobson, & Nilan, 1982). This suggests that finer grain discriminations of the audience may be necessary to ensure effective management communication.

As we have seen, perhaps the best strategy is to achieve a "match" between the information carriers managers choose to disseminate information with and the information-seeking profiles of individuals. Thus, the question becomes the much more sophisticated one of placing the most appropriate content, in the most appropriate channel, where it is most likely to be used by a predetermined audience.

Management efforts also suffer from unrealistic expectations. Most advertising campaigns would be happy with a level of change in their audience of 3–5 percent a year (Robertson & Wortzel, 1977). McGuire (1989) has also pointed out the very low probabilities of success of communication campaigns given the long string of steps that must be fulfilled (e.g, first get the audience's attention), each of which only has a moderate probability of success.

Modern views of managerial communication are more likely to stress a dialogic view of interaction, with both parties initiating and attending to messages in turn. These views also incorporate a much more specific role for information seeking, which in traditional views was almost totally ignored, at least on the worker's level. Management's most important role in these perspectives is as a stimulus or cue to action. They must define the most important issues that an organization needs to face. Thus, a letter from the president in a company newsletter may identify a top organizational priority (e.g., developing new products to meet increased competition). This is not an answer, it is an implied set of questions for information seeking: why are our competitors succeeding? What can we do in response? Successfully establishing this agenda will result in numerous proactive information-seeking behaviors by workers. Thus, a critical role of management in the innovation process is that of managing attention (Van de Ven, 1986).

While at its core almost every large organization has a bureaucracy, the issues that are emerging in modern organizations arise from a cluster of new technologies and horizontal coordination processes that many argue are resulting in a new organizational form: the networked organization (Nohria & Eccles, 1992). In this new organization, the principle function of management is not to extract information from ungrateful workers, nor to provide information from the top down. Management's role in a networked organization is to facilitate the flow of information and ensure that there is support for the organization's information infrastructure. Many organizations have realized that there are real strategic advantages, especially in enhancing quality and developing innovations, in investing in technologies that enable a networked form of highly collaborative organization that enhances needed coordination relationships.

As Porter and Millar (1985) point out, competitive advantages come not just from enhancing performance, but in giving organizations new ways to out-perform competitors and in developing new information businesses. Improving information management (White, 1985), associated analytic skills (Cronin & Davenport, 1993), and knowledge utilization (Menon & Varadarajan, 1992) should be a top priority of management (McGee & Prusak, 1993). However, too often, information systems are ignored by users because they are not accessible or user friendly (McKinnon & Bruns, 1992). But before we turn to these trends, we will examine the traditional view of information seeking on the part of managers.

Management's Search for Information

In Chapters 2 and 5, we detailed the powerful barriers that exist to management's search for information in traditional bureaucratic structures: segmentation, contrary individual motives, lack of trust, and so forth. Here we focus on strategies managers can use to acquire information in traditional organizational structures. Unfortunately, many organizations have dual structures: the networked collaborative structure existing side by side with the traditional formal one; with the former used for getting the work done, and the latter used for preserving and maintaining power and for the accomplishment of narrow productivity goals. The consistent use of some of the strategies discussed in this section may result in a tilt by management to the old ways, which prevent the coming of the new.

Much of the early sections of this book covered structures, like formal MIS systems, and communication channels, like e-mail, which managers use to support their information needs. Many of the strategies used by newcomers to uncover information, which we discussed in the preceding chapter, also can be used by managers. For example, browsing, especially because of its random, unstructured nature, can alert managers to potential problems that might exist in their organizations. Management by walking around is but one form of browsing, especially useful for the early stages of decision making (Saunders & Jones, 1990), that managers might employ (Peters & Waterman, 1982: Chang & Rice, 1993). So managers might set aside a couple of hours a week for seemingly random tours of facilities; they also might take a random walk through the paperwork done at lower levels, rather than relying on more formal, condensed reports.

Smart managers listen to and learn from their subordinates. While managers are walking around they might pause to "shoot the breeze" with workers. This conversation will do very little good in an information-seeking sense if a manager spends all the time talking or tries to persuade workers to adopt a new approach to work. A manager must be prepared to ask neutral questions and listen with care to responses. Thus, browsing is also a specific example of a more general strategy of going directly to the source of information rather than letting information be filtered by various intermediaries in the formal structure. Almost 90 percent of managers report learning of significant organizational problems through these sorts of informal information strategies (Katzer & Fletcher, 1992).

It helps managers to have key informants for particular domains of information (Mintzberg, 1976). Traditionally, these individuals have been described as gatekeepers because of their role in filtering information, often in a condensed and understandable fashion (Downs, 1967). The modern trend is to eliminate the middle-man, keeping the hierarchy flat, reflecting the need of managers to be closer to information sources if messages are not going to be distorted (Downs, 1967). Still, no manager can regularly go to the direct source of information, because there is not sufficient time. Here a manager can use many of the suggestions of Burt (1992) related to structural holes, developing a wide range of nonredundant sources strategically located so that they give the manager the widest possible view of the organization. In doing this, managers also should develop sources of information external to their organization (e.g., customers, suppliers, media) who can give them an idea of how their organization is functioning (Downs, 1967).

At the same time that managers are developing a breadth of ties, they need to ensure that they have sufficient redundant ties to give them alternative sources of information on critical issues (Burt, 1992). Creating competitive sources for the same information, with overlapping responsibilities, rewarding a diversity of views (Downs, 1967), also overcomes the disturbing tendency of many to distort information. While the carrot may be preferable to the stick, it helps to have a visible, even if unused, stick around. For example, performance appraisal systems should explicitly reward information sharing and punish hoarding. Employees should realize that there is the threat of investigation, that there will be a followup on problems (Downs, 1967), and that they will be corrected. Managers who have influence and contacts with those above them in the hierarchy are more likely to be the target of upward communication from their subordinates (Glauser, 1984), partly because this entails access to rewards and punishment. So, when someone passes information on to you, it is important that s/he know what you did with it (i.e., that it did have some impact).

While managers often have compelling reasons to hoard information, to not share it with others, the efficiency and effectiveness of modern organizations depends on information sharing. Managers should realize they have a vested interest in upgrading the information-seeking skills and capabilities of their subordinates if for no other reason than it will enhance the quality of information that they in turn pass on to their supervisors and any decisions they reach (More, 1990). However, as Marshall and Stoll (1993) found in their study of network participation and empowerment, managers often resist wide-scale worker involvement, seeing it as detracting from more narrow productivity goals.

FACILITATING INFORMATION SEEKING

Efficiency requires members of the audience to be treated amorphously and to bend to the institution. Effectiveness requires that individuals be helped on their own terms. (Dervin, 1989, p. 85)

The basic task of management is to change structures, information infrastructure and technology, and culture (e.g., transmission rules [Downs, 1967]) to promote information sharing and seeking. In effect, management should serve as a guide to what areas and sources are most likely to have valuable information. In more modern organizational forms, the basic job of management is not finding information, but rather facilitating the search for information by all members of the organization. Managers must serve as the chief designer of more effective information systems and organizational structures (Galbraith, 1995) which unfortunately have seldom been compatible with each other (More, 1990).

In this section, we will discuss several strategies managers can employ to this end, at times referring to specific software packages and technologies that are currently available. But, as even the most casually interested reader is aware, information technologies are rapidly changing. So, our task is to acquaint the reader with general concerns and issues. For specific discussions of current technology, the interested reader probably would be best served by such magazines as *Scientific American, Business Week, PC Computing*, and *PC Magazine*, among a host of others, which track more recent developments.

In part, enhanced information seeking can be accomplished by improving the climate of the organization. Satisfied, secure, high performing, and ambitious employees are less likely to distort communication messages (Glauser, 1984) and thus block the acquisition of information by others. A focus on information about what the organization should be doing in the future, rather than the ego-threatening that we have done in the past (Downs, 1967), contributes to the development of more positive climates. So does promoting a feeling of problem solving—encouraging feelings of experimentation and inquiry. The best managers in these new organizational environments are practical theorists who solve puzzles, focusing on quantitative, objective information whenever possible (Downs, 1967).

A cornerstone of any strategy to facilitate information seeking is the removal of various access barriers. Firms have to support the sharing and using of information (Menon & Varadarajan, 1992). Workers must have access to up-to-date, detailed, technical information. They should be able to self-serve themselves from a common pool of available information through modern tele-communication and database systems we will turn to in a moment. In creating such systems, management must be willing to let workers' inquiries go where they will. It is self-defeating to listen in on bulletin boards and other electronic forms of communication (Zuboff, 1988), since this defeats their primary infor-mation-sharing function.

Perhaps most importantly, management must be willing to share its inter-pretations of information and what types of information it considers to be the most critical to the organization's future. In short, managers must be willing objects/resources for information searches by organizational employees. A pre-cursor to a better dialogue would be to increase the organizational members' knowledge base. To provide better information, subordinates need to under-stand what messages are relevant to their supervisors and what is important to them (Glauser, 1984).

In the emerging market-based organizations, rewards are inherent in the search and exchange of information. Markets allow for the possibility of a few central rules governing relationships that can be easily enforced, that permit a delegation of authority to individuals to determine for themselves the ulti-mate value of any information exchange. Management must think carefully about the incentives for more active information seeking. In many organiza-tional contexts, sharing ideas is an "unnatural act," especially where individual performance is the sole focus of reward systems (*Business Week*, 1994). As a general rule, managers should encourage employees to develop weak ties to encourage information sharing throughout the organization. Traditionally, in-formation seeking has been punished in various ways. If you uncovered some-thing wrong in the organization, you were placed in the position of the classic messenger to the emperor whose head was chopped off for bringing bad news.

Educate Organizational Members on Capabilities of Information Carriers

Currently workers can easily "avoid" management communications because they often use channels and sources that are unfamiliar to them. Managers need to understand workers' normative expectations of information carriers; and where this is misguided, agencies may want to correct this with their training programs, since avoiding authoritative sources can impede individual performance, often resulting in individuals working at cross purposes to or-ganizational goals.

Increasing an individual's familiarity with possible authoritative sources of information should be one aspect of any training program. Even highly trained scientists may be unaware of sophisticated bibliographic tools (Brittain, 1970).

One objective of training in information seeking should be to sensitize individuals to other sources of communication (Robertson & Wortzel, 1977) and to increase their information-seeking capabilities (Evans & Clarke, 1983). Increasingly, when employees use sources like the Internet, which contains many conflicting voices, they need to be trained in how to weigh the credibility of various sources as well. Companies that successfully implement information technologies often must spend 3 dollars in training for every 1 dollar spent on hardware (Hoffman, 1994).

For enhanced information seeking, training and skill development are essential, but one major concern related to increased use of technology is deskilling, which is the use of information technology to reduce the level of expertise of human operators of a system. At its simplest level, this can often be seen in counter and clerical people in retail organizations who interface with increasingly sophisticated management information systems that do their work for them (e.g., scan for the price of individual items and automatically calculate the costs of a group of purchases for customers). These machines can monitor the pace of workers, ensuring they are performing at high levels. These systems provide for more managerial control; at the same time, they demand less from a worker (Palmquist, 1992). Offsetting these trends is the possibility of a system "informating" a work task, providing workers with constant feedback on their performance and, in doing so, upgrading skill levels. For example, computer monitoring of athletic performance can provide essential feedback on technique that can result in enhanced performance. In effect, the athlete is in partnership with an automatic trainer that provides him/her with an increasingly sophisticated view of his/her behaviors.

One key outcome of training programs should be the enhancement of decision making. The point is not just to acquire information, but to acquire information that is goal- or job-related. At one extreme, some high information users spend so much time communicating that they have very little time left over to be productive (Brittain, 1970; McGee & Prusak, 1993). At the other extreme, there are individuals who try to make the decision search as easy as possible, looking for a cause near its effect and looking for a solution near an old one (MacCrimmon & Taylor, 1976).

One approach to this problem is to combine training with new software and technology that further reinforces new information-seeking norms and enhances decision making. One clear example that has emerged in the last decade is Group Decision Support Systems (GDSS). GDSS essentially support group decision-making processes by using sophisticated computer software to facilitate the process of making a decision and providing ready access for group members to databases and data manipulation systems.

Typically, in the same room, group members are arranged in a horseshoe, with a focus on an open area where a public computer screen can be projected for the whole group. GDSS software is designed to systematically take members through each stage of the decision process, ensuring, for example, that multiple alternatives are weighed and evaluated. Once alternatives are assessed, they also permit various methods for reaching a decision from simple voting to a proportional weighting of various group members (e.g., upper managers, different divisions).

Recent attempts at Group Decision Support Systems and the general use of technology to support decision-making processes often appear to be attempts to reintroduce rationality into decision making, by shifting the focus away from people to ideas. GDSS systems are designed to overcome many problems symptomatic of groupthink by promoting critical thinking and removing status considerations. GDSS systems encourage consensus approaches to decision making and equality of participation. The resulting increased cohesiveness and competitiveness of their members also can act to promote information seeking (Smith & Jones, 1968). Thus, two different work teams could be charged with the task of seeking information related to a particular organizational problem. The group incentive arises from the sort of competitiveness characteristic of a scavenger hunt.

Their proponents make very strong claims about the improved decision making that would result from these rather expensive (with estimates ranging up to $500,000) systems (Hoffman, 1994). Unfortunately these claims have yet to be supported in research studies (Fulk & Boyd, 1991), in part because organizations modify these systems in use to reflect their cultures. However, in actual use they may also be limited in the same way that other processes are—by the limits of human decision making and the artificial boundaries imposed upon them by an organization's culture (Poole & DeSanctis, 1992). These are limits that should be kept in mind as we turn to the development of information infrastructures in organizations.

CREATING RICH INFORMATION FIELDS

By enabling top managers to obtain local information quickly and accurately, management information systems reduce ignorance and help managers make decisions that they, otherwise, may have been unwilling to make. (Huber, 1990, p. 56)

Everyone is entitled to their own opinion, but not their own data. (Galbraith, 1995, p. 94)

Another possible approach to enhancing information seeking is to increase the richness of an individual's information fields: for example, providing access to a corporate sales database on an individual's PC through a local area network (LAN). This is an especially appropriate strategy for individuals who are not normally active seekers, but who are interested and concerned about organizational issues. This strategy can potentially broaden awareness of larger corporate issues beyond someone's immediate job, since it removes barriers to the acquisition of information. It can also increase the knowledge base of individuals, making it more likely they can communicate effectively with managers when a problem develops. Conversely, it also has the effect of undermining the power of managers who depend on information hoarding for control (Hoffman, 1994).

Increasing the availability of information is particularly appropriate for individuals who are only casually motivated to seek out information. Allen's (1977) work in research and development laboratories suggests that increased familiarity with information carriers increases perceptions of accessibility, but this does little good if the information is not perceived as useful. These strategies are also essential to creating information equity (Siefert, Gerbner, & Fisher, 1989) that might serve to reduce critical gaps in the knowledge and awareness of organizational issues. Managers must make it easy for workers to change, since most individuals will resist change, especially change related to information technology (Hoffman, 1994).

Because of the unwillingness of individuals to devote much effort to information acquisition as noted earlier, it is important that managers arrange to have information easily available to target audiences. Two general strategies for accomplishing this will be reviewed in this section. The first is to increase the physical access to information in one's immediate work environment. Beyond one's immediate physical environment, access to information processing technologies becomes critical.

Physical Environment

As we have seen in Chapter 3, physical access provides the opportunity and occasion for interactions (Sykes, 1983). Both social density (or the number of interactants within a bounded space) and proximity act to determine the access of individuals to each other in organizations. In research and development laboratories considerable effort has been devoted to discovering the ideal physical layout to ensure there is a sharing of ideas (e.g., Allen, 1977). Open office landscaping, with common areas where people can meet and work together on projects, is arranged to facilitate the flow of information. Minimizing physical barriers increases ambient information that can be easily observed or overheard by physically proximate parties. Individuals may be stimulated to seek additional information not directly related to their narrow job by having physical access to information.

Access is also affected by the relative mobility of individuals in the work place. Increasing mobility may be a direct result of transport technologies, but the necessity for this mobility may stem from utilitarian technological imperatives associated with coordination and control as well (Johnson, 1993a). Therefore, spatial factors affect channels selected for information seeking in determinant ways; and channels, particularly electronic ones, can be viewed as the communicative surrogate of mobility.

Information Processing Technologies

Broadly, information systems perform several essential functions for organizations. First, they support the development of large-scale operations (and often increased efficiencies and profits that follow large-scale operations). Second, they perform basic business transactions (e.g., from scanning purchases to payments of accounts). Third, decision support systems often result from the combination of basic business transaction information with computer software that develops trend information, as well as reporting the current status of organizational operations. Fourth, they monitor the performance of organizational members. Fifth, information systems retain corporate memory through records held in corporate databases. Sixth, they maintain communication channels through which information is accessed and reported (Gurbaxani & Whang, 1991). They can specifically enhance the performance of executives by creating new channels for sending and receiving information, filtering information, reducing dependence on others, leveraging time to concentrate on the most important tasks, and diminishing complexity (Boone, 1991).

Electronic media have been found to diffuse leadership in groups, promote the formation of subgroups, and focus attention on the task (Culnan & Markus, 1987), all of which are factors that may promote information seeking by individuals. Communication technologies, like bulletin boards, permit the sending of messages to a communication space that is characterized by potential similarities of messages and communicators, rather than to specific individuals. This enhances participation and access by saying that all individuals who share a similar interest can come to the same electronic space to communicate (Culnan & Markus, 1987). New technologies, like bulletin boards and e-mail, also can reduce interpersonal coordination costs for management.

"Other things being equal, then, information technology should permit the development of more elaborate and complex organizational structures" (Pfeffer, 1978, p. 74). New forms of electronic communication often open new possibilities for communication within organizational structures (Culnan & Markus, 1987), with lower level organizational members having enhanced access to numerous others. As a result, decision processes move to lower levels of the organization and the organizational hierarchy is flattened (Fulk & Boyd, 1991). Thus, a key factor in the introduction of new technologies is the removal of constraints from organizational members (Rice, 1989). Many have argued that these new technologies create the possibilities for new organizational forms, like network organizations (Nohria, 1992) or for the full operation of markets within organizations (Malone, Yates, & Benjamin, 1987b).

In spite of often rosy predictions, the impact of information-processing technologies on organizational communication structure has been a matter of some controversy in recent years, as has its relationship to corporate productivity and profitability (Hoffman, 1994). While computerization of information should make it possible for organizations to deliver the right information, at the right time, to the right place, accomplishing this has proven to be much more difficult than it would appear on the surface (McGee & Prusak, 1993). While optimists wait for the next generation of computer software and hardware, realists are increasingly looking at the organization itself, especially its culture and structures, as the major impediment to improved information processing (McGee & Prusak, 1993). It also must be understood that information systems can only capture a small proportion (some have estimated as low as 10 percent) of the information available in organizations. The other 90 percent resides in people's heads, the social system, paper files, and so forth (McGee & Prusak, 1993).

Fulk and Boyd (1991) argue that organizations choose technologies that promote centralization (e.g., mainframes) depending on their current situations. Huber (1990) has argued for a contrary effect, with computer-assisted communication increasing centralization in decentralized forms and vice versa. While it appears obvious that the impact of technologies would be dramatic, both structurally and spatially (Morgan, 1986), especially in relation to the enhanced ability to control and coordinate organizational processes, this has not been the case in actual practice, with many promising technologies being used to do the old jobs in the old ways (Carter & Culnan, 1983; Johnson & Rice, 1987). For example, a word processor is treated as a fancier version of a typewriter and used for essentially the same functions. However, the promise of electronic media rests in the new capabilities they offer organizations, particularly in areas such as new ways of addressing communication (e.g., public bulletin boards); memory, storage, and retrieval of communication (e.g., automatic storage of transcripts of electronic meetings); and control over access to and participation in communication. There is a consensus that, eventually, often after a considerable lag time, new information technologies have an impact on organizational structures (Huber & McDaniel, 1988) often because of competitive pressures.

Rice et al. (1988) detail the sorts of impacts that one information-processing technology, electronic message systems, could possibly have on organizational communication structure and relatedly information seeking. First, it reduces the necessity for synchronous communication such as telephone calls. Second, it can increase the frequency of communication through a widening of professional and social connections. Third, it can increase efficiency by reducing media transformations (e.g., data files on disk to computer tape) and shadow functions (e.g., time wasted on unanswered telephone calls). Fourth, users may perceive they have greater control, improved communication, and greater access to information.

Centralization is one area where two competing positions concerning the impact of information-processing technologies has been fully articulated. Some have found support for the position that enhanced information-processing capabilities leads to greater centralization of decision making and control by management (Reif, 1968), while others have found a negative relationship between more centralized information-processing technologies and decentralization (Carter & Culnan, 1983) when size was controlled (Pfeffer & Leblebici, 1977) or when computers were geographically dispersed (Blau & Schoenherr, 1971). This issue is particularly critical since it relates directly to the information-processing capacity of management. Computers can serve to increase this capacity, if they present information in a comprehensible manner (Carter, 1984; Carter & Culnan, 1983), but there are real limits to the capacity of individual managers to process information, and computers also can serve to vastly increase overload problems for upper level management.

Computers might serve to decentralize decision making in two ways: by providing an extensive array of control mechanisms (e.g., automatic warnings when activities monitored by the computers go outside certain boundaries), and by routinizing work activities (Carter & Culnan, 1983). Some computer technologies do enhance administrative intensity by increasing the efficiency with which managers can monitor the activities of workers (Carter & Culnan, 1983). This raises the issue of what decentralization really is since management constrains activities in these instances (Pfeffer, 1978).

It is possible that both views may be simultaneously correct. Centralization may have increased—not at the level of upper management, but at lower levels with an especially functional locus. So, lower level decision makers in the MIS department or editors in a newspaper office, for example, may be at the nexus of organizational information flows (Carter & Culnan, 1983).

While decentralization moves decisions closer to the organizational action, it may move it further away from strategic issues emerging outside the firm and from the perspective of top decision makers (McGee & Prusak, 1993). So, some have called for a flattening of an organization's information environment so that key decision makers are not far from operations and vice versa. Traditionally, the discrepancy between these organizational components was ameliorated by middle managers who could serve a critical bridging function; but, as we have seen, their numbers are steadily declining (Cash et al., 1994). So the tension between general strategic information and specific, tactical operational information often directly relates to issues surrounding centralization and decentralization.

The effects of new technologies on centralization also relate to the more general arguments concerning the impact of new media on the democratization of the work place through changes in authority relationships. While it would appear that these technologies offer the potential to empower lower level organizational employees in a variety of ways, in actual practice existing rules and norms tend to limit the use of new technologies for this purpose (Komsky, 1989). Some have argued that the primary reason information technologies fail is that their designers do not recognize the information politics of their organizations (McGee & Prusak, 1993). Increasingly, it is argued that the optimal political structure is akin to a federalist system with many checks and balances and explicit negotiations between sovereign states within the organization (McGee & Prusak, 1993; Hoffman, 1994). Part of what is negotiated is who has access to what information.

In the following sections, however, we will look at the information-seeking *possibilities* created by new technologies in several areas. In essence, a corporation's information architecture has three primary components: data storage, data transport, and data transformation (Cash et al., 1994). While we will discuss these components separately, increasingly it is their blending and integration that is creating exciting new opportunities for information seeking.

Data Storage

Traditionally, in bureaucracies, data storage has meant physical storage of information in filing systems. Needless to say, modern ideas of storage have broadened conceptions of this function considerably to include verification and quality control of information entering a storage system. Security systems for the stored information, which directly relate to information seeking, are also increasingly important. For example, many electronic means of communication allow an organization to store for future retrieval what would have previously been unrecorded interactions, such as those that occur in electronic mail and group decision support systems. Who should have access to this often more informal and personal information?

Security issues, however, also involve means to ensure that no one can tamper with or change information residing in a database (Hoffman, 1994). The viability of information also includes issues like shelf life of data. The long-term ability of media like computer disks to store and to retrieve information physically is one aspect of this problem. Increasingly salient is the related issue of the meaningfulness of the keywords and software assumptions that categorized the original information. This also raises the issue of how old, irrelevant information is culled from any storage system. A not-so-apparent problem of public databases, like the Internet, is the lack of quality control in the information available to users. This is especially troublesome given the general lack of information-seeking sophistication detailed earlier.

Databases. Databases are repositories of information that become key elements of a corporation's memory. Essentially they provide a means for storing, organizing, and retrieving information. Shared databases are at the core of developing information systems, since they provide a common core of information to which all members of the organization have access (Malone et al., 1987a). As we will see in the next section, usually they must be combined with sophisticated electronic access, such as the Internet, to achieve their full potential for information seeking.

One of the earliest forms of databases, and one that has been a critical technology to the early development of bureaucracies, is the vertical file system. Files provide physical access to permanent records that are typically alphabetized by some topical system. For example, all personal records for a particular division are kept in alphabetic order and perhaps color coded by rank. As organizations grow, files become increasingly unwieldy and, as the sophistication of questions increases, they become unmanageable, in spite of cross referencing. So, if I am a manager at Ford and I want to link performance records for my international managers by purchase orders from particular suppliers, I have probably exceeded the capabilities of physical storage systems.

As anyone who has created a simple database (e.g., personal investments, recipes, bibliographic references) is fully aware, creating and maintaining a database requires considerable investments of time and energy and associated opportunity costs. The creator of a database hopes to achieve some advantage from this investment (e.g., more sophisticated reports produced in a more timely fashion). Making databases available to wide numbers of others raises several interesting dilemmas for their creators, since users often have very little investment in them, but often may reap substantial returns for their use. While this use by others does not diminish their value to the original creator, the developers may be envious that they did not think of this new application of their work (Connolly & Thorn, 1990). There is a human tendency to limit the free access of others to databases or to not create them in the first place, hoping to get a "free ride" from others. Managers can offset the cost side of the equation to some extent by separately rewarding contributions to the development of a common corporate information infrastructure, such as databases, beyond what an individual might expect for his/her own immediate application.

Electronic storage enhances the possibilities of linking various databases to create increasingly sophisticated searches. Until recently, these systems have often been inaccessible (available to only a few managers on corporate mainframes who might, on a discretionary basis, make them available to others [Connolly & Thorn, 1990]) and difficult to work with (e.g., awkward and non-natural language keyword systems). Modern databases, especially those available on CD-ROMs, provide the possibility for every organizational employee to have easy access to enormous amounts of information at their PC workstation. For academic literature searches, for example, ABI/INFORM provides information searches of over 1,000 important business publications providing 200-word abstracts for each citation. Increasingly these systems are user-friendly and portable. For example, police are issued laptops to carry in their vehicles with databases of outstanding warrants and stolen cars that permit them to search rapidly for information themselves. These systems are often augmented with wireless FAX for even more current information.

Databases, when coupled with powerful search engines and the linking capabilities of modern relational databases, also encourage ever more complex questions. On the immediate horizon are associative databases that automatically may search for information on increasingly remote or tenuous relationships to provide answers we never expected (or at least would have been unlikely to uncover). For example, whose third cousin in Arkansas is linked to the second cousin of a Whitewater indictee? Data mining programs, a form of artificial intelligence expert system, continually look for new statistical and visual representations of data, linked in ways that would be very difficult for even the most diligent human researcher to have the patience for.

Data Transport

The previously mundane world of data transport is increasingly the stuff of lead stories on the evening news, from providing easier access to information on the Internet through NETSCAPE software to providing new business opportunities through revised telecommunication laws. Essentially data transport involves the acquisition and exchange of information.

Telecommunications. Telecommunication systems, such as fiber optic cables and satellites, provide the hardware that links individuals, enhancing access to information. For information seeking, the critical issues here revolve around the carrying capacity of a particular system and the ease, range, and timeliness of access. Fiber optic systems are vastly superior to traditional metal wire systems because of their increased carrying capacity, permitting, for example, the transmission of moving visual images that eat up enormous volumes of information bits. Without this increase in carrying capacity, the current movement toward merging entertainment companies with cable and telephone companies would be impractical.

Similarly, satellite systems create new possibilities for instantaneous access to even the most seemingly mundane questions. For example, the answer to the simple question of "where am I?" can be given with amazing specificity from global positioning satellite systems. From one new technology whole new industries have been spun off, with associated hardware and software. For example, one traditional problem that trucking and delivery companies have had is keeping track of where their distant employees are. Now, if I want to know where truck X is at a particular time, I can receive a nearly instantaneous answer that is accurate to within 50 feet. This creates a quantum leap in my ability to control my operations and to maximize the use of my resources. So, if I get an order from a customer, and I know I have a nearby, empty truck dead-heading back to the warehouse, I can call up the driver on my cellular telephone and much more quickly respond to my customer.

Networks. Networks, like the Internet, usually combine enhanced telecommunication capabilities with software that permits the linkage and exchange of information between users (one of which is often a database). One reason for the excitement about the Internet is its easy access (both in terms of cost and the lack of other barriers) and the increasing user-friendliness of software like NETSCAPE and MOSAIC that permit access to web sites.

The proliferation of home pages and web sites, where users can obtain information related to specific topics, is proceeding at an incredible pace. For example, small businesses often have problems devoting resources to keeping pace with developments in information technology. There are several world-wide web sites that focus on their unique concerns. The Small Business Administration operates a U.S. Business Advisor site (http://www.business.gov) that gathers brochures, laws, and regulations from over 60 government agencies. Free e-mail services and contacts with other small business owners is also facilitated through the Small Business Administration (http://www.sbaonlin.sba.gov). Links to a variety of consultants, government agencies, lenders, used-equipment dealers, and other services are also available at the MCI Small Business Resource Center (http://www.mci.com).

In terms of academic sites, which touch on information seeking, there are a number of options. For example, Internet e-mail systems permit subscription to listserv addresses that facilitate the open exchange of information on specialized topics (e.g., teaching methods, data sources, analytic techniques) among participants. OCISNET (available at MAILSERV@BAYLOR.EDU), for example, has recently been established for public dialogue between members of the Organizational Communication and Information Systems Division of the Academy of Management. Similar listserv addresses are available for divisions ranging from Applied and Organizational Communication (subscribe at MAJORDOMO@CREIGHTON.EDU) to the TQM caucus (DAVE&UWYO.EDU).

Specialized information retrieval software allows the user to search more broadly on the WEB from literally hundreds of sites. For example, Dow Jones News/Retrieval is a relatively expensive on-line service that permits keyword searches of over 1800 databases, newspapers, magazines, and company reports. Its Custom Clip feature allows continuous monitoring of certain key words to keep current on business topics the user identifies. Profound delivers documents located by on-line search in their original format for printing or downloading a portion of a report or the whole document. (Overcoming the barrier represented by two-step systems that provide the user with a citation that they must look up themselves.) Profound's search engine, InfoSort, sifts through literally millions of information sources, including sophisticated market research surveys.

Data Transformation

Combining databases and telecommunications with software creates telematics that allow for the possibility of increasingly sophisticated searches for information and analysis/interpretation of it once it is compiled.

Expert Systems. Following the work of Galbraith (1973) on organizational information processing, work on expert systems has created an exciting hybrid of many of his classes of integrating mechanisms. These systems considerably enhance the ability of an organization to coordinate and control its operations.

In expert systems, rules derived from knowledge workers and/or experts (e.g., engineers, systems designers) are incorporated into computerized vertical information systems. Thus, "Expert systems are computer programs that couple a collection of knowledge with a procedure that can reason using that knowledge" (Feigenbaum, McCorduck, & Nii, 1988, p. 6).

These systems embody many of the characteristics of artificial intelligence systems. They can result in more thorough and consistent decision making. Expert systems have been used primarily in diagnosing problems, such as those associated with automobiles, steam turbines, or steel blast furnaces. They have also been used successfully on a wide array of additional tasks including processing medical claims, selecting the appropriate chemical formulation for a particular application, and filling sales orders for complex mini-computer configurations. Expert systems can be used in conjunction with other systems to automatically inform another part of the organization if something goes wrong, thus improving the speed of horizontal communication (Feigenbaum, McCorduck, & Nii, 1988).

Expert systems offer a whole host of new possibilities for information seeking, including intelligent search engines. The Internet has spawned many very flexible information search and retrieval services based on expert systems. For example, the World Wide Web Worm and the Web Crawler are new programs that regularly search every node they can reach and compile fresh databases of what they find. Queries to Internet databases result in a listing of hypertext links that users can be tied to with only a click of their mouse (Hayes, 1994).

Expert search engines, such as Knowledge Gateway Systems (KGS), try to accommodate different learning and search styles of users, adapting to specific individuals (Marchand & Horton, 1986). Intelligent information sharing systems filter information on several levels before it is sent to a user on electronic data systems (Malone et al., 1987a). Messages might be screened, sorted, and prioritized based on several categories: the urgency with which a response is needed, cognitive domains (e.g., key words), social dimensions (e.g., more attention given to friends, those higher in the hierarchy), future communication events (e.g., the agenda for an upcoming meeting), and so on.

In effect, expert systems, and their associated tools of simulation and econometric modeling, can overcome individual cognitive limits by providing humans with answers without concerning them with an enormous range of variables and potential scenarios/options that these programs automatically consider (Gurbaxani & Whang, 1991). These computer programs increasingly rely on powerful graphic images of data, assuming that for interpretation of information a picture is literally worth a thousand words.

Executive Information Systems. Specialized information systems have also been developed for particular groups within the organization. For example, increasingly sophisticated Executive Information Systems (EIS) are becoming available for top management (Matthews & Shoebridge, 1993). In part, these systems recognize the conflicting pressures relating to centralization we discussed earlier in this section. Well-developed EIS systems permit increasingly sophisticated monitoring of performance (McGee & Prusak, 1993), while not obtrusively interfering with the operations of lower level organizational employees.

Unlike more well-known MIS systems, which are primarily inflexible means of accumulating data, EIS systems focus on the analysis, presentation, and communication of data. EIS systems, such as Commander, Pilot, Lightship, and EIS-Track, contain several essential features: a briefing book overview, "drill-down" to allow users quick access to more in-depth information, information presented in graphic forms, flexible reporting of information along various dimensions and criteria (recognizing that organizational performance is multidimensional [McGee & Prusak, 1993]), monitoring of exceptional performance, and keeping track of trends. They also permit "what-if analyses" that determine the impact various changes might have on organizational performance.

Information Centers. Developing "information centers" is one strategy for enhanced information seeking often employed by larger organizations (Daft & Huber, 1987). These centers share many characteristics with traditional corporate libraries. Unfortunately corporate libraries seldom interact with the real users of information and, as a result, are becoming increasingly marginalized (Broadbent & Koenig, 1988; McGee & Prusak, 1993). Information and referral centers can take many forms, such as hotlines, switchboards, and units within organizations (e.g., micro-computer support groups) where an individual can go to get answers to pressing concerns. They serve three primary functions: educating and assisting people in making wise choices in sources and topics for searches; making information acquisition less costly; and accommodating a range of users (Doctor, 1992).

In many ways, the most useful thing referral services can provide is putting people within the organization who have the information in touch with those who seek to acquire it, thus the growth of corporate yellow pages (McGee & Prusak, 1993). These yellow pages essentially expand on the traditional organizational chart by listing specific areas of technical expertise. So, for example, organizational members may not understand that their information technology office also can conduct communication network analysis as a diagnostic tool for determining user telecommunication needs. A detailed listing of functions, rather than organizational titles, can often facilitate the searches for organizational members.

SUMMARY

All this suggests the increasing importance of information as a strategic asset to organizations that should be systematically incorporated in the planning of upper management (Marchand & Horton, 1986). Corporations also need to recognize the potential benefit of marketing unique corporate knowledge an-dexpertise (Marchand & Horton, 1986) to other information seekers. For example, large-scale agricultural enterprises may have developed unique ancillary knowledge related to weather prediction that could lead to new spinoff industries that others would like to acquire. Somewhat relatedly, Strategic Information Systems, such as American Airline's Sabre reservation system, can be marketed to other companies to the considerable advantage of the developing company (Cerveny, Pegels, & Sanders, 1993).

These trends also suggest a need to reintroduce organizational simplicity, partially by establishing more direct communication linkages with the primary source of information (Keen, 1990), and to think carefully about what information should be excluded from organizational information processing. While more and more information can be produced more efficiently, there is a concomitant increase in the costs of consuming (e.g., interpreting, analyzing) this information (More, 1990). Organizations increasingly will be organized as knowledge specialists reacting to a common theme, emulating many characteristics of symphony orchestras (Drucker, 1988). In orchestras there must be some common thread that all the members are working from if their individual efforts are not to become too discordant. Some simplifying melody is required so that the players can react to and build upon it in their solo performances, upon which the whole effort depends. Another variant of this approach is to identify a few Critical Success Factors (e.g., orders) that can be quantified and widely shared (McKinnon & Bruns, 1992).

Somewhat relatedly, to coordinate most effectively there must be compatibility among various information systems (Malone et al., 1987) and some form of organization-wide standards for information processing (Hoffman, 1994). Coordination costs increase with distributed work and more extensive lines of communication (Keen, 1990) and the problem of information asymmetries (e.g., quality) may be insurmountable in terms of creating totally open corporate information infrastructures (Connolly & Thorn, 1990). For example, in hospital settings, CEOs received twice as much decision-making information as their boards and three times as much as their medical staffs (Thomas, Clark, & Gioia, 1993). As a result, they have considerably different knowledge bases and interpretive frameworks. The type of information processed by functional specialties also differs, with production-based information more certain and quantifiable than the typical mix of marketing and sales information (McKinnon & Bruns, 1992). This fragmentation, which can be augmented and enhanced by information technology, makes it much harder for differing groups to communicate across their boundaries (Hoffman, 1994).

Until recently, most information-processing activities in organizations have targeted *automating* tasks; and increasingly computers are being used to augment human capabilities by *informating* tasks. The wave of the future may lie in restructuring tasks so that they are *transformed* (Cash et al., 1994). For example, the next wave of computers may quickly pass human capacities to simulate complex models, including many more variables than humans are capable of considering, to come up with scenarios of various degrees of plausibility for human decision makers. Increasingly, seeking and interpretation will be delegated to intelligent software (Maes, 1995). These software systems will not, however, be able to make policy and ethical decisions related to issues facing societies and the role of human beings within them. It has become a truism that computer-based information and decision systems excel at programmed tasks. They do not perform well, and may even be dangerous, for tasks that are ambiguous, or that need creativity and judgment (Keen & Morton, 1978). So, the relentless drive for efficiency, in part brought on by global economic trends, may directly confront human needs for more participation and democratization which open access to information encourages (Cheney, 1995).

EIGHT

SUMMING UP: INFORMATION SEEKING IN THE INFORMATION AGE

In this chapter, we bring together our central themes and we point to the future. A compelling feature of research on information-seeking is that it stands at the intersection of so many important theoretical and policy issues. It raises issues that have captured the attention of a new generation of political leaders in the United States, ranging from Al Gore to Newt Gingrich. As a pragmatic issue, it is the subject of cover story after cover story in the popular business press, with magazines like *Business Week* giving information technologies extensive coverage. It also raises compelling theoretical questions in many areas that have generally received inadequate attention in the social sciences, to which we now turn.

DEVELOPING A RECEIVER ORIENTATION

Communication research and theory have been dominated by a source perspective. If receivers have been examined, it usually is in the context of how we can better get our messages across to them. So, we focus on the imperfections in receivers, particularly their cognitive limits. We also focus on the question of what do receivers "really want anyway?" so that we can construct more effective persuasive communication campaigns (Dervin, 1980).

Particularly in areas relating to organizations, management concerns have been our predominant focus (e.g., Grunig, 1975). As Drucker (1974) has observed, traditionally most managerial communication aimed at conversion and implicitly demanded surrender to management views of the organization. It has almost become a cliché that the reason information technologies and systems fail is that they do not consider the needs of users (e.g., Johnson & Rice, 1987; Hoffman, 1994; Kuhlthau, 1991; More, 1990; Nath, 1994; Pinelli, 1991;

Rouse & Rouse, 1984; Steinke, 1991; Varlejs, 1986) with estimates of failure rates of 30 percent attributable to nontechnical factors (More, 1990). By and large, except for human resources and critical approaches, the nature and motives of receivers have been downplayed, and even the information needs of managers have been relatively ignored (McKinnon & Bruns, 1992; Choo & Auster, 1993). Information seeking may be the missing link in explaining information processing in organizations (Choo & Auster, 1993).

An emphasis on information seeking is also an emphasis on receivers of communication messages (Chen & Hernon, 1982) who are ultimately the arbiters of the value of any piece of information (Hall, 1981; Rowley & Turner, 1978). Thus, a balance is restored between the two sides of any communication relationship (Drucker, 1974; March, 1994). Focusing on the sender often leads management astray, because the assumption is that just because a message is uttered, it is attended to (Axley, 1984). However, how a message is perceived really determines the nature of a communication event (Drucker, 1974). It is the audience that ultimately interprets any message (Morley, 1993).

As the classic selective perception and selective attention literatures suggest (Katz, 1968), a fundamental property of communication relationships is that a receiver must attend to a communication message for any communication to occur (Drucker, 1974). This is perhaps the most poorly understood area of communication in modern research (Gans, 1993). Why do people communicate with some individuals and not others? Why do they seek out information on some topics and not others? Why do they recurrently structure their communication to attend to certain messages, from particular communication channels, from specific sources? The antecedents to communication events and the structure of an individual's daily communication contain many of the answers to these questions, but, with the exception by and large of the works cited in this book, generally the larger field of communication has ignored these issues that are fundamental to any theory of information seeking.

Focus on Behaviors

The attributes or attitudes of actors contribute little or nothing in explaining actions. What matters is the structural location of actors. (Nohria & Eccles, 1992, p. x)

Traditionally, the organizational literature has focused on psychological phenomenon involved in processing information, rather than on behaviors representing the search itself (Miller & Jablin, 1991; Smithson, 1989). But the structural approaches examined here offer compelling advantages over psychological approaches (Dervin, 1980; Pfeffer, 1982). If for no other reason than organizations are social collectivities, we must look beyond individual attributes. As we have seen, the constraints imposed by the collective often determine individual action, especially information-seeking ones. But the answers individuals acquire and disseminate can in turn shape the collective. A focus on collective activities, such as information seeking, offers many advantages for developing organizational communication theory, including the possibility of focusing on dynamic, interpretive properties of social systems as well (McPhee & Corman, 1995).

Individual Action in Social Context

Organizing consists of an unresolved dialectic between autonomy and interdependence, agency and constraint. (Contractor & Eisenberg, 1990, p. 147)

One persistent theoretical problem in the social sciences is accounting for individual action in a social context (Dervin, 1980; Poole & Van de Ven, 1989; Savolainen, 1993; Warriner, 1981). For example, in order to advance, network analysis research must explain what drives actors as purposeful, intentional agents (Nohria, 1993). While the larger framework of societal structures, norms, and values provides parameters for social action, it does not completely determine them. The problem then is to account for individual variation within social contexts, especially the impact of agency in organizations, since it is central to understanding management processes (DiMaggio, 1992; White, 1992).

Information seeking is one of many actions individuals can engage in. It cannot be separated from the specific context in which it occurs (Chen & Hernon, 1982). It is governed by available information fields and carriers, norms related to appropriate information-seeking behaviors, and individual beliefs concerning the efficacy of information seeking. Thus, it provides a focus for efforts to develop a more general theory of individual action.

In sum, information-seeking behaviors often represent individual motives and cognitive abilities. These behaviors result in a structure for the organization. Actions related to information seeking also represent an inherently dynamic view of human behavior that moves us further from traditional theoretical focus on a static world (DiMaggio, 1992). Information seeking is a dynamic process, with an often predictable sequencing of sources consulted, but with each additional step often determined by the answers received from preceding ones (Pescosolido, 1992; Savolainen, 1993).

Synthesizing Across Contexts

Increasingly, communication research has found itself divided by context domains: a person does research in interpersonal, organizational, mass media, and so forth. This increasing specialization within communication, as in other disciplines, hinders the development of research in areas like information seeking that cut across various contextual domains. Focusing on information seeking provides a promise of integrating increasingly fragmented areas of communication research.

Another issue that needs to be more systematically addressed is the varying levels (individual, group, and organizational) at which information seeking might occur within organizational contexts. Organizations inevitably have mixed-level processes (Rousseau, 1985). For example, a constant theme of the boundary spanning literature is the tension individual group members experience between the information they acquire and the conventional wisdom of their group. So, while an individual may be charged with seeking information on behalf of the group, group processes may ostracize him/her, if s/he returns with information that is discordant with accepted group norms (Johnson, 1993a; O'Reilly & Pondy, 1979), especially under conditions where the group feels threatened by external conditions (Staw, Sandelands, & Dutton, 1981).

Building Bridges

A focus on information seeking promises an increasingly central role for communication research in the work of other disciplines. For example, Ruben (1992) has argued there will be an increasing convergence of communication and information sciences research largely because of the "market pull" of societal trends. Unfortunately, historically, the real insights into communication phenomena generally have come not from communication researchers, but from other disciplines (Drucker, 1974).

Information-seeking research is a critical focus of inquiry in a variety of disciplines: decision-making research in organizational contexts, economics in relation to the operation of markets, sociology, information sciences, library and information sciences, computer science, systems engineering, and consumer behavior (Ray & Ward, 1975; Rouse & Rouse, 1984; Ward, 1987). Human cognitive abilities also play a critical role in the placement of individuals in particular communication structures (DiMaggio, 1992), and thus the human framework in which they can seek information. The central concepts of coordination and control in cybernetic systems theory also are directly related to information seeking—with enhanced information-seeking capacity promoting coordination, while diminishing control. While information seeking is critical to many divergent bodies of knowledge, a coherent approach to the phenomenon has yet to emerge.

FUTURE DIRECTIONS OF INFORMATION-SEEKING RESEARCH

Some have argued that there is a data glut, with not enough theory to guide us in this area of research (Brookes, 1980; Buckland, 1991b; Dervin & Nilan, 1986; Stonier, 1991), particularly as it relates to understanding the role of technology (Steinfeld & Fulk, 1990). In spite of literally thousands of studies on information technologies, this related area has not advanced substantially; it needs an organizing paradigm. While this has historically been true of almost all inquiries into the impact of new communication technologies on society (Wartella & Reeves, 1985), it is particularly troubling given their policy relevance and the accelerated pace of change. Information-seeking research is in a similar position with a number of descriptive, proscriptive models (e.g., Freimuth, Stein, & Kean, 1989), but few empirically tested ones.

A Comprehensive Model of Information Seeking

In recent years, Johnson and his colleagues have attempted to develop and to test a model of information seeking in both health and organizational contexts. This model, which was discussed in detail in Chapter 4, can serve to summarize some of the preceding themes of this book and to suggest future directions for research. To review, the Comprehensive Model of Information Seeking (CMIS) (see Figure 4.2) contains three primary classes of variables. The Antecedents provide the underlying imperatives to seek information, they activate individuals to seek information and determine the intensity of the search. Information Carrier Characteristics shape the nature of the specific intentions to seek information from particular carriers. Information Seeking Actions reflect the nature of the search itself and are the outcomes of the preceding classes of variables.

Research on the CMIS suggests it provides the "bare bones" of a causal structure, although the nature of the specific relationships contained in the model might be context dependent. Tests of the CMIS in health situations suggested the model worked best with authoritative channels, such as doctors, which were the object of intense, goal-directed searches (Johnson, 1993b; Johnson & Meischke, 1993). The revised CMIS, which was developed in a test focusing on informal channels and confirmed on formal, provided an excellent fit to the data in the organizational setting (Johnson et al., 1995). The most important paths in the model were those between media characteristics and Actions and cultural beliefs and media characteristics.

Antecedents had significant direct impacts on Actions in these empirical tests, suggesting that the mediating role of Information Carrier Factors may not be as encompassing as was originally thought. The general pattern of findings suggested that one central assumption of the original CMIS—that Antecedents activate a search, and that Information Carrier Factors determine the specific nature of the search—needs to be rethought. Especially for the individually based variables, there was a weak relationship between Antecedents and Information Carrier Factors. This general finding may be partially attributable to the nature of channel differences examined in the organizational test, which focused on issues of authority and the official nature of the channel, rather than more classic communicative attributes of the channel, which have been the focus of most prior research. Reflecting this, the path between Characteristics and Actions was not supported in either test, suggesting contingent channel differences that need to be explored in future research, perhaps incorporating some perspectives on channel usage discussed in Chapter 4.

One important limitation of this research stream lies in the general lack of development of adequate methodological tools to conduct research on information seeking. The level of development of scales, for example, is primitive compared to other areas of research in organizations. Particularly important are more sophisticated views of Information Seeking Actions, beyond simply the number of contacts an individual might have, especially related to underlying cognitive factors, styles, competence, search strategies (e.g., browsing [O'Conner, 1993; Overhage & Harmon, 1965], and berrypicking [Bates, 1989]).

The pattern of results for the CMIS suggests the characteristics of subformal organizations (Downs, 1967), where a mix of formal and informal factors was important. This is reflected in the relative importance of interpersonal interdependence and is similar to the informal problem solving approach often found for technical problems in health organizations (Stevenson & Gilly, 1991). Most importantly, from the personal interviews that were conducted, it was clear that professional knowledge and credibility were important in potential sources of information, so some individuals in informal channels had as much authority as formally assigned managers. Still, this was a bureaucratic organization, where official sanction was needed for project approval. So, individual information seeking was often a patchwork quilt of formal and informal ties, with a strong cultural commitment to the goals of the organization as well. These factors may account for the lack of clear differentiation between formal and informal channels in the test results. The findings of the CMIS also point to several other specific directions for future research in information seeking.

Active versus Passive Information Acquisition

The failure of some CMIS paths also reflects their linkage to general predispositions to communicate, rather than being linked to specific information-seeking problems. Operationally, disentangling passive acquisition of information, not to mention retrieval of information from memory for experienced workers (Connolly, 1977) from information that has been actively sought, has been one of the most ticklish tasks for information-seeking research.

In part to confront this problem, in his research stream on information seeking in interpersonal contexts, Berger (1979) identified three general strategies individuals have for information acquisition: passive (e.g., unobtrusive observation), active (e.g., reading a corporate report), and interactive (e.g., talking to the author of the report). While it could be argued that individuals have more investment in active and interactive strategies, and that, therefore, any information that was gathered by them would also be more likely to be relevant (Connolly, 1977), very little research has addressed the issue of the varying impact of information acquired under these different conditions.

In one of the few studies that directly measured both passive and actively gathered information, Morrison (1993b) found that passive acquisition of information by newcomers had an impact on task mastery and role clarity, but the effects were generally modest when considered next to the active information seeking of newcomers and the amount of the organizational investment in formal socialization programs. In addition, active information acquisition might have a secondary impact on an individual, such as promoting a sense of efficacy and control, that just being the passive recipient of information may not provide (Morrison, 1993b).

This feeling of mastery also may raise interesting questions of when the seeker becomes the sought-after. At what point do newcomers, for example, gather, synthesize, and interpret enough information so that they can mentor even newer arrivals than themselves? One of the most interesting findings from the liaison literature is that liaisons often occupy their positions not because of what they do, but because others initiate interactions with them. Similar patterns have been found in information acquisition in informal status networks (e.g., Blau, 1954) and are contained in Burt's (1992) conceptions of prominence and power. Interestingly, elite academic departments and research laboratories operate in such rich information environments that they often exhibit considerable nonchalance in information searching, feeling that anything that is of value will reach them spontaneously (Paisley, 1980). These factors may lead to the findings that managers in information-rich environments do less scanning of the environment than those in information poor ones (Zmud, 1990).

Those who have occupied a position of authority, or one where they can publicize wrongdoing, have probably encountered their own "deep throat," who has an interest in disseminating information through them. So, for example, when I was chairperson of an academic governance committee charged with disbandment of academic departments, often my most effective information-seeking strategy was to wait for the phone to ring and then listen carefully to the caller. Somewhat akin to the scientist who serendipitously discovers something in his/her laboratory, while conducting research on another topic, perhaps the most effective information seekers are those who are prepared to be surprised and to consider the unique value of unexpected pieces of information that they stumble across in their regular activities.

Ironically, then, the most overtly active information seekers may be those most unlikely to use the information for organizational rather than individual purposes. Newcomers and lower status individuals appear to have the most interest in acquiring information, and are less likely to passively receive information. On the other hand, experienced hands, who are bombarded with information (and influence attempts), may have more requests and opportunities to make use of information than they have time, leaving little incentive to seek out new information. So, those most likely to seek information may be those who can do the least in an organizational sense (e.g., implementing a new information technology) with any information they acquire.

Reintroducing Rationality and Objectivity

As we have seen, a major trend of the decision making literature has been to more and more irrational views of human behavior. Somewhat similarly, a major trend in organizational communication over the last decade has been to more subjective, post-modern conceptions of organizations (e.g., Corman, in press; Eisenberg & Goodall, 1993). A focus on the technological tools available for modern information searches, however, may reintroduce the logical and rational, since these systems often demand very logical approaches (e.g., key word searches) by users (Corman, in press). Information-as-thing, as commodity, may be the only sense of information that makes sense for information systems (Buckland, 1991a). In fact, information systems are often very mechanistic, an approach to organizations that clearly has gone out of fashion. As Drucker (1974) has argued, information may be inherently rational, but it is the perception and interpretation of it that is subjective.

The Boundaryless Organization

Establishing boundaries around organizations has been a continuing problem, with tasks like trying to identify the invisible college of researchers in particular areas nearly boundaryless in conventional organizational terms (Johnson, 1993a). Increasingly, organizational information seeking is a boundaryless phenomenon. Professionals seek answers to their questions wherever they may easily be available, whether inside or outside the organization (Johnson et al., 1995). Sophisticated search agents and brokers will only accelerate this trend. Therefore, it will be much harder to define the limited domain of any one organization as the context for information seeking; in fact, linkages between knowledge workers may further encourage alliances between firms (Corman, in press). Already organizations are forming consortiums where the dissemination of information and knowledge generation and synthesis are the focus. In doing this, they often partner with think tanks and key university personnel.

Context

Despite repeated appeals for contextual inquiry and sensitivity to context . . . no one is exactly sure what is being requested or how to produce it. (Weick, 1983, p. 27)

Fundamentally all communication must occur within a context. While context is an integral part of information seeking, the extent to which it can be systematically related to it is limited by the dearth of literature dealing with this linkage at any meaningful level. Determining clear linkages to contextual factors offers the potential of moving information-seeking research from the descriptive level it has generally operated on to a more theoretical level. Greater understanding of context isolates crucial explanatory variables and thereby suggests theoretical propositions between contextual and information-seeking variables generalizable across organizational situations.

Most of the prior research on the CMIS has focused on cancer-related information seeking by the general population (Johnson, 1993b; Johnson & Meischke, 1993). Needless to say, for most individuals, this is a nonrecurring problem, which is novel and fraught with emotional complications. In many ways, this situation is analogous to the nonprogrammed organizational decision processes discussed earlier, which led many to emphasize the irrationality and subjectivity of organizational decisions.

However, tests of the CMIS in the defined context of a technical organization suggested critical differences in the more rational and programmed task faced by engineers. The critical mediating factor of channel in the prior tests was not as crucial in this organizational context, with individuals instead gathering information wherever it might be available, regardless of the characteristics of the channel. The results of the CMIS suggested there were few dramatic differences between channels, thus calling into question the current academic fascination with processes of channel selection in organizations (e.g., Rice, 1993; Sitkin, Sutcliffe, & Barrios-Choplin, 1992). The results in the organizational context also suggested that individual differences related to education and interpersonal work interdependence play a more direct role, and the general pattern of findings suggested a more sophisticated, complex understanding of information seeking among technically trained respondents.

Specifying the Linkage between Social Context and Individual Action

As we have seen, one historical reason for the failure of downward communication has been a failure to consider a complete range of the motivations that impel individual actors. This has in turn led to perceptions of an obstinate and irrational audience that is blamed for thwarting well-meaning and beneficial campaigns (Dervin, 1980). (People just don't understand what's good for them.) However, an approach that has information seeking as its focus inherently tries to picture the world of the actor and the self-interests that motivate him/her (Dervin, 1980). But individuals, of course, are not totally free of constraints which govern their actions. They depend on others for information and for services, and the general societal framework in which they are embedded restricts the range of questions and alternatives that can be pursued.

These questions, then, lie at the heart of any future efforts in information seeking: how is individual agency limited and shaped by the larger information fields and carriers that compose an individual's information environment? This problem is also fundamental to explanations of the larger question of the development of communication structures in organizations (Poole & Van de Ven, 1989).

As we have seen, organizations are faced with a fundamental dilemma: bureaucracy, stemming from efficiency needs and the need to maintain existing power positions, often limits the access of individuals to information. Yet, structural designs are often flawed and circumstances change, requiring individuals to seek information normally unavailable to them. Innovation, and often survival, depend on allowing free and open access to information for those individuals who seek it. How these conflicting imperatives are resolved is a critical dilemma for the modern organization. Unfortunately, while volumes have been written on formal organizational design, comparatively little is known about the forces that shape individual information seeking within organizations.

These issues are summarized in Figure 8.1, which specifies an overarching conceptual framework for future information-seeking research. Contextual constraints affect and shape all three elements of this framework: the gap, the CMIS, and sense-making. The start of any search is the perception of a gap in existing knowledge. Dervin and her colleagues (Dervin, 1980; Dervin, Jacobsen, & Nilan, 1982; Dervin, 1989) have found that information seeking is related to "gap-bridging:" individuals ask questions that are directed at determining the implications of events for themselves directly and/or are related to their future activities. The actor's current need for drive reduction, or gaps, and their related information purposes are critical triggers to information seeking. As Kulthau (1991) has suggested, gap bridging moves beyond just uncertainty reduction and often encompasses considerable anxiety evoked in the individual when they face unknowns.

An actor's search for information would be guided by his/her strategies and underlying criteria for determining the type of information that will fill the gaps in his/her current understanding (Dervin, 1989). In a decision situation, individuals have clear goals and are free to choose their own information-seeking strategies for attaining them. In a barrier situation, individuals feel that they cannot attain their information goals because of factors such as an organizational policy of confidentiality. In worry situations, individuals do not know clearly what their goals are nor do they have a clear idea of what strategies to pursue. In an observing situation, individuals monitor a situation, but do not actively engage in a search for any particular type of information.

In the framework presented in Figure 8.1, perceptions of gaps in knowledge (usually known unknowns) of various sorts trigger an information-seeking process, represented by the CMIS, the outcomes of that process, the information gathered, are then interpreted by sense-making processes (e.g., Savo-

Figure 8.1
A Conceptual Framework for Future Information-Seeking Research

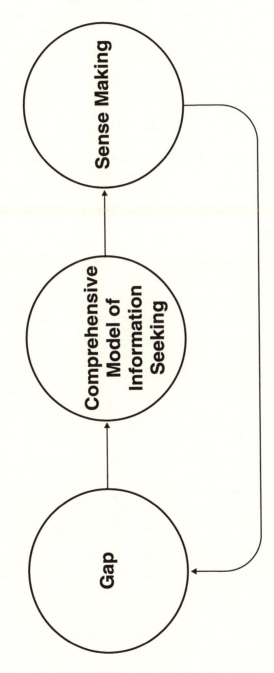

lainen, 1993; Thomas, Clark, & Gioia, 1993). Most prior research has focused on how information is processed, rather than on how it is acquired (Miller & Jablin, 1991). The answers obtained are then compared to the original problem represented by the gap. If the gap remains (or if a new one has been created by the search), then the process continues, until time has expired (or exhaustion sets in). Information seeking is clearly a dynamic process, with an individual's level of knowledge changing as it goes on (Kuhlthau, 1991). Interestingly, in one of the few studies that has examined newcomer information seeking over time, Morrison (1993b) found that the amount of information seeking was relatively stable; however, she suggested that the type of information sought changed considerably over time. The processual nature of information seeking, especially in terms of its sequencing and staging, will be a rich area for future information-seeking studies.

POLICY IMPORTANCE OF INFORMATION-SEEKING RESEARCH

Information is the product of the information society and information management is its major problem. (Marchionini, 1992, p. 156)

The information processing industry is evolving as the basic or core industry of the information economy. (Marchand & Horton, 1986, p. 28)

The concept of technological change has been widely discussed and debated. . . . For each argument that information technology provides greater prosperity . . . , there is a counter argument that it can enslave the individual and degrade the quality of life. (Palmquist, 1992, p. 5)

Americans have long cherished the notion that democratic political participation requires an informed citizenry, and that to be informed we must have ready access to the information we need. (Lievrouw, 1994, p. 350)

A democratic society depends on an informed and educated public. (Thomas Jefferson)

The concepts of an "information gap" and the "information poor" have been advanced in recent years as important policy issues, generally in terms of their broad societal ramifications (Chen & Hernon, 1982; Dervin, 1980; Doctor, 1991, 1992; Siefert, Gerbner, & Fisher, 1989). In general, it has been argued that there is a growing difference in access to information for different segments of our society and that increasingly this gap also reflects other demographic classifications, such as socioeconomic status. Perhaps even more importantly, "informational have-nots" in many respects represent the average U.S. citizen, not a small minority of the population (Dervin, 1989; Doctor, 1992), and these individuals risk becoming members of a permanent underclass.

New technologies, such as personal computers, and hookups to information services, such as Prodigy and Compuserve, create an increasingly fragmented and privatized information environment, as opposed to the more mass, public access technologies represented by television and radio (Siefert, Gerbner, & Fisher, 1989). Instead of being equalizers, new information technologies may serve to increase the information gaps among organizational members (Rubin-yi, 1989).

In response to these trends, governmental agencies are adopting policies to promote information equity among various segments of our society (Doctor, 1992). Often universal telephone service is used as an exemplar for the emerging uses of the Internet, but some question whether access to information resources can ever truly be universal, in spite of the best intentions of our policy makers (Fortner, 1995). This is partly because of the unwillingness of potential users to avail themselves of information resources. At a societal level, very few people use our existing information infrastructure (Dervin, 1980; Dervin & Nilan, 1986) and managers tend not to use libraries and online databases for environmental scanning (Choo & Auster, 1993).

Beyond use, there is the general concern for need, with several user studies of the general populace finding users have few information needs, at least ones they can't satisfy informally (e.g., Beal, 1979). All this raises the policy question of what level of support should be given to an information infrastructure which receives little general use; especially since, for specialized concerns (e.g., legal, medical libraries), there has been an explosion of for-profit libraries, with 28,000 established since the 1980s (Varian, 1995).

The knowledge gap hypothesis (Tichenor, Donohue, Olien, 1970) argues that over time, gaps will increase since more highly educated individuals assimilate new information faster than more poorly educated ones; they also have more relevant social contacts who are likely to discuss issues with them. In addition, technology and software access is likely to be greater for privileged groups. Still, it has also been argued that the use of mass media can act to reduce gaps relating to issues that are of interest to normally disadvantaged groups (Freimuth, Stein, & Kean, 1989), and, further, at some point the haves become satiated and the poor can catch up (Dervin, 1980).

Inevitably, differential access to information produces differential participation rates in any collectivity (Lievrouw, 1991), whether it is an organization or society. Classically our mass media infrastructures have produced information fields that are *informing*. They are geared to providing information they select that is then consumed by their audiences. Increasingly, information technologies offer the possibility of *involving* audience members through their interactive capabilities and enhanced possibilities for information seeking (Lievrouw, 1991). Differential access to information sources has direct implications for the involvement of individuals in democratic processes (Braman, 1994; Doctor, 1991, 1992; Palmquist, 1992; Siefert, Gerbner, & Fisher, 1989). It has been suggested that policy makers should strive to create information equity among different segments of our society (Siefert, Gerbner, & Fisher,

1989). One underlying reason for creating equity is that the wider the range of ideas available to individuals, the more likely it is that a plurality will gravitate toward the correct one.

Disconcertingly, it is also possible that people will become so overloaded with information they will "escape," turning to demagogues who offer simple solutions to increasingly complex problems. The dark side of the quest for uncertainty reduction is that once an answer is arrived at and a decision made, blockage from future information seeking may occur (Smithson, 1989). As we have seen, disastrous consequences often arise from situations where group ideas become accepted as truth, discouraging even the possibility of seeking discordant information.

It is also likely, especially in organizations, that pressing for open access to information will only drive it underground. For example, in part because of privacy concerns, some organizational members are using unofficial, nonsanctioned public carrier e-mail systems (e.g., Prodigy), enabling coalitions to informally develop.

One step in reducing information gaps is greater knowledge of the factors affecting information seeking. However, a major impediment to information seeking for some groups is a lack of necessary skills, some as fundamental as a lack of literacy. Information seeking clearly differs by the educational levels of individuals (Chen & Hernon, 1982; Doctor, 1992). So, it is important not only to provide access to the information superhighway—people also must receive the training necessary to use it (Doctor, 1992). Rather than stressing simple access to ideas, it may be better to stress access to playful intellectual tools that allow individuals to make sense of an overwhelming information environment (Entman & Wildman, 1992).

Even if there is not a knowledge gap, there is a utilization gap. This utilization gap arises, in part, because some individuals are consciously deciding to decline membership in the information society (Fortner, 1995). Some people have just reached a saturation point; they cannot spend any more time communicating (Fortner, 1995). Some groups, such as unions, have historically mistrusted the application of new technologies (Palmquist, 1992) and deliberately rejected "establishment" positions. Others decide, for aesthetic or lifestyle reasons, not to adopt new information technologies. So instead of surfing the Internet, they might prefer more civil discourse with their friends (Fortner, 1995). Others prefer old and familiar information sources. For example, in researching this book, I did use computer databases and search engines, but I often gained as much useful information browsing through our campus library, which is a very old technology indeed.

We have always had among us Luddites who reject new technologies because they are socially and economically disadvantaged by them. We also have many individuals, whom we typically don't like to talk about, who really don't want to know things, who are more interested in "vegging out" and being entertained (Fortner, 1995). While over and over again corporations emphasize their need for individuals who will constantly grow and develop into perpetual learners, it must be acknowledged that some individuals would prefer a comfortable world where they do not need to change nor expend the necessary effort to become full-fledged participants in the information society.

Indeed, it has been estimated that as little as 10 percent of top executives use the information technologies currently available to them (Fortner, 1995). Some more cynical observers of information seeking in the professions suggest that perhaps the most powerful motivation for doctors and lawyers to keep up-to-date is the ever-present threat of a malpractice suit (Paisley, 1993). Most other professions do not have similarly compelling external motivations to keep current; they do not have sanctions for "remediable ignorance," for actions which duplicate or overlook existing knowledge (Paisley, 1980). These professions can in effect conspire to say it is pointless to try to keep up.

Most of the people who write about, think about, and implement information technologies are information junkies who have very little understanding of (or tolerance for) these individuals. Some exhibit pathologies on the other extreme and become so concerned with acquiring information that it becomes an end in itself, rather than serving any particular organizational purpose. These individuals, who are often information professionals, tend to overburden information systems they design, providing users with too much information and too many options. They fail to distinguish between what people "need to know" and what it would be "nice to know," if you had unlimited time (Paisley, 1993).

Even more disturbing than the information gap is the *understanding gap* that is developing between individuals who have access to a rich array of diverse information sources and the resources necessary to synthesize information: "bad ideas spread more rapidly among the ignorant than among the informed, and good ideas spread more rapidly among the informed than the ignorant" (March, 1994, p. 246). Our elites, both institutions and individuals, are developing a considerably different view of the world than other members of our society, in part because of their differential levels of information-seeking capacities and skills. Even between elites, constant self-selection of information sources is producing different views of the world. The information revolution is contributing to the accelerating fragmentation of our culture (Fortner, 1995).

Increasingly there are organizational analogues for these societal trends. Most organizations do not have the resources to support elaborate information infrastructures, which can be very expensive (Fortner, 1995). As we have seen, a variety of governmental programs have arisen to assist organizations, especially small businesses, in their information needs. Larger enterprises, with sufficient resources, are increasingly finding competitive advantage in the growing gap between themselves and other organizations. This has led to considerable concern that individuals and organizations with resources and access will perpetuate (or even widen) gaps in information to preserve or enhance their power and economic advantages (Doctor, 1991, 1992; Lievrouw, 1994).

Ironically, the same technologies that can serve to increase democratic participation in the workforce also can heighten control and centralization depending on how they are implemented (Cheney, 1995). Traditionally, new organizational forms have emerged from changes in how information is processed and distributed, with the operations of modern multinationals made possible by advances in telematics (Braman, 1994). It is likely that the organizations that exist ten years from now will be considerably different in their communication structures, reflecting new organizational forms, such as the virtual organization (Galbraith, 1995). So, while commentators dwell on the societal ramifications of information seeking, similar trends are playing out in organizational contexts (Palmquist, 1992).

In sum, information seeking is at the center of many theoretic and pragmatic issues facing our society. Maybe in the end Kant will be proven correct again and there will be nothing so useful as a good theory that promotes deeper understanding of these issues (Stonier, 1991). The task ahead is a daunting one for, as we have seen, information seeking is "the result of a complex set of interactions among multiple variables each with differing capacities to predict information source use" (Summers, Matheson, & Conry, 1983, p. 85). As this book has illustrated, on many levels, information seeking is a compelling focus for future study and research in organizations.

BIBLIOGRAPHY

Acker, S. R., & Calabrese, A. M. (1987). *The changing environment for scholarly research: Media technologies and the velocity of information.* Paper presented at the annual meeting of the International Communication Association, Montreal.

Adams, J. S. (1980). Interorganizational processes and organizational activities. In S. B. Bacharach (Ed.), *Research in organizational behavior, Volume 2* (pp. 321–355). Greenwich, CT: JAI Press.

Adelman, M. B., Parks, M. R., & Albrecht, T. L. (1987). Beyond close relationships: Support in weak ties. In T. L. Albrecht & M. B. Adelman (Eds.), *Communicating social support* (pp. 126–147). Newbury Park, CA: Sage.

Aiken, M., & Hage, J. (1971). The organic model and innovation. *Sociology, 5,* 63–82.

Alba, R. D. (1982). Taking stock of network analysis: A decade's results. In S. B. Bacharach (Ed.), *Research in the sociology of organizations* (pp. 39–74). Greenwich, CT: JAI Press.

Albrecht, T. L. (1979). The role of communication in perceptions of organizational climate. In D. Nimmo (Ed.), *Communication yearbook 3* (pp. 343–357). New Brunswick, NJ: Transaction Books.

Albrecht, T. L., & Adelman, M. B. (1987a). Communicating social support: A theoretical perpective. In T. L. Albrecht & M. B. Adelman (Eds.), *Communicating social support* (pp. 18–39). Newbury Park, CA: Sage.

Albrecht, T. L., & Adelman, M. B. (1987b). Communication networks as structures of social support. In T. L. Albrecht & M. B. Adelman (Eds.), *Communicating social support* (pp. 40–63). Newbury Park, CA: Sage.

Albrecht, T. L., & Ropp, V. A. (1984). Communicating about innovation in networks of three U.S. organizations. *Journal of Communication, 34,* 78–91.

Allen, I. L. (1969). Social relations and the two-step flow: A defense of the tradition. *Journalism Quarterly, 46,* 492–498.

Allen, T. J. (1966). Performance of information channels in the transfer of technology. *Industrial Management Review, 8,* 87–98.

Allen, T. J. (1977). *Managing the flow of technology: Technology transfer and the dissemination of technological information within the R&D organization.* Cambridge, MA: MIT Press.

American Heritage Dictionary. (1976). *The American Heritage Dictionary of the English Language.* Boston: Houghton Mifflin.

Archea, J. (1977). The place of architectural factors in behavioral theories of privacy. *Journal of Social Issues, 33,* 16–37.

Armenikas, A. A., Harris, S. G., & Mossholder, K. W. (1993). Creating readiness for organizational change. *Human Relations, 46,* 681–703.

Ashford, S. J. (1986). Feedback seeking in individual adaptation: A resource perspective. *Academy of Management Journal, 29,* 465–487.

Ashford, S. J. (1989). Self-assessments in organizations: A literature review and integrative model. In S. B. Bacharach (Ed.), *Research in organizational behavior, Volume 11* (pp. 133–174). Greenwich, CT: JAI Press.

Ashford, S. J., & Cummings, L. L. (1985). Proactive feedback seeking: The instrumental use of the information environment. *Journal of Occupational Psychology, 58,* 67–79.

Ashford, S. J., & Tsui, A. S. (1991). Self-regulation for managerial effectiveness: The role of active feedback seeking. *Academy of Management Journal, 34,* 251–280.

Astley, W. G., & Zajac, E. J. (1991). Intraorganizational power and organizational design: Reconciling rational and coalitional models of organization. *Organization Science, 2,* 399–411.

Atkin, C. (1973). Instrumental utilities and information seeking. In P. Clarke (Ed.), *New models for mass communication research* (pp. 205–242). Beverly Hills, CA: Sage.

Atkin, C. (1979). Research evidence on mass mediated health communication campaigns. In D. Nimmo (Ed.), *Communication Yearbook 3* (pp. 655–668). New Brunswick, NJ: Transaction Books.

Atkin, C. K. (1981). Mass communication research principles for health education. In M. Meyer (Ed.), *Health education by television and radio: Contributions to an international conference with a selected bibliography* (pp. 41–55). New York: K. G. Saur.

Axley, S. R. (1984). Managerial and organizational communication in terms of the conduit metaphor. *Academy of Management Review, 9,* 428–437.

Babrow, A. S. (1992). Communication and problematic integration: Understanding diverging probability and value, ambiguity, ambivalence and impossibility. *Communication Theory, 2,* 95–130.

Baliga, B. R., & Jaeger, A. M. (1984). Multinational corporations: Control systems and delegation issues. *Journal of International Business Studies, 14,* 25–40.

Bates, M. J. (1989). The design of browsing and berrypicking techniques for the online search interface. *Online Review, 13,* 407–424.

Bates, M. J. (1990). Information as an economic good: A reevaluation of theoretical approaches. In B. D. Ruben & L. A. Lievrouw (Eds.), *Information and Behavior, Volume 3* (pp. 379–394). New Brunswick, NJ: Transaction Books.

Bauer, R. A. (1972). The obstinate audience: The influence process from the point of view of social communication. In W. Schramm & D. F. Roberts (Eds.), *The process and effects of mass communication* (pp. 326–346). Urbana, IL: University of Illinois Press.

Beal, C. (1979). Studying the public's information needs. *Journal of Librarianship, 11*, 130–151.

Beetham, D. (1987). *Bureaucracy*. Milton Keynes, UK: Open University Press.

Bellah, R. N., Madsen, R., Sullivan, W. M., Swidler, A., & Tipton, S. M. (1991). *The good society*. New York: Knopf.

Bellin, D. (1993). The economic value of information. *Knowledge: Creation, Diffusion, Utilization, 15*, 233–240.

Beninger, J. R. (1990). Conceptualizing information technology as organization, and vice versa. In J. Fulk & C. Steinfield (Eds.), *Organizations and communication technology* (pp. 29–45). Newbury Park, CA: Sage.

Berger, C. R. (1979). Beyond initial interactions: Uncertainty, understanding, and the development of interpersonal relationships. In H. Giles & R. S. Clair (Eds.), *Language and social psychology*. Oxford, UK: Basil Blackwell.

Berger, C. R., & Calabrese, R. J. (1975). Some explorations in initial interaction and beyond: Toward a developmental theory of interpersonal communication. *Human Communication Research, 1*, 99–112.

Berger, C. R., & Chaffee, S. H. (Eds.) (1987). *Handbook of communication science*. Newbury Park, CA: Sage.

Berger, P. L., & Luckmann, T. (1967). *The social construction of reality*. Garden City, NY: Anchor Books.

Berlo, D. K. (1960). *The process of communication: An introduction to theory and practice*. New York: Holt, Rinehart and Winston.

Blair, R., Roberts, K. H., & McKechnie, P. (1985). Vertical and network communication in organizations: The present and the future. In R. D. McPhee & P. K. Tompkins (Eds.), *Organizational communication: Traditional themes and new directions* (pp. 55–78). Beverly Hills, CA: Sage.

Blau, P. M. (1954). Patterns of interaction among a group of officials in a government agency. *Human Relations, 7*, 337–348.

Blau, P. M. (1955). *The dynamics of bureaucracy: A study of interpersonal relations in two government agencies*. Chicago: University of Chicago Press.

Blau, P. M., & Schoenherr, R. (1971). *The structure of organizations*. New York: Basic Books.

Boone, M. E. (1991). *Leadership and the computer*. Rocklin, CA: Prima Publishing.

Borgman, C. L. (1986). Human-computer interaction with information retrieval systems: Understanding complex communication behavior. In B. Dervin & M. J. Voight (Eds.), *Progress in communication sciences, Volume VII* (pp. 91–122). Norwood, NJ: Ablex.

Boulding, K. E. (1966). The economics of knowledge and the knowledge of economics. *American Economic Review, 56*, 1–13.

Bradach, J. L., & Eccles, R. G. (1989). Price, authority, and trust: From ideal types to plural forms. *Annual Review of Sociology, 15*, 97–118.

Braman, S. (1994). The autopoietic state: Communication and democratic potential in the net. *Journal of the American Society for Information Science, 45*, 358–368.

Brass, D. J. (1985). Men's and women's networks: A study of interaction patterns and influence in an organization. *Academy of Management Journal, 28*, 327–343.

Brenner, M. H., & Sigband, N. B. (1973). Organizational communication: An analysis based on empirical data. *Academy of Management Journal, 16*, 323–325.

Brett, J. M., Feldman, D. C., & Weingart, L. R. (1990). Feedback-seeking behavior of new hires and job changers. *Journal of Management, 16*, 737–749.

Brittain, J. M. (1970). *Information and its users: A review with special reference to the social sciences*. Claverton Down, Bath, UK: Bath University Press.

Broadbent, M., & Koenig, M. E. D. (1988). Information and information technology management. In M. E. Williams (Ed.), *Annual review of information science and technology, Volume 23* (pp. 237–270). Amsterdam: Elsevier Science.

Brody, M. (1986). NASA's challenge: Isolation at the top. *Fortune* (May 12), 26–32.

Brooks, B. C. (1980). The foundations of information science: Part I. Philosophical aspects. *Journal of Information Science, 2*, 125–133.

Brown, M. H., & McMillan, J. J. (1988). *Constructions and counterconstructions: Organizational power revisited*. Paper presented at the annual convention of the Speech Communication Association, New Orleans, LA.

Buckland, M. (1991a). *Information and information systems*. Westport, CT: Greenwood Press.

Buckland, M. (1991b). Information as thing. *Journal of American Society for Information Science, 42*, 351–360.

Burgoon, J. K., & Burgoon, M. (1980). Predictors of newspaper readership. *Journalism Quarterly, 57*, 589–596.

Burgoon, M., & Burgoon, J. K. (1979). Predictive models of satisfaction with a newspaper. In D. Nimmo (Ed.), *Communication yearbook 3* (pp. 271–281). New Brunswick, NJ: Transaction Books.

Burgoon, M., Burgoon, J. K., & Wilkinson, M. (1981). Newspaper image and evaluation. *Journalism Quarterly, 58*, 411–419, 433.

Burke, R. J., & Bolf, C. (1986). Learning within organizations: Sources and content. *Psychological Reports, 59*, 1187–1196.

Burt, R. S. (1983). A note on inference concerning network subgroups. In R. S. Burt & M. J. Minor (Eds.), *Applied network analysis: A methodological introduction* (pp. 283–301). Beverly Hills, CA: Sage.

Burt, R. S. (1992). *Structural holes: The social structure of competition*. Cambridge, MA: Harvard University Press.

Business Week. (1994). The information revolution. Special issue. *Business Week*, p. 107.

Caldwell, D. F., & O'Reilly, III, C. A. (1985). The impact of information on job choices and turnover. *Academy of Management Journal, 28*, 934–943.

Canter, D., & Kenny, C. (1975). The spatial environment. In D. Canter & P. Stringer (Eds.), *Environmental interaction: Psychological approaches to our physical surroundings* (pp. 127–163). New York: International University Press.

Carley, K. (1986). An approach for relating social structure to cognitive structure. *Journal of Mathematical Sociology, 12*, 137–189.

Carlson, E. R. (1960). Psychological satisfaction and interest in news. *Journalism Quarterly, 37*, 547–551.

Carter, N. M. (1984). Computerization as a predominate technology: Its influence on the structure of newspaper organizations. *Academy of Management Journal, 27*, 247–271.

Carter, N. M., & Culnan, J. B. (1983). *The computerization of newspaper organizations: The impact of technology on organizational structuring*. Lanham, MD: University Press of America.

Cash, J. I., Jr., Eccles, R. G., Nohria, N., & Nolan, R. L. (1994). *Building the infor-mation-age organization: Structure, control, and information technologies.* Boston: Irwin.

Cerveny, R. P., Pegels, C. C., & Sanders, G. L. (1993). Introduction to strategic information systems. In R. P. Cerveny, C. C. Pegels, & G. L. Sanders (Eds.), *Strategic information systems for strategic, manufacturing, operations, marketing, sales, financial and human resources management* (pp. 1–12). Greenwich, CT: JAI Press.

Chaffee, S. H., & McCleod, J. M. (1973). Individual vs. social predictors of information seeking. *Journalism Quarterly, 50,* 237–245.

Chang, S.-J., & Rice, R. E. (1993). Browsing: A multidimensional framework. In M. E. Williams (Ed.), *Annual review of information science and technology, Volume 28* (pp. 231–276). Medford, NJ: Learned Information.

Chen, C., & Hernon, P. (1982). *Information seeking: Assessing and anticipating user needs.* New York: Neal-Schuman Publishers.

Cheney, G. (1995). Democracy in the workplace: Theory and practice from the perspective of communication. *Journal of Applied Communication Research, 23,* 167–200.

Cheng, J. L. C. (1983). Interdependence and coordination in organizations: A role-system analysis. *Academy of Management Journal, 26,* 156–162.

Choo, C. W., & Auster, E. (1993). Environmental scanning: Acquisition and use of information by managers. *Annual review of information science and technology, Volume 28* (pp. 279–314). Medford, NJ: Learned Information.

Clayton, C. (1974). Communication and spatial structure. *Tijdschrift voor Economische en Sociale Geografie, 65,* 221–227.

Cleveland, H. (1985). The twilight of hierarchy: Speculations on the global information society. In S. R. Corman, S. P. Banks, C. R. Bantz, & M. E. Mayer (Eds.), *Foundations of organizational communication* (pp. 370–374). White Plains, NY: Longman.

Cline, T. R. (1983). *Work group communication in word processing.* Paper presented at the annual meeting of the Speech Communication Association, Washington, DC.

Cole, C. (1994). Operationalizing the notion of information as a subjective construct. *Journal of the American Society for Information Science, 45,* 465–476.

Comer, D. R. (1991). Organizational newcomers' acquisition of information from peers. *Management Communication Quarterly, 5,* 64–89.

Connolly, T. (1977). Information processing and decision making in organizations. In B. M. Staw & G. R. Salancik (Eds.), *New directions in organizational behavior* (pp. 205–234). Chicago, IL: St. Clair Press.

Connolly, T., & Thorn, B. K. (1990). Discretionary databases: Theory, data, and implications. In J. Fulk & C. Steinfield (Eds.), *Organizations and communication technology* (pp. 219–234). Newbury Park, CA: Sage.

Conrad, C. (1985). *Strategic organizational communication.* New York: CBS College Publishing Co.

Contractor, N. S., & Eisenberg, E. M. (1990). Communication networks and new media in organizations. In J. Fulk & C. Steinfield (Eds.), *Organizations and communication technology* (pp. 143–172). Newbury Park, CA: Sage.

Corman, S. R. (in press). The reticulation of quasi-agents. In G. A. Barnett (Ed.), *Organizational communication: Emerging perspectives*. Norwood, NJ: Ablex.

Cronin, B., & Davenport, E. (1993). Social intelligence. In M. E. Williams (Ed.), *Annual review of information science and technology, Volume 28* (pp. 3–44). Medford, NJ: Learned Information.

Culnan, M. J. (1983). Environmental scanning: The effects of task complexity and source accessibility on information gathering behavior. *Decision Sciences, 14*, 194–206.

Culnan, M. J., & Markus, M. L. (1987). Information technologies. In F. M. Jablin, L. L. Putnam, K. H. Roberts, & L. W. Porter (Eds.), *Handbook of organizational communication: An interdisciplinary perspective* (pp. 420–443). Beverly Hills, CA: Sage.

Cushman, D. P., King, S. S., & Smith, T. I. (1988). The rules perspective on organizational communication research. In G. M. Goldhaber & G. A. Barnett (Eds.), *Handbook of organizational communication* (pp. 55–94). Norwood, NJ: Ablex.

Cushman, D. P., & Whiting, G. C. (1972). An approach to communication theory: Toward consensus on rules. *Journal of Communication, 22*, 217–238.

Cyert, R. M., Simon, H. A., & Trow, D. B. (1956). Observation of a business decision. *Journal of Business, 29*, 237–248.

Czepiel, J. A. (1975). Patterns of interorganizational communications and the diffusion of a major technological innovation in a competitive industrial community. *Academy of Management Journal, 18*, 6–24.

D'Aprix, R. (1988). Communication as process: The managers' view. In G. M. Goldhaber & G. A. Barnett (Eds.), *Handbook of organizational communication* (pp. 265–272). Norwood, NJ: Ablex.

Daft, R. L. (1978). A dual-core model of organizational innovation. *Academy of Management Journal, 21*, 193–210.

Daft, R. L., & Huber, G. P. (1987). How organizations learn: A communication framework. In N. D. Tomoso & S. B. Bacharach (Eds.), *Research in organizational behavior* (pp. 1–36). Greenwich, CT: JAI Press.

Daft, R. L., & Lengel, R. H. (1986). Organizational information requirements: Media richness and structural design. *Management Science, 32*, 554–571.

Daft, R. L., & Macintosh, N. B. (1981). A tentative exploration into the amount and equivocality of information processing in organizational work units. *Administrative Science Quarterly, 26*, 207–224.

Dalton, D. R., Todor, W. D., Spendolini, M. J., Fielding, G. J., & Porter, L. W. (1980). Organization structure and performance: A critical review. *Academy of Management Review, 5*, 49–64.

Dance, F. E. X., & Larson, C. H. (1976). *The functions of human communication*. New York: Holt, Rinehart & Winston.

Dansereau, F., & Markham, S. E. (1987). Superior-subordinate communication: Multiple levels of analysis. In F. M. Jablin, L. L. Putnam, K. H. Roberts, & L. W. Porter (Eds.), *Handbook of organizational communication: An interdisciplinary perspective* (pp. 343–388). Newbury Park, CA: Sage.

Darnell, D. K. (1972). Information theory: An approach to human communication. In R. W. Budd & B. D. Ruben (Eds.), *Approaches to human communication* (pp. 156–169). New York: Spartan Books.

Davidow, W. H., & Malone, M. S. (1992). *The virtual corporation: Structuring and revitalizing the corporation for the 21st century*. New York: HarperCollins.

Davis, T. R. (1984). The influence of the physical environment in offices. *Academy of Management Review, 9*, 271–283.

de Chardin, P. (1961). *The phenomenon of man*. New York: Harper.

Dean, J. W., Jr., & Bowen, D. E. (1994). Management theory and total quality: Improving research and practice through theory development. *Academy of Management Review, 19*, 392–418.

Dervin, B. (1980). Communication gaps and inequities: Moving toward a reconceptualization. In B. Dervin & M. J. Voight (Eds.), *Progress in communication sciences, Volume II* (pp. 74–112). Norwood, NJ: Ablex.

Dervin, B. (1989). Users as research inventions: How research categories perpetuate inequities. *Journal of Communication, 39*, 216–232.

Dervin, B., Jacobson, T. L., & Nilan, M. S. (1982). Measuring aspects of information seeking: A test of quantitative/qualitative methodogy. In M. Burgoon (Ed.), *Communication yearbook 6* (pp. 419–444). Beverly Hills, CA: Sage.

Dervin, B., & Nilan, M. S. (1986). Information needs and uses. In M. A. Williams (Ed.), *Annual review of information science and technology, Volume 21* (pp. 3–33). Medford, NJ: Knowledge Industry Publications.

DeTocqueville, A. (1966). *Democracy in America*. New York: Harper & Row.

DeVito, A. J., Bogdanowicz, J., & Reznikoff, M. (1982). Actual and intended health-related information seeking and health locus of control. *Journal of Personality Assessment, 46*, 63–69.

Dewhirst, H. D. (1971). Influence of perceived information-sharing norms on communication channel utilization. *Academy of Management Journal, 14*, 205–315.

DiMaggio, P. (1992). Nadel's Paradox revisited: Relational and cultural aspects of organizational structure. In N. Nohria & R. G. Eccles (Eds.), *Networks and organizations: Structure, form, and action* (pp. 118–142). Boston: Harvard Business School Press.

Dobos, J. (1988). Choices of new media and traditional channels in organizations. *Communication Research Reports, 5*, 131–139.

Doctor, R. D. (1991). Information technologies and social equity: Confronting the revolution. *Journal of the American Society for Information Science, 42*, 216–228.

Doctor, R. D. (1992). Social equity and information technologies: Moving toward information democracy. In M. E. Williams (Ed.), *Annual review of information science and technology* (pp. 44–96). Medford, NJ: Learned Information.

Donohew, L., Helm, D. M., Cook, P. L., & Shatzer, M. J. (1987). *Sensation seeking, marijuana use, and response to prevention messages: Implications for public health campaigns*. Paper presented at the International Communication Association, Montreal, Canada.

Donohew, L., Tipton, L., & Haney, R. (1978). Analysis of information-seeking strategies. *Journalism Quarterly, 55*, 25–31.

Douglas, W. (1985). Anticipated interaction and information seeking. *Human Communication Research, 12*, 243–258.

Dow, G. K. (1988). Configurational and coactivational views of organizational structure. *Academy of Management Review, 13*, 53–64.

Downs, A. (1967). *Inside bureaucracy*. Boston: Little, Brown.

Downs, C. W., Clampitt, P. G., & Pfeiffer, A. L. (1988). Communication and organizational outcomes. In G. M. Goldhaber & G. A. Barnett (Eds.), *Handbook of organizational communication* (pp. 171–212). Norwood, NJ: Ablex.

Drucker, P. F. (1974). *Management—Tasks, responsibilities, practices*. New York: Harper and Row.

Drucker, P. F. (1988). The coming of the new organization. *Harvard Business Review, 66* (January/February), 45–53.

Dunegan, K. J., Green, S. G., & Baker, N. R. (1987). *Coordination, critical resources, and R&D performance: A contextual profile*. Paper presented at the Academy of Management annual convention, New Orleans, LA.

Durlak, J. T. (1987). A typology of interactive media. In M. L. McLaughlin (Ed.), *Communication yearbook 10* (pp. 743–757). Beverly Hills, CA: Sage.

Eccles, R., & White, H. (1988). Price and authority in inter-profit center transactions. *American Journal of Sociology, Supplement, 94*, S17–S51.

Eisenberg, E. M. (1984). Ambiguity as strategy in organizational communication. *Communication Monographs, 51*, 227–242.

Eisenberg, E. M. (1990). Jamming: Transcendence through organizing. *Communication Research, 17*, 139–164.

Eisenberg, E. M., & Goodall, H. L., Jr. (1993). *Organizational communication: Balancing creativity and constraint*. New York: St. Martin's Press.

Eisenberg, E. M., & Riley, P. (1988). Organizational symbols as sense-making. In G. M. Goldhaber & G. A. Barnett (Eds.), *Handbook of organizational communication* (pp. 131–150). Norwood, NJ: Ablex.

Eisenberg, E. M., & Whetten, M. G. (1987). Reconsidering openness in organizational communication. *Academy of Management Review, 12*, 418–426.

Ellis, D. (1989). A behavioral model for information retrieval system design. *Journal of Information Science, 15*, 237–247.

Emery, F., & Trist, E. (1965). The causal texture of organizational environment. *Human Relations, 18*, 21–32.

Entman, R. M., & Wildman, S. S. (1992). Reconciling economic and non-economic perspectives on media policy: Transcending the "marketplace of ideas." *Journal of Communication, 42*, 5–19.

Evans, S. H., & Clarke, P. (1983). When cancer patients fail to get well: Flaws in health communication. In R. N. Bostrom (Ed.), *Communication yearbook 7* (pp. 225–248). Beverly Hills, CA: Sage.

Fairhurst, G. T. (1986). Male-female communication on the job: Literature review and commentary. In M. L. McLaughlin (Ed.), *Communication yearbook 9* (pp. 83–116). Beverly Hills, CA: Sage.

Fairhurst, G. T., & Snavely, B. K. (1983). A test of the social isolation of male tokens. *Academy of Management Journal, 26*, 353–361.

Farace, R. V., & Johnson, J. D. (1974). *Comparative analysis of human communication networks in selected formal organizations*. Paper presented at the International Communication Association annual convention, New Orleans, LA.

Farace, R. V., & Mabee, T. (1980). Communication network analysis methods. In P. R. Monge & J. N. Cappella (Eds.), *Multivariate techniques in human communication research* (pp. 365–391). New York: Academic Press.

Farace, R. V., Monge, P. R., & Russell, H. (1977). *Communicating and organizing.* Reading, MA: Addison-Wesley.

Farace, R. V., Taylor, J. A., & Stewart, J. P. (1978). Criteria for evaluation of organizational communication effectiveness: Review and synthesis. In D. Nimmo (Ed.), *Communication yearbook 2* (pp. 271–292). New Brunswick, NJ: Transaction Books.

Feigenbaum, E., McCorduck, P., & Nii, H. P. (1988). *The rise of the expert company: How visionary companies are using artificial intelligence to achieve higher productivity and profits.* New York: Times Books.

Feldman, D. C., & Brett, J. M. (1983). Coping with new jobs: A comparative study of new hires and job changers. *Academy of Management Journal, 26,* 258–272.

Feldman, M. S., & March, J. G. (1981). Information in organizations as signal and symbol. *Administrative Science Quarterly, 26,* 171–186.

Fidler, L. A., & Johnson, J. D. (1984). Communication and innovation implementation. *Academy of Management Review, 9,* 704–711.

Form, W. H. (1972). Technology and social behavior of workers in four countries: A sociotechnical perspective. *American Sociological Review, 37,* 727–738.

Fortner, R. S. (1995). Excommunication in the information society. *Critical Studies in Mass Communication, 12,* 133–154.

Frances, J., Levacic, R., Mitchell, J., & Thompson, G. (1991). Introduction. In G. Thompson, J. Frances, R. Levacic, & J. Mitchell (Eds.), *Markets, hierarchies & networks: The coordination of social life* (pp. 1–19). Newbury Park, CA: Sage.

Freimuth, V. S. (1987). The diffusion of supportive information. In T. L. Albrecht & M. B. Adelman (Eds.), *Communicating social support* (pp. 212–237). Newbury Park, CA: Sage.

Freimuth, V. S., Stein, J. A., & Kean, T. J. (1989). *Searching for health information: The Cancer Information Service model.* Philadelphia: University of Pennsylvania Press.

Friedkin, N. (1980). A test of structural features of Granovetter's strength of weak ties theory. *Social Networks, 2,* 411–422.

Friedkin, N. E. (1982). Information flow through strong and weak ties in intraorganizational social networks. *Social Networks, 3,* 273–285.

Froehlich, T. J. (1994). Relevance reconsidered—Towards an agenda for the 21st century: Introduction to special topic issue on relevance research. *Journal of the American Society for Information Science, 45,* 124–134.

Fry, L. W., & Smith, D. A. (1987). Congruence, contingency, and theory building. *Academy of Management Review, 12,* 117–132.

Fulk, J. (1993). Social construction of communication technology. *Academy of Management Journal, 36,* 921–950.

Fulk, J., & Boyd, B. (1991). Emerging theories of communication in organizations. *Journal of Management, 17,* 407–446.

Fulk, J., Schmitz, J. W., & Steinfield, C. W. (1990). A social influence model of technology use. In J. Fulk & C. Steinfield (Eds.), *Organizations and communication technology.* (pp. 117–140). Newbury Park, CA: Sage.

Fulk, J., Steinfield, C. W., Schmitz, J., & Power, J. G. (1987). A social information processing model of media use in organizations. *Communication Research, 14,* 529–552.

Galbraith, J. R. (1973). *Designing complex organizations*. Reading, MA: Addison-Wesley.

Galbraith, J. R. (1974). Organizational design: An information processing view. *Interfaces, 4*, 28–36.

Galbraith, J. R. (1995). *Designing organizations: An executive briefing on strategy, structure, and process*. San Francisco: Jossey-Bass.

Gans, H. J. (1993). Reopening the black box: Toward a limited effects theory. *Journal of Communication, 43*, 29–35.

Geertz, C. (1978). The bazaar economy: Information and search in peasant marketing. *American Economic Review, 68*, 28–37.

Gerstberger, P. G., & Allen, T. J. (1968). Criteria used by research and development engineers in the selection of an information source. *Journal of Applied Psychology, 52*, 272–279.

Glauser, M. J. (1984). Upward information flow in organizations: Review and conceptual analysis. *Human Relations, 37*, 613–643.

Goldenson, R. M. (1984). *Longman Dictionary of Psychology and Psychiatry*. New York: Longman.

Goldhaber, G. M., Yates, M. P., Porter, T. D., & Lesniak, R. (1978). Organizational communication: 1978. *Human Communication Research, 5*, 76–96.

Gould, C. C., & Pearce, K. (1991). *Information needs in the sciences: An assessment*. Mountain View, CA: The Research Libraries Group.

Granovetter, M. (1982). The strength of weak ties: A network theory revisited. In P. V. Marsden & N. Lin (Eds.), *Social structure in network analysis* (pp. 105–130). Beverly Hills, CA: Sage.

Granovetter, M. (1985). Economic action and social structure: The problem of embeddedness. *American Journal of Sociology, 91*, 481–510.

Granovetter, M. S. (1973). The strength of weak ties. *American Journal of Sociology, 78*, 1360–1380.

Greider, W. (1992). *Who will tell the people: The betrayal of American democracy*. New York: Simon & Schuster.

Grunig, J. E. (1975). A multi-systems theory of organizational communication. *Communication Research, 2*, 99–136.

Guetzkow, H. (1965). Communication in organizations. In J. G. March (Ed.), *Handbook of organizations* (pp. 534–573). Chicago, IL: Rand-McNally.

Guetzkow, H., & Simon, H. A. (1955). The impact of certain communication nets upon organization and performance in task-oriented groups. *Management Science, 1*, 233–250.

Gupta, A. K., & Govindarajan, V. (1991). Knowledge flows and the structure of control within multinational organizations. *Academy of Management Review, 16*, 768–792.

Gurbaxani, V., & Whang, S. (1991). The impact of information systems on organizations and markets. *Communications of the ACM, 34*, 59–73.

Hackman, J. (1983). Group influences on individuals. In M. Dunette (Ed.), *Handbook of industrial and organizational psychology* (pp. 1455–1525). New York: Wiley.

Hagarstrand, T. (1953). *Innovation diffusion as a spatial process*. Chicago, IL: University of Chicago Press.

Hage, J. (1974). *Communication and organizational control: Cybernetics in health and welfare settings*. New York: Wiley.

Hage, J., & Aiken, M. (1970). *Social change in complex organizations.* New York: Random House.

Hage, J., Aiken, M., & Marrett, C. B. (1971). Organization structure and communications. *American Sociological Review, 36,* 860–871.

Halberstam, D. (1986). *The reckoning.* New York: William Morrow.

Hall, H. J. (1981). Patterns in the use of information: The right to be different. *Journal of the American Society for Information Science, 32,* 103–112.

Hanser, L. M., & Muchinsky, P. M. (1978). Work as an information environment. *Organizational Behavior and Human Performance, 21,* 47–60.

Hanson, R., Porterfield, R. I., & Ames, K. (1995). Employee empowerment at risk: Effects of recent NLRB rulings. *Academy of Management Executive, 9,* 45–54.

Hayes, B. (1994). The world wide web. *American Scientist, 82,* 416–420.

Hayes, R. M. (1993). Measurement of information. *Information Processing & Management, 29,* 1–11.

Heeter, C. (1989). Classifying mediated communication systems. In J. A. Anderson (Ed.), *Communication yearbook 12* (pp. 477–489). Newbury Park, CA: Sage.

Hewins, E. T. (1990). Information need and use studies. In M. E. Williams (Ed.), *Annual review of information science and technology, Volume 25* (pp. 145–172). Amsterdam: Elsevier Science Publishers.

Hickson, D. J. (1987). Decision-making at the top of organizations. *Annual Review of Sociology, 13,* 165–192.

Hiemstra, G. (1982). Teleconferencing, concern for face, and organizational culture. In M. Burgoon (Ed.), *Communication yearbook 6* (pp. 874–904). Beverly Hills, CA: Sage.

Hoffman, E., & Roman, P. M. (1984). The effect of organizational emphasis upon diffusion of information about innovations. *Journal of Management, 10,* 277–291.

Hoffman, G. M. (1994). *The technology payoff: How to profit with empowered workers in the information age.* New York: Irwin.

Holsapple, C. W., & Whinston, A. B. (1988). *The information jungle: A quasi-novel approach to managing corporate knowledge.* Homewood, IL: Dow Jones-Irwin.

Huber, G. P. (1990). A theory of the effects of advanced information technologies on organizational design, intelligence, and decision making. *Academy of Management Review, 15,* 47–71.

Huber, G. P., & Daft, R. L. (1987). The information environment in organizations. In F. M. Jablin, L. L. Putnam, K. H. Roberts, & L. W. Porter (Eds.), *Handbook of organizational communication: An interdisciplinary perspective* (pp. 130–164). Newbury Park, CA: Sage.

Huber, G. P., & McDaniel, R. R., Jr. (1988). Exploiting information technologies to design more effective organizations. In M. Jarke (Ed.), *Managers, micros and mainframes* (pp. 221–236). New York: Wiley.

Hudson, J., & Danish, S. J. (1980). The acquisition of information: An important life skill. *Personnel and Guidance Journal, 59,* 164–167.

Huff, C., Sproull, L., & Kiesler, S. (1989). Computer communication and organizational commitment: Tracing the relationship in a city government. *Journal of Applied Social Psychology, 19,* 1371–1391.

Hyman, H. H., & Sheatsley, P. B. (1947). Some reasons why information campaigns fail. *Public Opinion Quarterly, 11,* 412–423.

Inman, T. H., Olivas, L., & Golen, S. P. (1986). Desirable communication behaviors of managers. *Business Education Forum, 40,* 27–28.

Jablin, F. M. (1978). Message response and "openness" in superior-subordinate communication. In B. D. Ruben (Ed.), *Communication yearbook 2* (pp. 293–309). New Brunswick, NJ: Transaction Books.

Jablin, F. M. (1985). Task/work relationships: A life-span perspective. In G. R. Miller & M. L. Knapp (Eds.), *Handbook of interpersonal communication* (pp. 615–654). Beverly Hills, CA: Sage.

Jablin, F. M. (1987). Formal organization structure. In F. M. Jablin, L. L. Putnam, K. H. Roberts, & L. W. Porter (Eds.), *Handbook of organizational communication: An interdisciplinary perspective* (pp. 389–419). Newbury Park, CA: Sage.

Jablin, F. M., & Krone, K. J. (1987). Organizational assimilation. In C. R. Berger & S. H. Chaffee (Eds.), *Handbook of communication science* (pp. 711–746). Newbury Park, CA: Sage.

Jablin, F. M., & Sussman, L. (1983). Organizational group communication: A review of the literature and model of the process. In H. H. Greenbaum, R. L. Falcione, & S. A. Hellweg (Eds.), *Organizational communication: Abstracts, analysis, and overview* (pp. 11–50). Beverly Hills, CA: Sage.

Janis, I. L. (1971). Groupthink. *Psychology Today* (November), 43–76.

Johnson, B. M., & Rice, R. E. (1987). *Managing organizational innovation: The evolution of word processing to office information systems.* New York: Columbia University Press.

Johnson, J. D. (1983). A test of a model of magazine exposure and appraisal in India. *Communication Monographs, 50,* 148–157.

Johnson, J. D. (1984a). International communication media appraisal: Tests in Germany. In R. N. Bostrom (Ed.), *Communication yearbook 8* (pp. 645–658). Beverly Hills, CA: Sage.

Johnson, J. D. (1984b). Media exposure and appraisal: Phase II, tests of a model in Nigeria. *Journal of Applied Communication Research, 12,* 63–74.

Johnson, J. D. (1987). A model of international communication media appraisal: Phase IV, generalizing the model to film. *International Journal of Intercultural Relations, 11,* 129–142.

Johnson, J. D. (1992). Approaches to organizational communication structure. *Journal of Business Research, 25,* 99–113.

Johnson, J. D. (1993a). *Organizational communication structure.* Norwood, NJ: Ablex.

Johnson, J. D. (1993b). *Tests of a comprehensive model of cancer-related information seeking.* Paper read at the Speech Communication Association annual convention, Miami, FL.

Johnson, J. D., Donohue, W. A., Atkin, C. K., & Johnson, S. H. (1995). A comprehensive model of information seeking: Tests focusing on a technical organization. *Science Communication, 16,* 274–303.

Johnson, J. D., & Meischke, H. (1993). A comprehensive model of cancer-related information seeking applied to magazines. *Human Communication Research, 19,* 343–367.

Johnson, J. D., & Meyer, M. (1995). *Office of Admissions & Scholarships Network Analysis Project.* Unpublished report. E. Lansing, MI: Department of Communication.

Johnson, J. D., & Oliveira, O. S. (1988). A model of international communication media appraisal and exposure: A comprehensive test in Belize. *World Communication, 17*, 253–277.

Johnson, J. D., & Tims, A. R. (1981). Magazine evaluations and levels of readership: A cross-national comparison. *Journalism Quarterly, 58*, 96–98.

Kanter, R. M. (1977). *Men and women of the corporation.* New York: Basic Books.

Kanter, R. M. (1983). *The change masters: Innovation and entrepreneurship in the American corporation.* New York: Simon & Schuster.

Kasperson, C. J. (1978). An analysis of the relationship between information sources and creativity in scientists and engineers. *Human Communication Research, 4*, 113–119.

Katz, D., & Kahn, R. L. (1978). *The social psychology of organizations.* New York: Wiley.

Katz, E. (1957). The two-step flow of communication: An up-to-date report on an hypothesis. *Public Opinion Quarterly, 21*, 61–78.

Katz, E. (1968). On reopening the question of selectivity in exposure to mass communications. In R. P. Abelson (Ed.), *Theories of cognitive consistency* (pp. 788–796). New York: Rand McNally.

Katz, E., Gurevitch, M., & Haas, H. (1973). On the use of the mass media for important things. *American Sociological Review, 38*, 164–181.

Katz, E., & Lazarsfeld, P. F. (1955). *Personal influence: The part played by people in the flow of mass communications.* New York: The Free Press.

Katz, R., & Allen, T. J. (1982). Investigating the Not Invented Here (NIH) syndrome: A look at the performance, tenure, and communication patterns of 50 R & D project groups. *R&D Management, 12*, 7–19.

Katzer, J., & Fletcher, P. T. (1992). The information environment of managers. In *Annual review of information science and technology, Volume 27* (pp. 227–263). Medford, NJ: Learned Information.

Keen, P. G. W. (1990). Telecommunications and organizational choice. In J. Fulk & C. Steinfield (Eds.), *Organizations and communication technology* (pp. 295–312). Newbury Park, CA: Sage.

Keen, P. G. W., & Morton, M. S. S. (1978). *Decision support systems: An organizational perspective.* Reading, MA: Addison-Wesley.

Kellerman, K. (1986). Anticipation of future interaction and information exchange in initial interaction. *Human Communication Research, 13*, 41–75.

Kellerman, K., & Reynolds, R. (1990). When ignorance is bliss: The role of motivation to reduce uncertainty in uncertainty reduction theory. *Human Communication Research, 17*, 5–75.

Kerwin, A. (1993). None too solid: Medical ignorance. *Knowledge: Creation, Diffusion, Utilization, 15*, 166–185.

Keyton, J. (1987). *Meta analysis of experimental studies using teleconferencing and mediated modes of communication.* Paper presented at the annual meeting of the International Communication Association, Montreal, Quebec, Canada.

Kling, R. (1980). Social analyses of computing: Theoretical perspectives in recent empirical research. *Computing Surveys, 12*, 61–110.

Komsky, S. H. (1989). *Electronic mail and democratization of organizational communication.* Paper presented at the annual meeting of the International Communication Association, San Francisco, CA.

Korzenney, F. (1978). A theory of electronic propinquity: Mediated communication in organizations. *Communication Research, 5,* 3–24.

Krackhardt, D. (1989). *Graph theoretical dimensions of informal organizations.* Paper presented at the national meeting of the Academy of Management, Washington, DC.

Krikelas, J. (1983). Information seeking behavior: Patterns and concepts. *Drexel Library Quarterly, 19,* 5–20.

Krippendorf, K. (1986). *Information theory: Structural models for qualitative data.* Newbury Park, CA: Sage.

Krizner, I. M. (1973). *Competition and entrepreneurship.* Chicago: University of Chicago Press.

Kuhlthau, C. C. (1991). Inside the search process: Information seeking from the user's perspective. *Journal of the American Society for Information Science, 12,* 361–371.

Kuhn, T. S. (1970). *The structure of scientific revolutions,* 2nd ed. Chicago: University of Chicago Press.

Kurke, L. B., Weick, K. E., & Ravlin, E. C. (1989). Can information loss be reversed? Evidence for serial construction. *Communication Research, 16,* 3–24.

LaFollette, M. C. (1993). Editorial. *Knowledge: Creation, Diffusion, Utilization, 15,* 131–132.

Larson, J. R., Jr. (1989). The dynamic interplay between employees' feedback-seeking strategies and supervisor's delivery of performance feedback. *Academy of Management Review, 14,* 408–422.

Lawrence, P. R., & Lorsch, J. W. (1967). *Organization and environment: Managing differentiation and integration.* Boston: Harvard Business School.

Lee, A. M. (1970). *Systems analysis frameworks.* London, UK: McMillan.

Lengel, R. H., & Daft, R. L. (1988). The selection of communication media as an executive skill. *Academy of Management Executive, 2,* 225–232.

Lenz, E. R. (1984). Information seeking: A component of client decisions and health behavior. *Advance in Nursing Science, 6,* 59–72.

Levacic, R. (1991). Markets: Introduction. In G. Thompson, J. Frances, R. Levacic, J. Mitchell (Eds.), *Markets, hierarchies & networks: The coordination of social life* (pp. 21–23). Newbury Park, CA: Sage.

Levitt, S. R. (1989). *Formal and informal communication in the diffusion and implementation of an organization-wide innovation: "They heard it through the grapevine."* Paper presented at the annual conference of the International Communication Association, San Francisco, CA.

Lewis, R. S. (1988). *Challenger: The final voyage.* New York: Columbia University Press.

Lievrouw, L. A. (1994). Information resources and democracy: Understanding the paradox. *Journal of the American Society for Information Science, 45,* 350–357.

Likert, R. (1967). *The human organization: Its management and value.* Hightstown, NJ: McGraw-Hill.

Littlejohn, S. W. (1992). *Theories of human communication,* 4th ed. Belmont, CA: Wadsworth.

Longenecker, C. O., Gioia, D. A., & Sims, H. P., Jr. (1987). Behind the mask: The politics of employee appraisal. *Academy of Management Executive, 1,* 183–194.

Lord, R. G., & Maher, K. J. (1990). Alternative information-processing models and their implications for theory, research, and practice. *Academy of Management Review, 15,* 9–28.

Lorenz, E. H. (1989). Neither friends nor strangers: Informal networks of subcontracting in French industry. In D. Gambetta (Ed.), *Trust: Making and breaking of cooperative relations* (pp. 194–210). Oxford, UK: Basil Blackwell.

Lukasiewicz, J. (1994). *The ignorance explosion: Understanding industrial civilization.* Ottawa, Canada: Carlton University Press.

MacCrimmon, K. R., & Taylor, R. N. (1976). Decision making and problem solving. In M. D. Dunnette (Ed.), *Handbook of industrial and organizational psychology.* (pp. 1397–1453). Chicago, IL: Rand McNally.

Maes, P. (1995). Intelligent software. *Scientific American* (September), 84–86.

Maguire, C., & Kench, R. (1984). The introduction and diffusion of technological innovation in industry: An information research perspective. In B. Dervin & M. J. Voight (Eds.), *Progress in communication sciences* (pp. 163–204). Norwood, NJ: Ablex.

Malone, T. W., Grant, K. R., Turbak, F. A., Brobst, S. A., & Cohen, M. D. (1987a). Intelligent information-sharing systems. *Communications of the ACM, 30,* 390–402.

Malone, T. W., Yates, J., & Benjamin, R. I. (1987b). Electronic markets and electronic hierarchies. *Communications of the ACM, 30,* 484–497.

March, J. G. (1994). *A primer on decision making: How decisions happen.* New York: Free Press.

March, J. G., & Simon, H. A. (1958). *Organizations.* New York: Wiley.

Marchand, D. A., & Horton, J. F. W. (1986). *Infotrends: Profiting from your information resources.* New York: Wiley.

Marchionini, G. (1992). Interfaces for end-user information seeking. *Journal of the American Society for Information Science, 43,* 156–163.

Markus, M. L. (1987). Toward a 'critical mass' theory of interactive media: Universal access, interdependence and diffusion. *Communication Research, 14,* 491–511.

Markus, M. L. (1994). Electronic mail as the medium of managerial choice. *Organization Science, 5,* 502–527.

Marshall, A. A., & Stohl, C. (1993). Participating as participation: A network approach. *Communication Monographs, 60,* 137–157.

Matthews, R., & Shoebridge, A. (1993). The strategic importance of Executive Information Systems. In R. Ennals & P. Molyneaux (Eds.), *Managing with information technology* (pp. 23–36). New York: Springer-Verlag.

McGee, J. V., & Prusak, L. (1993). *Managing information strategically.* New York: Wiley.

McGuinness, T. (1991). Markets and managerial hierarchies. In G. Thompson, J. Frances, R. Levacic, & J. Mitchell (Eds.), *Markets, hierarchies, and networks: The coordination of social life* (pp. 66–81). Newbury Park, CA: Sage.

McGuire, W. J. (1989). Theoretical foundations of campaigns. In R. E. Rice & C. K. Atkin (Eds.), *Public communication campaigns* (pp. 43–66). Newbury Park, CA: Sage.

McIntosh, J. (1974). Processes of communication, information seeking and control associated with cancer: A selective review of the literature. *Social Science and Medicine, 8,* 167–187.

McKinnon, S. M., & Bruns, W. J., Jr. (1992). *The information mosaic*. Boston: Harvard Business School Press.

McNeil, K., & Thompson, J. D. (1971). The regeneration of social organizations. *American Sociological Review, 36*, 624–637.

McPhee, R. D. (1985). Formal structure and organizational communication. In R. D. McPhee & P. K. Tompkins (Eds.), *Organizational communication: Traditional themes and new directions* (pp. 149–178). Beverly Hills, CA: Sage.

McPhee, R. D. (1988). Vertical communication chains: Toward an integrated approach. *Management Communication Quarterly, 1*, 455–493.

McPhee, R. D., & Corman, S. R. (1995). An activity-based theory of communication networks in organizations, applied to the case of a local church. *Communication Monographs, 62*, 132–151.

Menon, A., & Varadarajan, P. R. (1992). A model of marketing knowledge use within firms. *Journal of Marketing, 56*, 53–71.

Metoyer-Duran, C. (1993). Information gatekeepers. In M. E. Williams (Ed.), *Annual review of information science and technology, Volume 28* (pp. 111–150). Medford, NJ: Learned Information.

Milgrom, P., & Roberts, J. (1988). An economic approach to influence activities in organizations. *American Journal of Sociology, 94*, S154–S179.

Miller, D. (1993). The architecture of simplicity. *Academy of Management Review, 18*, 116–138.

Miller, G. R. (1969). Human information processing: Some research guidelines. In R. J. Kibler & L. L. Barker (Eds.), *Conceptual frontiers in speech-communication* (pp. 51–68). New York: Speech Communication Association.

Miller, G. R., & Steinberg, M. (1975). *Between people: A new analysis of interpersonal communication*. Chicago, IL: Science Research Associates.

Miller, V. D., & Jablin, F. M. (1991). Information seeking during organizational entry: Influences, tactics, and a model of the process. *Academy of Management Review, 16*, 92–120.

Miller, V. D., Johnson, J. R., & Grau, J. (1994). Antecedents to willingness to participate in a planned organizational change. *Journal of Applied Communication Research, 22*, 59–80.

Minor, M. J. (1983). New directions in multiplexity analysis. In R. S. Burt & M. J. Minor (Eds.), *Applied network analysis: A methodological introduction* (pp. 223–244). Beverly Hills, CA: Sage.

Mintzberg, H. (1975a). *Impediments to the use of management information*. New York: National Association of Accountants.

Mintzberg, H. (1975b). The manager's job. *Harvard Business Review, 53* (July/August), 49–61.

Mintzberg, H. (1976). Planning on the left side and managing on the right. *Harvard Business Review, 54* (July/August), 49–58.

Mitchell, J. (1991). Hierarchies: Introduction. In G. Thompson, J. Frances, R. Levacic, & J. Mitchell (Eds.), *Markets, hierarchies & networks: The coordination of social life* (pp. 105–107). Newbury Park, CA: Sage.

Mitchell, J. C. (1969). The concept and use of social networks. In J. C. Mitchell (Ed.), *Social networks in urban situations: Analyses of personal relationships in Central African towns* (pp. 1–50). Manchester, UK: Manchester University Press.

Mitchell, O. S. (1988). Worker knowledge of pensions provisions. *Journal of Labor Economics, 6,* 21–39.

Moch, M. K. (1980). Job involvement, internal motivation, and employees' integration into networks of work relationships. *Organizational Behavior and Human Performance, 25,* 15–31.

Monge, P. R. (1987). The network level of analysis. In C. R. Berger & S. H. Chaffee (Eds.), *Handbook of communication science* (pp. 239–270). Newbury Park, CA: Sage.

Monge, P. R., & Eisenberg, E. M. (1987). Emergent communication networks. In F. M. Jablin, L. L. Putnam, K. H. Roberts, & L. W. Porter (Eds.), *Handbook of organizational communication: An interdisciplinary perspective* (pp. 304–342). Newbury Park, CA: Sage.

Moore, W. E., & Tumin, M. M. (1949). Some social functions of ignorance. *American Sociological Review, 14,* 787–795.

More, E. (1990). Information systems: People issues. *Journal of Information Science, 16,* 311–320.

Morgan, G. (1986). *Images of organization.* Beverly Hills, CA: Sage.

Morley, D. (1993). Active audience theory: Pendulums and pitfalls. *Journal of Communication, 43,* 13–19.

Morris, G. H. (1988). *Grounding media richness theory: An interpretive/critical viewpoint.* Paper presented at the annual meeting of the International Communication Association, New Orleans, LA.

Morrison, E. W. (1993a). Longitudinal study of the effects of information seeking on newcomer socialization. *Journal of Applied Psychology, 78,* 173–183.

Morrison, E. W. (1993b). Newcomer information seeking: Exploring types, modes, sources, and outcomes. *Academy of Management Journal, 36,* 557–589.

Morrison, E. W., & Bies, R. J. (1991). Impression management in the feedback-seeking process: A literature review and research agenda. *Academy of Management Review, 16,* 522–541.

Nass, C., & Mason, L. (1990). On the study of technology and task: A variable-based approach. In J. Fulk & C. W. Steinfield (Eds.), *Organizations and communication technology* (pp. 46–68). Newbury Park, CA: Sage.

Nath, R. (1994). Difficulties in matching emerging information technologies with business needs: A management perspective. *Information Processing & Management, 30,* 437–444.

Nayyar, P. R. (1993). Performance effects of information asymmetry and economies of scope in diversified service firms. *Academy of Management Journal, 36,* 28–57.

Noam, E. (1993). Reconnecting communications study with communications policy. *Journal of Communication, 43,* 199–206.

Nohria, N. (1992). Is a network perspective a useful way of studying organizations. In N. Nohria & R. G. Eccles (Eds.), *Networks and organizations: Structure, form, and action* (pp. 1–22). Boston: Harvard Business School Press.

Nohria, N., & Eccles, R. (1992). Face-to-face: Making network organizations work. In N. Nohria & R. Eccles (Eds.), *Networks and organizations: Structure, form, and action* (pp. 288–308). Boston, MA: Harvard Business School Press.

Nutt, P. C. (1984). Types of organizational decision processes. *Administrative Science Quarterly, 29,* 414–450.

O'Conner, B. C. (1993). Browsing: A framework for seeking functional information. *Knowledge: Creation, Diffusion, Utilization, 15,* 211–232.

O'Neill, B. (1984). Structures for nonhierarchical organizations. *Behavioral Science, 29,* 61–77.

O'Reilly, C. A., III (1978). The intentional distortion of information in organizational communication: A laboratory and field investigation. *Human Relations, 31,* 173–193.

O'Reilly, C. A., III (1980). Individuals and information overload in organizations: Is more necessarily better? *Academy of Management Journal, 23,* 684–696.

O'Reilly, C. A., III (1982). Variations in decision makers' use of information sources: The impact of quality and accessibility of information. *Academy of Management Journal, 25,* 756–771.

O'Reilly, C. A., III, Chatham, J. A., & Anderson, J. C. (1987). Message flow and decision making. In F. M. Jablin, L. L. Putnam, K. H. Roberts, & L. W. Porter (Eds.), *Handbook of organizational communication: An interdisciplinary perspective* (pp. 600–623). Newbury Park, CA: Sage.

O'Reilly, C. A., III, & Pondy, L. R. (1979). Organizational communication. In S. Kerr (Ed.), *Organizational behavior* (pp. 119–150). Columbus, OH: Grid.

Overhage, C. F., & Harman, R. J. (Eds.) (1965). *INTREX: Report on a planning conference on information transfer experiments.* Cambridge, MA: MIT Press.

Paisley, W. (1980). Information and work. In B. Dervin & M. J. Voight (Eds.), *Progress in communication sciences, Volume II* (pp. 114–165). Norwood, NJ: Ablex.

Paisley, W. (1993). Knowledge utilization: The role of new communication technologies. *Journal of the American Society for Information Science, 44,* 222–234.

Palmquist, R. A. (1992). The impact of information technology on the individual. In M. E. Williams (Ed.), *Annual review of information science and technology, Volume 27* (pp. 3–42). Medford, NJ: Learned Information.

Pelikan, J. (1992). *The idea of the university: A reexamination.* New Haven, CT: Yale University.

Penley, L. E. (1977). Organizational communication: Its relationship to the structure of work groups. In R. C. Huseman, C. M. Logue, & D. L. Freshley (Eds.), *Readings in interpersonal and organizational communication* (pp. 112–130). Boston: Holbrook Press.

Penley, L. E. (1982). An investigation of the information processing framework of organizational communication. *Human Communication Research, 8,* 348–365.

Perin, C. (1991). Electronic social fields in bureaucracies. *Communications of the ACM, 34,* 75–82.

Perrow, C. (1972). *Complex organizations: A critical essay.* Glenview, IL: Scott, Foresman.

Perse, E. M., & Courtright, J. A. (1993). Normative images of communication media: Mass and interpersonal channels in the new media environment. *Human Communication Research, 19,* 485–503.

Pescosolido, B. A. (1992). Beyond rational choice: The social dynamics of how people seek help. *American Journal of Sociology, 97,* 1096–1138.

Peters, T. J., & Waterman, R. H., Jr. (1982). *In search of excellence: Lessons from America's best-run companies.* New York: Harper & Row.

Pettigrew, L. S., & Logan, R. (1987). The health care context. In C. R. Berger & S.

H. Chaffee (Eds.), *Handbook of communication science* (pp. 675–709). Newbury Park, CA: Sage.

Pfeffer, J. (1978). *Organizational design*. Arlington Heights, IL: AHM Publishing.

Pfeffer, J. (1982). *Organizations and organization theory*. Boston: Pitman.

Pfeffer, J., & Leblebici, H. (1977). Information technology and organizational structure. *Pacific Sociological Review, 20*, 241–259.

Picot, A., Klingenberg, H., & Kranzle, H. P. (1982). Office technology: A report on attitudes and channels selection from field studies in Germany. In M. Burgoon (Ed.), *Communication yearbook 6* (pp. 674–693). Beverly Hills, CA: Sage.

Pinelli, T. E. (1991). The information seeking habits and practices of engineers. In C. Steinke (Ed.), *Information seeking and communicating behavior of scientists and engineers* (pp. 5–25). New York: Haworth Press.

Poole, M. S., & DeSanctis, G. (1992). Microlevel structuration in computer-supported group decision making. *Human Communication Research, 19*, 5–49.

Poole, M. S., & McPhee, R. D. (1983). A structurational analysis of organizational climate. In L. L. Putnam & M. E. Pacanowsky (Eds.), *Communication and organizations: An interpretive approach* (pp. 195–220). Beverly Hills, CA: Sage.

Poole, M. S., & Van de Ven, A. H. (1989). Using paradox to build management and organization theories. *Academy of Management Review, 14*, 562–578.

Porter, L. W., Allen, R. W., & Angle, H. L. (1981). The politics of upward influence in organizations. In S. M. Bacharach (Ed.), *Research in organizational behavior* (pp. 109–149). Greenwich, CT: JAI Press.

Porter, M. E., & Millar, V. E. (1985). How information gives you competitive advantage. *Harvard Business Review, 63*, 149–160.

Powell, W. W. (1990). Neither market nor hierarchy: Network forms of organization. In S. B. Bacharach (Ed.), *Research in organizational behavior* (pp. 295–336). Greenwich, CT: JAI Press.

Presthus, R. (1962). *The organizational society*. New York: Random House.

Randolph, W. A. (1978). Organizational technology and the media and purpose dimension of organization communications. *Journal of Business Research, 6*, 237–259.

Ravetz, J. R. (1993). The sin of silence: Ignorance of ignorance. *Knowledge: Creation, Diffusion, Utilization, 15*, 157–165.

Ray, M. L., & Ward, S. (1975). Introduction: The relevance of consumer information processing studies to communication research. *Communication Research, 2*, 195–202.

Reder, S., & Conklin, N. F. (1987). *Selection and effects of channels in distributed communication and decision making tasks: A theoretical review and a proposed research paradigm.* Paper presented at the International Communication Association annual conference, Montreal, Canada.

Reif, W. E. (1968). *Computer technology and management organization*. Iowa City, IA: University of Iowa.

Reinsch, N. L. J., & Beswick, R. W. (1990). Voice mail versus conventional channels: A cost minimization analysis of individual's preferences. *Academy of Management Journal, 33*, 801–816.

Reynolds, E. V., & Johnson, J. D. (1982). Liaison emergence: Relating theoretical perspectives. *Academy of Management Review, 7*, 551–559.

Rice, R. E. (1989). Issues and concepts in research on computer-mediated communication systems. In J. A. Anderson (Ed.), *Communication yearbook 12* (pp. 436–476). Newbury Park, CA: Sage.

Rice, R. E. (1993). Media appropriateness: Using social presence theory to compare traditional and new organizational media. *Human Communication Research, 19,* 451–484.

Rice, R. E., & Associates (1984). *The new media: Communication, research and technology.* Beverly Hills, CA: Sage.

Rice, R. E., & Aydin, C. (1991). Attitudes towards new organizational technology: Network proximity as a mechanism for social information processing. *Administrative Science Quarterly, 36,* 219–244.

Rice, R. E., Grant, A., Schmitz, J., & Torobin, J. (1988). *Organizational information processing, critical mass and social influence: A network approach to predicting the adoption and outcomes of electronic messaging.* Paper presented at the annual meeting of the International Communication Association, New Orleans, LA.

Rice, R. E., & Manross, G. G. (1987). The case of the intelligent telephone: The relationship of job category to the adoption of an organizational communication technology. In M. L. McLaughlin (Ed.), *Communication yearbook 10* (pp. 727–742). Beverly Hills, CA: Sage.

Rice, R. E., & Shook, D. E. (1990). Relationships of job categories and organizational levels to use of communication channels, including electronic model: A meta-analysis and extension. *Journal of Management Studies, 27,* 196–229.

Richards, W. D. (1985). Data, models, and assumptions in network analysis. In R. D. McPhee & P. K. Tompkins (Eds.), *Organizational communication: Traditional themes and new directions* (pp. 109–128). Beverly Hills, CA: Sage.

Riley, M. W., & Riley, J. W. (1951). A sociological approach to communications research. *Public Opinion Quarterly, 15,* 445–460.

Roberts, K. H., & O'Reilly, C. A., III (1979). Some correlations of communication roles in organizations. *Academy of Management Journal, 4,* 283–293.

Robertson, T. S., & Wortzel, L. H. (1977). Consumer behavior and health care change: The role of mass media. *Consumer Research, 4,* 525–527.

Robertson, T. S., & Wortzel, L. H. (1979). Consumer behavior and health care change: The role of mass media. In P. D. Cooper (Ed.), *Health care marketing: Issues and trends* (pp. 167–174). Germantown, MD: Aspen Systems Corporation.

Rogers, E. M. (1983). *Diffusion of innovations.* New York: Free Press.

Rogers, E. M., & Agarwala-Rogers, R. (1976). *Communication in organizations.* New York: Free Press.

Rogers, E. M., & Kincaid, D. L. (1981). *Communication networks: Toward a new paradigm for research.* New York: Free Press.

Rogers, E. M., & Shoemaker, F. F. (1971). *Communication of innovations.* New York: Free Press.

Rogers, E. M., & Storey, J. D. (1987). Communication campaigns. In C. R. Berger & S. H. Chaffee (Eds.), *Handbook of Communication Science* (pp. 817–846). Newbury Park, CA: Sage.

Rosenstock, I. M. (1974). Historical origins of the Health Belief Model. In M. H. Becker (Ed.), *The Health Belief Model and personal health behavior* (pp. 1–8). Thorofare, NJ: Charles B. Slack.

Rouse, W. B., & Rouse, S. H. (1984). Human information seeking and design of information systems. *Information Processing and Management, 20*, 129–138.

Rousseau, D. M. (1985). Issues of level in organizational research: Multi-level and cross-level perspectives. In S. M. Bacharach (Ed.), *Research in organizational behavior, Volume 7* (pp. 1–37). Greenwich, CT: JAI Press.

Rowley, J. E., & Turner, C. M. D. (1978). *The dissemination of information*. Boulder, CO: Westview Press.

Ruben, B. D. (1992). The communication-information relationship in system-theoretic perspective. *Journal of the American Society for Information Science, 43*, 15–27.

Rubin, A. M. (1986). Uses, gratifications, and media effects research. In J. Bryant & D. Zillman (Eds.), *Perspectives on media effects* (pp. 281–301). Hillsdale, NJ: Lawrence Erlbaum Associates.

Rubinyi, R. M. (1989). Computers and community: The organizational impact. *Journal of Communication, 39*, 110–123.

Salancik, G. R., & Pfeffer, J. (1977). An examination of need-satisfaction models of job attitudes. *Administrative Science Quarterly, 22*, 427–453.

Salancik, G. R., & Pfeffer, J. (1978). A social information processing approach to job attitudes and task design. *Administrative Science Quarterly, 23*, 224–253.

Saracevic, T. (1975). Relevance: A review of and a framework for the thinking on the notion in information science. *Journal of the American Society for Information Science, 26*, 321–343.

Saunders, C., & Jones, J. W. (1990). Temporal sequences in information acquisition for decision making: A focus on source and medium. *Academy of Management Review, 15*, 29–46.

Saunders, C. S., Robey, D., & Vaverek, K. A. (1994). The persistence of status differentials in computer conferencing. *Human Communication Research, 20*, 443–472.

Savolainen, R. (1993). The sense-making theory: Reviewing the interests of a user-centered approach to information seeking and use. *Information Processing & Management, 29*, 13–28.

Schall, M. S. (1983). A communication-rules approach to organizational culture. *Administrative Science Quarterly, 28*, 557–581.

Schamber, L. (1994). Relevance and information behavior. In M. E. Williams (Ed.), *Annual review of information science and technology, Volume 29* (pp. 3–48). Medford, NJ: Learned Information.

Schein, E. H. (1965). *Organizational psychology*. Englewood Cliffs, NJ: Prentice-Hall.

Schmitz, J., & Fulk, J. (1991). Organizational colleague, media richness, and electronic mail. *Communication Research, 18*, 487–523.

Schneider, L. A. (1962). The role of public relations in four organizational types. *Journalism Quarterly, 62*, 567–576, 594.

Schramm, W. S. (1973). *Men, messages, and media*. New York: Harper & Row.

Schreiman, D. B., & Johnson, J. D. (1975). *A model of cognitive complexity and network role*. Paper presented to the International Communication Association, Chicago, IL.

Schroder, J. M., Driver, J. J., & Streufert, S. (1967). *Human information processing*. New York: Holt, Rinehart and Winston.

Scott, J. (1991). *A social network analysis: A handbook*. Newbury Park, CA: Sage.

Senge, P. M. (1990). *The fifth discipline: The art and practice of the learning organi-zation*. New York: Doubleday Currency.

Sept, R. (1989). *Bureaucracy, communication, and information system design*. Paper presented at the annual meeting of the International Communication Associa-tion, San Francisco, CA.

Shannon, C. E., & Weaver, W. (1949). *A mathematical theory of communication*. Chi-cago: University of Illinois Press.

Shaw, M. E. (1971). *Group dynamics: The psychology of small group behavior*. New York: McGraw-Hill.

Shimanoff, S. B. (1980). *Communication rules: Theory and research*. Beverly Hills, CA: Sage.

Siefert, M., Gerbner, G., & Fisher, J. (Eds.) (1989). *The information gap: How com-puters and other new communication technologies affect the social distribution of power*. New York: Oxford University Press.

Simon, H. A. (1960). "The executive as decision maker" and "Organizational design: Man-machine systems for decision making." In H. A. Simon (Ed.), *The new science of management decision making* (pp. 1–8). New York: Harper & Row.

Simon, H. A. (1987). Making management decisions: The role of intuition and emotion. *Academy of Management Executive, 1*, 57–64.

Simpson, R. L. (1952). Vertical and horizontal communication in formal organizations. *Administrative Science Quarterly, 2*, 188–196.

Sitkin, S. B., Sutcliffe, K. M., & Barrios-Choplin, J. R. (1992). A dual-capacity model of communication media choice in organizations. *Human Communication Re-search, 18*, 563–598.

Smelser, N. J. (1963). *The sociology of economic life*. Englewood Cliffs, NJ: Prentice-Hall.

Smith, C. G., & Jones, G. (1968). The role of the interaction-influence system in planned organizational change. In A. S. Tannebaum (Ed.), *Control in organi-zations* (pp. 165–184). New York: McGraw-Hill.

Smith, K. G., Caroll, S. J., & Ashford, S. J. (1995). Intra- and interorganizational cooperation: Toward a research agenda. *Academy of Management Journal, 38*, 7–23.

Smith, R. L., Richetto, G. M., & Zima, J. P. (1972). Organizational behavior: An ap-proach to human communication. In R. Budd & B. Ruben (Eds.), *Approaches to human communication* (pp. 269–289). New York: Spartan Books.

Smithson, M. (1989). *Ignorance and uncertainty: Emerging paradigms*. New York: Springer-Verlag.

Smithson, M. (1993). Ignorance and science: Dilemmas, perspectives, and prospects. *Knowledge: Creation, Diffusion, Utilization, 15*, 133–156.

Spekman, R. E. (1979). Influence and information: An exploratory investigation of the boundary role person's basis of power. *Academy of Management Journal, 22*, 104–117.

Stasser, G., Taylor, L. A., & Hanna, C. (1989). Information sampling in structured and unstructured discussions of three- and six-person groups. *Journal of Personality and Social Psychology, 57*, 67–78.

Stasser, G., & Titus, W. (1985). Pooling of unshared information in group decision making: Biased information sampling during discussion. *Journal of Personality and Social Psychology, 48*, 1467–1478.

Staw, B. M., Sandelands, L. E., & Dutton, J. E. (1981). Threat-rigidity effects in organizational behavior: A multilevel analysis. *Administrative Science Quarterly*, *26*, 501–524.

Steinfield, C. W., & Fulk, J. (1990). The theory imperative. In J. Fulk & C. Steinfield (Eds.), *Organizations and communication technology* (pp. 13–25). Newbury Park, CA: Sage.

Steinfield, C. W., Jin, B., & Ku, L. L. (1987). *A preliminary test of a social information processing model of media use in organizations*. Paper presented at the annual meeting of the International Communication Association, Montreal, Quebec, Canada.

Steinke, C. (1991). Introduction. In C. Steinke (Ed.), *Information seeking and communicating behavior of scientists and engineers* (pp. 1–3). New York: Haworth Press.

Stevenson, W. B., & Gilly, M. C. (1991). Information processing and problem solving: The migration of problems through formal positions and networks of ties. *Academy of Management Journal*, *34*, 918–926.

Stigler, G. J. (1961). The economics of information. *Journal of Political Economy*, *69*, 213–225.

Stocking, S. H., & Holstein, L. W. (1993). Constructing and reconstructing scientific ignorance: Ignorance claims in science and journalism. *Knowledge: Creation, Diffusion, Utilization*, *15*, 186–210.

Stonier, T. (1991). Towards a new theory of information. *Journal of Information Science*, *17*, 257–263.

Strobel, L. P. (1980). *Reckless homicide? Ford's Pinto trial*. South Bend, IN: and books.

Sullivan, C. B. (1995). Preferences for electronic mail in organizational communication tasks. *Journal of Business Communication*, *32*, 49–65.

Summers, E. G., Matheson, J., & Conry, R. (1983). The effect of personal, professional, and psychological attributes, and information seeking behavior on the use of information sources by educators. *Journal of the American Society for Information Science*, *34*, 75–85.

Sundstrom, E., Burt, R. E., & Kamp, D. (1980). Privacy at work: Architectural correlates of job satisfaction and job performance. *Academy of Management Journal*, *23*, 101–117.

Sutton, H., & Porter, L. W. (1968). A study of the grapevine in a government organization. *Personnel Psychology*, *21*, 223–230.

Swinehart, J. W. (1968). Voluntary exposure to health communications. *American Journal of Public Health*, *58*, 1265–1275.

Sykes, R. E. (1983). Initial interaction between strangers and acquaintances: A multivariate analysis of factors affecting choice of communication partners. *Human Communication Research*, *10*, 27–53.

Szilagyi, A. D., & Holland, W. E. (1980). Changes in social density: Relationships with functional interaction and perceptions of job characteristics, role stress, and work satisfaction. *Journal of Applied Psychology*, *65*, 28–33.

Tan, A. S. (1985). *Mass communication theories and research*, 2nd ed. New York: Wiley.

Taylor, R. S. (1968). Question-negotiation and information seeking in libraries. *College & Research Libraries*, *29*, 178–194.

Thayer, L. (1988). How does information "inform." In B. D. Ruben (Ed.), *Information and behavior, Volume 2* (pp. 13–26). New Brunswick, NJ: Transaction Books.

Thomas, J. B., Clark, S. M., & Gioia, D. A. (1993). Strategic sensemaking and organizational performance: Linkages among scanning, interpretation, action, and outcomes. *Academy of Management Journal, 36,* 239–270.

Thompson, G., Frances, J., Levacic, R., & Mitchell, J. (Eds.) (1991). *Markets, hierarchies & networks: The coordination of social life.* Newbury Park, CA: Sage.

Thompson, J. D. (1967). *Organizations in action.* New York: McGraw-Hill.

Tichenor, P. J., Donohue, G. A., & Olien, C. N. (1970). Mass media and differential growth in knowledge. *Public Opinion Quarterly, 34,* 158–170.

Trevino, L. K., Daft, R. L., & Lengel, R. H. (1990). Understanding managers' media choices: A symbolic interactionist perspective. In J. Fulk & C. Steinfield (Eds.), *Organizations and communication technology* (pp. 71–94). Newbury Park, CA: Sage.

Trevino, L. K., Lengel, R., & Daft, R. L. (1987). Reasons for media choice in management communication: A symbolic interactionist perspective. *Communication Research, 14,* 553–574.

Trevino, L. K., & Webster, J. (1992). Flow in computer-mediated communication: Electronic mail and voice mail evaluation and impacts. *Communication Research, 19,* 539–573.

Tsui, A. S., & O'Reilly, C. A. I. (1989). Beyond simple demographic effects: The importance of relational demography in superior-subordinate dyads. *Academy of Management Journal, 32,* 402–423.

Van de Ven, A. H. (1986). Central problems in the management of innovation. *Management Science, 32,* 590–607.

Van de Ven, A. H., Delbecq, A. L., & Koenig, R. (1976). Determinants of coordination modes within organizations. *Administrative Science Quarterly, 41,* 322–338.

Varian, H. R. (1995). The information economy: How much will two bits be worth in the digital marketplace. *Scientific American* (September), 200–202.

Varlejs, J. (1986). Information seeking: Changing perspectives. In J. Varlejs (Ed.), *Information seeking: Basing services on users' behaviors* (pp. 67–82). London, UK: McFarland & Co.

Victor, B., & Blackburn, R. S. (1987). Interdependence: An alternative conceptualization. *Academy of Management Review, 12,* 486–498.

von Hayek, F. (1989). Spontaneous ("grown") order and organized ("made") order. In N. Modlovsky (Ed.), *Order—With or without design* (pp. 101–123). London, UK: Centre for Research into Communist Economies.

Wales, M., Rarick, G., & Davis, H. (1963). Message exaggeration by the receiver. *Journalism Quarterly, 40,* 339–342.

Wallack, L. (1989). Mass communication and health promotion: A critical perspective. In R. E. Rice & C. K. Atkin (Eds.), *Public communication campaigns* (pp. 87–104). Newbury Park, CA: Sage.

Walther, J. B. (1994). Anticipated ongoing interaction versus channel effects on relational communication in computer-mediated interaction. *Human Communication Research, 20,* 473–501.

Walton, E. (1975). Self-interest, credibility, and message selection in organizational communication; A research note. *Human Communication Research, 1,* 180–181.

Wang, G. (1977). Information utility as a predictor of newspaper readership. *Journalism Quarterly, 54,* 791–794.

Ward, S. (1987). Consumer behavior. In S. H. Berger & S. H. Chaffee (Eds.), *Handbook of communication science* (pp. 651–674). Newbury Park, CA: Sage.

Warriner, C. K. (1981). Levels in the study of social structure. In P. M. Blau & R. K. Merton (Eds.), *Continuity in structural inquiry*. Beverly Hills, CA: Sage.

Wartella, E., & Reeves, B. (1985). Historical trends in research on children and the media: 1900–1960. *Journal of Communication, 35,* 118–133.

Weick, K. E. (1969). *The social psychology of organizing*. Reading, MA: Addison-Wesley.

Weick, K. E. (1983). Organizational communication: Toward a research agenda. In L. L. Putnam & M. E. Pacanowsky (Eds.), *Communication and organizations: An interpretive approach* (pp. 13–29). Beverly Hills, CA: Sage.

Weimann, G. (1983). The strength of weak conversational ties in the flow of information and influence. *Social Networks, 5,* 245–267.

White, H. C. (1992). Agency as control in formal networks. In N. Nohria & R. G. Eccles (Eds.), *Networks and organizations: Structure, form, and action* (pp. 92–117). Boston: Harvard Business School Press.

White, M. (1985). Intelligence management. In B. Cronin (Ed.), *Information management: From strategies to action* (pp. 21–35). Oxon, UK: ASLIB.

Wilensky, H. L. (1968). Organizational intelligence. In D. L. Sills (Ed.), *The international encyclopedia of the social sciences* (pp. 319–334). New York: Free Press.

Wilson, D. O., & Malik, S. D. (1995). Looking for a few good sources: Exploring the intraorganizational communication linkages of first line managers. *Journal of Business Communication, 32,* 31–48.

Wilson, P. (1977). *Public knowledge, private ignorance: Toward a library and information policy*. Westport, CT: Greenwood Press.

Womack, S. M. (1984). *Toward a clarification of boundary spanning*. Paper presented at the Speech Communication Association annual convention, Denver, CO.

Zajonc, R. B., & Wolfe, D. M. (1966). Cognitive consequences of a person's position in a formal organization. *Human Relations, 19,* 139–150.

Zaltman, G., Duncan, R., & Holbek, J. (1973). *Innovations and organizations*. New York: Wiley.

Zenger, T. R., & Lawrence, B. S. (1989). Organizational demography: The differential effects of age and tenure distributions on technical communication. *Academy of Management Journal, 32,* 353–376.

Zmud, R. W. (1990). Opportunities for strategic manipulation through new information technology. In J. Fulk & C. Steinfield (Eds.), *Organizations and communication technology* (pp. 95–116). Newbury Park, CA: Sage.

Zuboff, S. (1988). *In the age of the smart machine: The future of work and power*. New York: Basic Books.

INDEX

About the Author

J. DAVID JOHNSON is Professor and Chairperson of the Department of Communication, Michigan State University. He is author of numerous articles and reviews in refereed journals on his research interests, which focus on organizational communication structure, information seeking, and health communication. Dr. Johnson is and has been a consulting editor for major journals in his fields and is author of a previous book, *Organizational Communication Structure* (1993).